THE
HIDDEN PLACES

of
The Cotswolds
Gloucestershire and Wiltshire

Second Edition
Edited by Shane Scott
Front Cover: Castle Combe Wiltshire
By Les Darlow

Acknowledgements

This book would not have been compiled without the dedicated help of the following: Elaine & Adele, Administration; Albert, Les & Sarah, Artists; Bob, Jody, Simon, Harvey, Gerald, Jim, Clare & Debbie, Research; Hattie, Writing; Jennie, Production; and finally Shane, Editing.

OTHER TITLES IN THIS SERIES

The Hidden Places of East Anglia
The Hidden Places of Somerset, Avon and Dorset
The Hidden Places of Southern and Central Scotland
The Hidden Places of Notts, Derby and Lincolnshire
The Hidden Places of the Thames and Chilterns
The Hidden Places of Northumberland and Durham
The Hidden Places of Hampshire and Isle of Wight
The Hidden Places of Lancashire and Cheshire
The Hidden Places of Hereford and Worcester
The Hidden Places of Devon and Cornwall
The Hidden Places of Yorkshire and Humberside
The Hidden Places of the South East
The Hidden Places of the Lake District and Cumbria

Printed and bound by Guernsey Press Channel Islands
© M&M PUBLISHING LTD.
Tryfan House, Warwick Drive, Hale, Altrincham, Cheshire, WA15 9EA

THE HIDDEN PLACES
OF
Gloucestershire and Wiltshire

CONTENTS

1.	Salisbury to Stonehenge	1
2.	Westbury to the Dorset border	27
3.	Trowbridge to Chippenham	47
4.	East Wiltshire	79
5.	Marlborough to the River Thames	107
6.	North West Wiltshire	129
7.	Tetbury to the River Severn	159
8.	The Cotswolds	189
9.	Gloucester and Cheltenham to the Hereford and Worcester border	233
10.	South West Gloucestershire	291
	Tourist Information Centres	323
	Town Index	325

CHAPTER ONE

Salisbury to Stonehenge

Wilton House

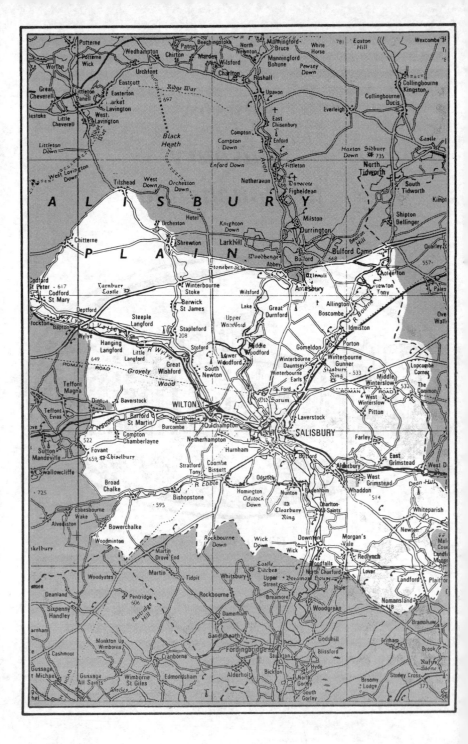

CHAPTER ONE

Index

Cozens House Self Catering and B&B, Orcheston St. Mary, Salisbury

The Fox and Goose Inn and Restaurant, Coombe Bissett, Salisbury

Grasmere House B&B, 70 Harnham Road, Salisbury

The Green Dragon Inn, Alderbury, Salisbury

"Harvest Moon" B&B, East Gomeldon, Salisbury

"Hillside" B&B, Odstock, Salisbury

The Homestead B&B, Pitton, Salisbury

Manor Farm B&B, Burcombe, Salisbury

The Old Bakery B&B, Netton, Nr Salisbury

The Queen's Head Inn and B&B, Broadchalke, Salisbury

Stratford Lodge Guest House, Castle Road, Salisbury

Templemans Farmhouse B&B, Red Lynch, Nr Salisbury

The Warren Guest House, Downton, Salisbury

Salisbury Cathedral

CHAPTER ONE

Salisbury to Stonehenge

We began our tour of central Wessex in the southeasternmost corner of Wiltshire, leaving the M27 at junction 1 and travelling northwest along the B3078 and B3080 towards the valley of the River Avon. We crossed into Wiltshire near the charmingly-named village of **Lover**, before making our first stop in **Redlynch**, a pleasant community noted for its fine brick-built mansion, **Newhouse**, which lies a short distance to the east of the village. This has a Jacobean core dating from 1619 and two Georgian wings which are arranged in the classic 'trinity' configuration. Inside, there is an interesting display of historic costumes, as well as a collection of relics relating to Admiral Nelson. We also found some excellent accommodation near Redlynch at Templeman's Old Farmhouse. *Redlynch   0725 20331*

The East End
Of Salisbury Cathedral

Templeman's Old Farmhouse is the delightful country home of June and Peter Dabell, two fine hosts who takes great delight in sharing it with their guests. Set high on the Downs on the edge of the New Forest, this makes a peaceful relaxing base from which to tour the surrounding area. Situated on the edge of the village, Salisbury is only eight miles away. Inside, the guest rooms are spacious and elegant; all are beautifully

5

furnished and are equipped with good facilities. To ensure they feel totally relaxed and at home, guests are even brought tea or coffee in bed each morning.

Continuing westwards, our next port of call was **Downton**, an ancient village which is spread out on both sides of the River Avon. The nearby earthwork was originally constructed by the Ancient Britons and was later occupied by the Saxons who established a meeting place or 'moot' on the site. This event was commemorated in the 18th-century when the present **Moot House** was constructed on the old castle foundations. The building and its garden stand opposite a small 18th-century amphitheatre which was built to resemble the original Saxon meeting place. In 1955, a Roman villa comprising of seven rooms and a bathhouse was discovered near here which is believed to date from around 300 AD.

The Borough, Downton

The mediaeval centre of Downton, with its broad main street and distinctive grassy strip, is known locally as **The Borough** and was laid out by the Bishop of Winchester in 1205. Many of the thatched brick-built houses which can be seen here today date from the 18th-century. We were surprised to find a working tannery beside the river at the heart of the village; this was built in 1918 and is still in use today. The village church of St Lawrence stands of the site of a Saxon church which is believed to have been consecrated by St Birinus in 638. The present-day building was originally constructed in the 1100s, although it has been much altered over the centuries. Inside, there are some fine carved monuments by the 18th-century Dutch sculptor, Peter Scheemaker. Downton's old manor house is the former home of the Raleigh family and for many years Sir Walter's brother, Carew, was the local member of parliament.

The Warren   Downton   0725 20263

Those wishing to stay in Downton should make a point of finding **The Warren**. Situated in the heart of this historic New Forest village, the Warren is a charming mediaeval longhouse which is owned by John and Elizabeth Baxter. Here, Elizabethan panelling and oak beams are complemented by antique furniture and furnishings which help to retain the property's original character, whilst modern comforts such as central heating ensure guests enjoy a restful stay. There are six well-equipped bedrooms, two en suite, plus a comfortable guest lounge, but the highlight of your stay is likely to be Elizabeth's wholesome breakfast which is enjoyed in a beautiful room overlooking the large walled garden with the Norman village church beyond. With Salisbury Plain, Stonehenge and many other places of interest within easy reach, the Warren makes a lovely base for touring this beautiful corner of England.

On leaving Downton, we crossed the River Avon and turned north onto the A338 Salisbury road. This road passes a couple of miles to the west of Eyre's Folly, a unique 17th-century octagonal tower which is believed to one of the earliest follies to have been built in Britain. More commonly known as **The Pepperbox**, this unusual slate-roofed structure was built in 1606 and enjoys magnificent views over Salisbury and southwest Wiltshire. The tower is surrounded by 72 acres of juniper-filled downland which now belongs to the National Trust.

The village of **Alderbury** lies a couple of miles to the northwest of the Pepperbox and four miles from the centre of Salisbury. Thankfully now bypassed the main A36 Salisbury to Southampton road, this delightful village possesses a renowned inn and eating place, the Green Dragon.

The Green Dragon   Alderbury   0722 710263

Standing on the old Southampton Road, the **Green Dragon** was originally built in the 14th-century as a chapel. Now Grade II listed, the interior of this charming country inn is magnificent, with superb oak-beamed ceilings adding to its charm and character. The proprietors, Jeremy and Flora Bowers, have built up an excellent reputation for serving first-class food and drink. There are two very comfortable, welcoming bars and the menu is varied and delicious, yet very reasonably priced. Jeremy is the chef responsible for such delights as platter of fish, tortillas, and the 'Green Dragon special', ensuring whatever your tastes, you will leave feeling satisfied and eager to return.

Our journey northwards along the A338 took us close by **Longford Castle**, a largely 16th-century structure which stands near the confluence of the Rivers Ebble and Avon. The building is constructed to an unusual triangular design and houses is an interesting collection of paintings.

From here, we drove back across the A338 to reach **Nunton**, an attractive village of thatched cottages and brick residences, the most notable of which is Nunton House. We were now in the lower valley of the Ebble, a delightful river which is said to contain some of the finest trout in the country. A mile or so upstream, we stopped in the pleasant riverside community of **Odstock**. Here, we made a point of visiting the village church which, according to local legend, is the subject of an infamous gypsy curse. The curse surrounds the figure of Joshua Scamp, a notorious local character whose grave lies in the southeast corner of the churchyard. Scamp was a gypsy who in 1801 was wrongfully hanged for stealing horses. This made him a martyr-figure among the Romany people and each year a disorderly crowd would assemble around his grave to commemorate his death, usually after having already toasted to his memory in the nearby Yew Tree Inn.

One year, the rector resolved to put an end to the unruly gathering; he locked the door of the church and dug up a wild rose which Scamp's family had planted beside his grave. This action so incensed the gypsy people that they placed a curse on anyone who dared to bar them from the church again. Not long after, two men defying the curse met with an untimely end, occurrences which led the rector to take the key of the church and throw it into the River Ebble where it is said to remain to this day. A briar rose was then replanted on Scamp's grave which can still be seen beside his crumbling headstone. Other noteworthy buildings in the village include the manor farm and a 17th-century parsonage where Oliver Cromwell is rumoured to have stayed when the building functioned as an inn.

"Hillside"   *Odstock*   *0722 329746*

Present-day travellers looking for an excellent place to stay in the ancient village of Odstock should try **Hillside**. Set in a beautiful tranquil spot and lying only a couple of miles from Salisbury, this appropriately-named bed and breakfast establishment is the home of Carol and Jeffrey Dodd, two fine hosts who provide first-class hospitality. Their en suite guest rooms are all superbly equipped and located in a separate wing with its own entrance. As well as enjoying magnificent views over the surrounding countryside, this charming hillside house has a wonderful private garden. This is inhabited by a splendid peacock whose plumage adds a brilliant splash of colour to the lovely open lawns. All in all, this true haven of peace and tranquillity is an ideal place to enjoy Wiltshire at its best.

The charming village of **Coombe Bissett** lies a couple of miles further upstream at the point where the A354 Blandford Forum to Salisbury road crosses the River Ebble. This is where we found the first-rate pub and restaurant, the Fox and Goose.

9

The Fox and Goose is situated in the heart of Coombe Bissett, just across the road from the village pond. The pub is a focal point for visitors and locals alike. Your friendly host, Mike Chapman, has been in the catering industry all his working life and has built this charming pub and eating place into a charming establishment which is full of character and charm. Customers can choose from a fine selection of ales, wines and first-class food. The menu is varied and imaginative and is sure to satisfy. It includes such mouthwatering dishes as deep-fried Brie or spicy chicken wings, followed by mixed grill or pork fillet. There is also a special children's menu and an excellent outdoor play area.

The Fox and Goose   Coombe Bissett   0722 77437

From Coombe Bissett, we continued northeastwards along the A354 towards Salisbury. The charming hamlet of **Britford** lies within the branches of the River Avon a mile-and-a-half to the south of the city. Here, we discovered a moated country house and the fine Saxon church of St Peter's which predates Salisbury Cathedral by several centuries. Inside, there are some fine stone carvings in the nave which are thought to date from around 800 AD, three carved door surrounds from before the Norman Conquest, and an unusual and elaborately decorated tomb believed to belong to the Duke of Buckingham who was beheaded in Salisbury in 1483. A fine view of the Salisbury's cathedral spire, which lies a couple of miles to the northwest, can be had from Britford's water meadows.

Salisbury stands at the confluence of the rivers Avon, Wylye, Bourne and Nadder. Originally called New Sarum, the town grew up around the cathedral which was erected on a sheltered site two miles south of its predecessor at Old Sarum. Over the centuries, the townspeople gradually followed the clergy down from the windswept hillside and today, Salisbury is a flourishing town with a twice weekly open-air market (Tuesdays and Saturdays), a corn exchange and a cattle market.

The new cathedral was the inspiration of Bishop Herbert Poole who wanted to distance the church from the Norman authorities who occupied a castle on the original site. Sadly, the bishop died before his dream was realised and it fell to his brother Richard to implement his plan. Work on the new building began on Easter Monday 1220 and was completed 38 years later, a remarkably short construction period considering the scale of the project and building methods of the day. As a result, the structure has a uniformity of style which is unmatched by any other mediaeval cathedral in England. The spire were added in 1334 and, at a height of 404 feet, is the tallest in the country. Its construction was a remarkable architectural achievement considering the central piers stand on foundations which go down less than ten feet into marshy ground.

Salisbury Cathedral

Set into the floor beneath the spire is a brass plate with the inscription, 'AD 1737 The Centre of the Tower'. This marks the spot where, fifty years earlier, Sir Christopher Wren calculated that the tower was leaning almost two-and-a-half feet off-centre. His answer to the problem was to insert iron tie-rods, and when these were replaced in the 1950s, it was discovered that the lean had not worsened in over 250 years.

The cathedral is said to contain a door for each month of the year, a window for each day and a column for each hour (8760 in total). The elaborately decorated west front includes a series of niches, each of which at one time contained a statue; over the centuries many were destroyed by weathering and the ones that can be seen today are 19th-century replacements. A small statue of Salisbury's 'Boy Bishop' stands inside the cathedral's west door. According to the custom of the day, a chorister was elected 'bishop' by his comrades for a period lasting from St Nicholas Day to Holy Innocents' Day (6-28 December) each year. On one occasion during the 17th-century, the incumbent was said to have been 'tickled to death' by the other choirboys, and because he had died 'in office', a statue was made showing him in his bishop's regalia.

The oldest working clock in Britain (and possibly in the world) can be found in the cathedral's fan-vaulted north transept. It was built in 1386 to strike the hour and has no clock face. Look out also for the recently-restored 13th-century roof paintings in the choir, and the 200-or-so carved stone figures illustrating scenes from the Old Testament on the walls of the octagonal chapter house.

There are also several magnificent tombs in the cathedral, the oldest of which is that of William Longespere, Earl of Salisbury, whose reclining armour-clad effigy has lain here since 1226. Eleven years before, he witnessed the sealing of the **Magna Carta** by his half-brother, King John, and indeed one of the four remaining copies of this historic document is on display in the Charter House. This is located in the library above the east walk of the cathedral's magnificent cloisters, the largest of their type in England.

As the cathedral was built before the town, it was necessary to construct housing for the clergy at the same time. This were arranged around a walled square which is now considered to be the finest **cathedral close** in the country. To enter the close it is necessary to pass through one of its mediaeval gateways, the least congested of which are Harnham Gate to the south and St Ann's Gate to the east. Just to the south of the cathedral lies the **Bishop's Palace** which was constructed in the 13th-century and now houses the cathedral choir school. During the Great Plague of 1665, Charles II based his court here for several months to the escape the pestilence which was sweeping London. The bishop's residence was also made famous by John Constable who painted his famous landscape of Salisbury Cathedral in the palace gardens; it now hangs in the Victoria and Albert Museum in London.

The pathway along the western side of the cathedral close, West Walk, passes two noteworthy establishments. The award-winning **Salisbury and South Wiltshire Museum** is located in the mediaeval King's House and contains a large collection of historic artefacts, including relics from Stonehenge, pottery fragments from Old Sarum and tiles from a Roman mosaic. There is also an interesting display of English china, pottery and glassware, and a mounted group of great bustards, the majestic birds which at one time were found on Salisbury Plain. Open Mondays to

Saturdays (and summer Sunday afternoons), 10am to 5pm, all year round. Admission charge payable. A few doors away, the splendid Bishop's Wardrobe houses the **Duke of Edinburgh's Royal Regiment Museum**; this contains an interesting collection of regimental militaria which documents the history of the Royal Berkshire and Wiltshire Regiments since 1743. Open daily, 10am to 4.30pm between June and October (restricted opening at other times; closed December and January).

Mompesson House

One of the finest buildings in the cathedral close stands on the northern side of Choristers' Green. The elegant **Mompesson House** was constructed for a wealthy Wiltshire merchant around 1701 and is now owned by the National Trust. Inside, there is a delicately carved oak staircase, a splendid collection of period furniture and some fine plaster ceilings and overmantels. The Turnbull Collection of 18th-century English china and glassware is also housed here, and to the rear, there is a delightful walled garden. Open Saturdays to Wednesdays, 12 noon to 5.30pm between 1st April and 1st November. Admission charge payable (free to National Trust members).

Malmesbury House on the northwestern side of the cathedral close has a 14th-century core and an interior and façade which were regularly updated between 1640 and 1749. This also contains some fine 18th-century furnishings and is open to the public on Tuesdays, Wednesdays, Thursdays and Bank Holiday Mondays between April and early-October. A row of handsome 17th-century almshouses can also be seen nearby

13

which were built on the instructions of the Bishop Seth Ward.

Beyond the walls of the cathedral close, a walk around Salisbury's city centre reveals a wonderful range of historic inns, shops and houses which chronicle the city's development from the 13th-century to the present day. Many are half-timbered or have overhanging gables or bow-windowed fronts. One of the most distinctive can be found in Queen Street, the three-storey house built in 1425 for six-times mayor **John A'Port**. Restoration of this half-timbered structure during the 1930s revealed that, astonishingly, none of the original 15th-century timbers needed replacing. It now operates as a retail shop, although visitors are welcome to view the interior with its Jacobean wood panelling, stone fireplace and carved oak mantelpiece.

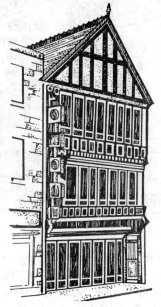

The Odeon Cinema, Salisbury

Other buildings in Salisbury worth mentioning are the octagonal **Poultry Cross** which was constructed in the 15th-century to provide shelter for the market traders, and the nearby church of **St Thomas of Canterbury** which occupies the site of a church which was completed twenty years before the cathedral. The present-day building contains a highly unusual 16th-century wall-painting which can be found above the chancel arch. Restored in the 19th-century, this remarkable work of primitive art depicts Christ on a rainbow, the Virgin Mary, St John the Baptist, and a whole collection of saints condemning the unworthy to eternal damnation. Even the local cinema is housed in a former merchants hall dating from the 15th century.

14

Leaving the city centre behind, we went in search of accommodation and were fortunate enough to discover the aptly-named **Grasmere**, an impressive Victorian bed and breakfast establishment which is set back off Harnham Road on the edge of Salisbury. (The literal meaning of *Grasmere* is lake or pond bordered by grassland.) Standing in beautiful grounds near the confluence of the Rivers Nadder and Avon, the atmosphere is one of elegant luxury; all the rooms are beautifully furnished yet still retaining a homely feel. The five guest rooms are all en suite, with three enjoying superb views of the rivers and the majestic cathedral beyond. There is a croquet lawn in the garden which guests are welcome to use, whilst those wishing to venture further afield will find the heart of historic Salisbury only a ten minute walk away.

Grasmere House   Salisbury   0722 338388

Before leaving Salisbury behind, we decided to have a look at the windswept hillside that formed the site of the original city. **Old Sarum** can be found a couple of miles north of the present city centre and just to the west of A345. This ancient stronghold was successively an Iron Age hill fort, a Roman settlement called *Sorviodunum*, and a mediaeval cathedral town. The Saxons named it *Searobyrg* meaning 'dry place', and this is perhaps another reason why the bishops decided to move their cathedral to another more hospitable site in the 13th-century. Today, Old Sarum is deserted. All that remains of the once-glorious 56-acre fortifications are some ruined castle walls and an outline of the cathedral's original foundations. However, it still has a distinctive atmosphere and is well worth a visit.

Despite having an electorate which at one time numbered only ten, Old Sarum returned two MPs to Westminster before the 1832 Reform Act put an end to the so-called 'rotten boroughs'. A plaque on the site commemorates the constituency's most illustrious MP, the 18th-century orator and statesman William Pitt the Elder. Below Old Sarum lies

Stratford-sub-Castle, a tranquil community of 17th- and 18th-century houses lying on the banks of the River Avon.

We all know that word of mouth is the best possible form of advertising, and that is how we heard of Jill Bayly and her beautiful Victorian home, **Stratford Lodge**. Salisbury is filled with hotels and guesthouses, but we doubt if you will find a quieter or more pleasant place to stay than Stratford Lodge. It is tucked away in Park Lane and has all the charm and grace of the Victorian era. Jill takes great care to ensure that her guests are well cared for; her cooking is second to none, and dinner in the lovely restaurant really is a special meal. Such dishes as 'roast duckling with black cherry and port sauce' are accompanied by fresh vegetables, straight from the garden. Dessert, often simple but always delicious, is also often prepared from fruit grown in the garden.

Stratford Lodge   Salisbury   0722 325177

This is a four-star guest house offering every comfort. The bedrooms are furnished to a very high standard, using pretty pastel colours and matching fabrics. Flowers, antique furniture and pictures adorn every room, and there are lots of books to help you plan your day's sightseeing. Jill is always on hand to let you know what's going on and to advise you of the best places to visit, or if you are feeling lazy and are loath to venture far, the garden is very sheltered and secluded. Guests are very welcome to make use of it and will find it a super place to curl up with a book and just enjoy the sunshine. Jill provides an excellent breakfast and she always tries to offer some slightly unusual dish which may tempt you away from the usual egg and bacon. Mushrooms on toast or smoked haddock kedgeree make a wonderful change and will set you up for the day.

We finally left Salisbury in a northeasterly direction and joined the A338 for a couple of miles before turning east onto the A30. After another two miles, we came to **Figsbury Ring**, a National Trust-owned Iron Age

16

hill fort which enjoys some excellent views over Salisbury and the Avon Valley. The country lanes to the southeast of here led us to the quiet hamlet of **Stockbottom**, near Pitton.

The Homestead   Stockbottom   0980 611160

Here, Cliff and Joan Lodge offer excellent bed and breakfast accommodation at their lovely 18th-century home, **The Homestead**. Renovated and refurbished to a very high standard, this lovely old house enjoys a beautiful setting with the Downs literally just over the garden fence. The guest rooms are all attractively furnished and have hot and cold washbasins and beverage making facilities, whilst the Stable and the Cart Shed, provide superb en suite accommodation in a converted barn. The highlight of your stay is likely to be the fresh farmhouse food which is personally prepared by Cliff and Joan. Their four-course breakfasts and superb dinners are highly recommended by locals and visitors alike.

Finding our way back onto the A30, we drove across the main road and continued northwest along the edge of the top secret military establishment, **Porton Down**. Except on rare occasions, this unusual area of chalk downland has remained hidden to the public for over fifty years. Ironically, this has led to it becoming a unique nature conservation area containing a wide variety of rare plants, flowers and birds. Indeed, the great bustard has successfully been reintroduced here following its local extinction in the early 19th-century. This large long-legged bird is a feature in the country's coat of arms and was once common on Salisbury Plain before before it was wiped out by over-enthusiastic riflemen.

On reaching the village of **Porton**, we turned southwest and followed the course of the River Bourne downstream towards the hamlet of **East Gomeldon**. This is where we discovered the **Harvest Moon**, a delightful bed and breakfast establishment run by Mike and Jan Sainsbury. This is a very special place with hosts who go out of their way to care for their guests. Amongst their many other talents, Jan is a first-class cook and

Mike is an excellent wood turner; many fine examples of his craft can be seen on display around the house. Guests are invited to enjoy the attractive garden which backs onto open countryside. This contains a well-stocked fish pond, owls, rabbits and a superb aviary beside the patio. Mike and Jan's other interests, bonsai and pottery-making, provide added attractions, making a stay at Harvest Moon one you will remember with great affection.

"Harvest Moon"   East Gomeldon   0980 610126

Driving westwards along the small country roads once again, we climbed onto the ridge which carries the main A345 before descending into the Avon Valley. The seven-mile stretch of river between Salisbury and Amesbury is known locally as the **Woodford Valley**. It contains some of the loveliest and most peaceful villages in Wiltshire, including **Great Durnford** with its Norman church, restored mill and picturesque cricket pitch, **Lake** with its impressive Tudor mansion, and **Middle Woodford** with its exceptional **Heale House Gardens and Plant Centre**. These beautifully landscaped gardens lie within the eight-acre grounds of Heale House, an elegant mansion dating from the late 16th-century which was built in an idyllic position beside the River Avon. Open daily, 10am to 5pm, all year round.

Two narrow roads, one on the east bank, one on the west, follow almost every bend in the river which along this stretch is shallow, wide and fast-flowing. We headed for the only bridge which connects the villages of **Netton** and **Upper Woodford**. Before crossing, however, we made a point of calling in at the Old Bakery in Netton.

Now the charming home of Valerie Dunlop, the **Old Bakery** offers first-rate bed and breakfast accommodation. As its name suggests, the house was converted from the former village bakery. The garden here is lovely. Guests look out on some of the few remaining water meadows in England to be properly worked, and an evening stroll across the meadows

18

to the village pub proves an enchanting experience. Valerie is a friendly hostess and excellent cook whose breakfasts are renowned. All three guest rooms are cosy and extremely comfortable, making this a marvellous place to stay and explore the many places of interest in the area.

The Old Bakery   Netton   0722 73351

Having crossed onto the western bank of the River Avon, we drove north along the Woodford Valley towards the A303 trunk road where we turned west towards Stonehenge.

Heale House

For one of the most famous Megalithic sites in Europe, **Stonehenge** appears strangely dwarfed by the open expanse of Salisbury Plain, and it's not until it is approached on foot through the tunnel under the A360 that the true scale of this spectacular Bronze Age monument becomes clear. In fact, some of its great stones stand over twenty feet high and are embedded up to eight feet in the ground. The central area consists of an inner horseshoe and an outer ring of massive sarsen (or 'foreign') stones with lintels which are thought to have been brought all the way from the Marlborough Downs. Some time earlier, a double outer circle of eighty 'bluestones' had been erected which are believed have been quarried in the Preseli Hills in Dyfed and then transported over 200 miles to Salisbury Plain.

Stonehenge

The largest bluestone, the Alter Stone, is set at the very centre of the formation and from here, the Heel Stone can be seen some 256 feet away. On the longest day each year, the sun rises over this stone leading experts to conclude that the site was constructed for the purpose of observing ancient sun worshipping rituals. Stonehenge is owned and managed by English Heritage and is open daily, all year round. Admission charge payable (free to English Heritage and National Trust members).

The A360 Amesbury to Devizes road is one of the few routes across the central expanse of Salisbury Plain. Four miles northwest of Stonehenge and just to the north of this road, we discovered the village of **Orcheston**, a remote community lying at the head of a small river on the edge of Salisbury Plain.

It is here that we discovered the charming accommodation at **Cozens House**. The hosts, Penelope and Antony Smith, are two real country lovers who offer their many guests peace and tranquillity at their detached, self-contained cottage which is fully equipped for self-catering as well as bed and breakfast. There are twin bedrooms, one of which is en suite, and bed and breakfast is also available in the main house. The surrounding gardens are delightful and feature a superb Grade II listed grain store. As a peaceful haven from which to explore nearby Salisbury, Stonehenge, the New Forest and other such places of interest, Cozens House is hard to beat.

Cozens House   Orcheston St. Mary   0980 620257

From Orcheston, we decided to head south once again and retraced our steps onto the A303 near **Winterbourne Stoke**. This village can be easily missed, being tucked away off the main road down a cul-de-sac; however, its charming stone-built cottages, 13th-century church and flint-and-stone-fronted manor house are well worth a detour to see. A series of about twenty burial mounds, or barrows, can be found to the east of the village, most of which were constructed by the Beaker people who migrated here from continental Europe around 2000 BC.

Three miles to the west of Winterbourne Stoke, and just to the north of the A303, lies the spectacular but little-visited Iron Age hill fort of **Yarnbury Castle**. Dating from the 2nd-century BC, the fort's series of grassy banks and ditches enclose an area of some 28 acres which are a haven of tranquillity compared with the organised commotion of Stonehenge. The fort has an earlier earthwork fortification at its centre and enjoys spectacular views over the southern fringe of Salisbury Plain.

A couple of miles to the southwest, the village of **Wylye** was once an important junction and staging post on the London to Exeter coaching route. At one time, the village boasted nine inns although today, only the 14th-century Bell Inn remains. A statue near the bridge over the River Wylye (from which Wilton and Wiltshire get their names) commemorates a post-boy who was sadly drowned after rescuing several passengers

21

from a stagecoach which overturned at this point during a flood.

On leaving Wylye, we joined a minor road which runs parallel to the A36 along the southwestern bank of the river. The six-mile stretch to the southeast of the village contains some delightful unspoilt communities, including the three **Langfords** (Little, Steeple and Hanging) with their chequered flint houses and thatched brick cottages, and **Great Wishford** with its 17th-century almshouses, 18th-century village fire engine and unusual sign on the churchyard wall recording the price of bread at various points in the last 200 years (in 1800 the cost was 3s 4d a gallon, in 1904 only 10d, and in 1924 2s 8d). Each year on Oak Apple Day (May 29th), the citizens of Great Wishford celebrate their ancient right to cut and gather timber in nearby Grovely Wood by marching onto the wooded ridge and returning with freshly cut branches. Later in the day, a party from the village dance on the green in front of Salisbury Cathedral carrying bundles of sticks known as 'nitches'.

Wilton

A little upstream from Great Wishford lies the attractive village of **Stapleford**, site of the Norman castle which once was owned by William the Conqueror's chief huntsman, Waleran. The village church dates from the same period and contains some impressive banded columns. A stone bench can be seen in the church porch which is marked out with the grid of the mediaeval board game, nine men's Morris.

Wilton, the capital of Saxon Wessex and third oldest borough in England, lies on the River Wylye midway between Stapleford and

Salisbury. The town is renowned throughout the world for its carpets which are still woven at the **Royal Wilton Carpet Factory**, an enterprise which was given a royal charter by William III in 1699. The carpets are manufactured along traditional lines from local wool and indeed, four sheep fairs continue to be held each year in the town between August and November. The old part of Wilton is centred around the market square which contains a number of interesting buildings, including an 18th-century town hall and the half-ruined Church of St Mary.

The Royal Wilton Carpet Factory

On the western edge of town, **Wilton House** stands on a site originally occupied by an abbey which was founded by Alfred the Great. After the abbey was dissolved by Henry VIII, this superb piece of land was given to Sir William Herbert who was created Earl of Pembroke in 1551; it has remained in his family ever since. After a devastating fire destroyed the original building in 1647, the house was rebuilt by Inigo Jones who was responsible for creating the magnificent single and double 'cube' rooms with their lavish gilt decorations. At the beginning of last century, the north and west fronts were remodelled by James Wyatt who also designed the Gothic-style cloisters.

Today, Wilton House contains an outstanding collection of works of art including furniture by Chippendale and Kent, and paintings by Rembrandt, Van Dyke, Rubens and Tintoretto. There is also a famous collection of over 7000 model soldiers and a magnificent Tudor kitchen. During World War II, the house was used as an operations centre for southern command and the Normandy landings are believed to have been planned here. The grounds of Wilton House are also well worth discovering. Originally laid out by Isaac de Caus, they are known for their distinctive cedar trees, Roger Morris' Palladian bridge of 1737, and Sir William Chambers' casino. Open daily, 11am (12 noon Sundays) to 6pm between Easter and mid-October. Admission charge payable.

The lovely small village of **Burcombe** lies a couple of miles west of Wilton on the banks of the River Nadder. Those looking for an exceptional place to stay in this attractive part of Wiltshire should make a point of finding Manor Farm.

Wilton House

Situated at the foot of the Downs just a quarter-of-a-mile from the A30 with Salisbury, Stonehenge and the New Forest all within an hour's drive, **Manor Farm** makes a superb touring base. Your friendly hostess, Sue Combes, takes great pride in offering her guests top class accommodation and excellent home cooking. Her enthusiasm and *joie de vivre* is infectious and a stay at here is sure to leave you revitalised and refreshed. Breakfasts here are wonderful; Sue uses only fresh local produce and provides a tasty and substantial meal that sets you up perfectly for the day. The farmhouse's walled garden is a delight, particularly in spring and autumn, as are the walks across the farm onto the Downs.

Four miles to the southwest of Burcombe, the A30 passes close to the famous **Fovant Hill Regimental Badges** which were carved into the side of the chalk escarpment by soldiers stationed nearby during the two

24

World Wars. After taking a look at these, we turned north in Fovant village to reach the two National Trust-owned properties which are located near the lovely hillside village of **Dinton**. The first, **Little Clarendon**, is a small, yet impressive early-Tudor manor house which is located quarter-of-a-mile east of Dinton church; it is open to the public by prior written appointment only. Admission charge payable (free to National Trust members).

Manor Farm   Burcombe   0722 742177

The second property is situated to the west of the village on the northern side of the B3089. **Philipps House** is a handsome white-fronted neo-Grecian residence which was designed by architect Jeffry Wyattville in the early 19th-century. It stands within the attractive landscaped grounds of Dinton Park and is administered and maintained by the Young Women's Christian Association as an arts and cultural centre. Open to the public by prior arrangement only (contact the Warden). Admission charge payable (free to National Trust members). Dinton village also contains the 17th-century **Lawes Cottage** which is the former home of composer and associate of John Milton, William Lawes. Part of his score for Milton's *Masque of Comus* is believed to have been written here in 1634.

The final area we wished to explore in this part of Wiltshire was the delightful upper **Ebble Valley**, so we retraced our steps back to Fovant before continuing southwards along a small country lane towards the Saxon village of **Broad Chalke**. This is the former home of the 17th-century diarist, John Aubrey, whose family owned a small estate in the village. Aubrey was a warden at the parish church and lived in the Old Rectory; he was also a keen angler and wrote of his beloved River Ebble, 'there are not better trouts in the Kingdom of England than here'.

Broad Chalke is also the home of the first-rate **Queen's Head Inn**. The ambience here is best described as one of peace and plenty; there is

25

a lovely inglenook fireplace which adds warmth and character to the bar, and outside, there is a secluded patio garden where customers can enjoy a quiet drink on a fine summer's day. The superb restaurant menu often features local fish and game along with old-fashioned dishes such as jugged hare or game pie, followed by mouthwatering homemade desserts such as chocolate ripple cheesecake or walnut and treacle tart. Finally, having satisfied your appetite, what could be better than to retire to one of the four excellently equipped, self-contained guest rooms which are situated off the rear courtyard.

The Queen's Head   Broadchalke   0722 780344

The gentle landscape of the Ebble Valley contains a number of other pleasant settlements, many of which (Stratford Tony, Stoke Farthing, Fifield Bavant, Ebbesborne Wake) seem to have particularly charming names . Another of these, **Berwick St John**, was the first stop in our next chapter.

CHAPTER TWO

Westbury to the Dorset Border

Chalcot House

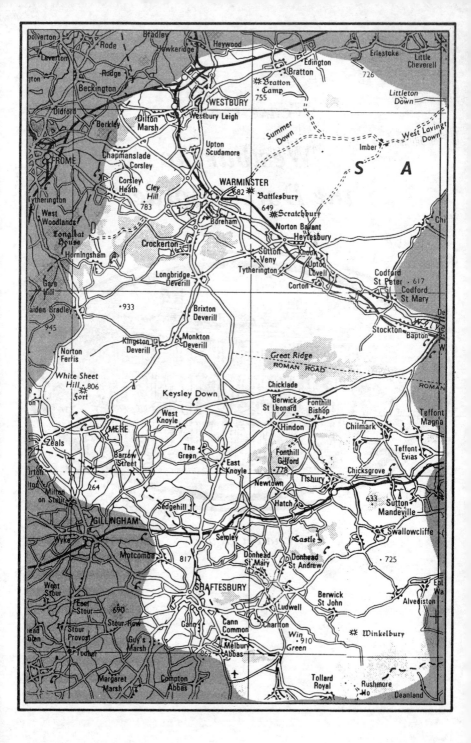

CHAPTER TWO

Index

The Angel Coaching Inn, Heytesbury, Nr Warminster
The Bridge House Restaurant, Nunney, Frome
The George Hotel Inn and B&B, Codford, Nr Warminster
Hurlingpot Farmhouse B&B, Chelynch, Shepton Mallet
Mill Farm B&B, Horningsham, Nr Warminster
Prince Leopold Restaurant and B&B, Upton Lovell, Nr Warminster
Southfield Farm B&B, Rodden, Nr Frome

The Great Portal Entrance to the Main Hall at Wardour Castle

CHAPTER TWO

Westbury To The Dorset Border

The village of **Berwick St John** lies at the head of the Ebble Valley and just to the north of the steep ridge of chalk downland known as Cranborne Chase. According to local legend, it is possible to summon the Devil by cursing at the top of one's voice whilst walking seven times around Winkelbury Camp, the ancient Iron Age hill fort which lies to the north of the village. When called in this manner, Satan is said to appear riding a black horse and will grant his summoner one wish.

The possible appearance of the Devil is perhaps at the root of one of Berwick St John's less unnerving customs. Thanks to a legacy left by the vicar for this purpose, the church bells were tolled for ten minutes at eight o'clock each night to direct travellers lost on the downs to safety, a custom which lasted for over 200 years between the mid-18th-century and the Second World War.

On leaving Berwick St John, we drove westwards towards Ludwell on the A30, before turning south onto the country road which connects with the B3081 Shaftesbury to Tollard Royal road. This road runs along the western edge of the National Trust-owned **Win Green Hill**, the highest point in Cranborne Chase (and indeed, in Wiltshire) which is crowned by a copse of beech trees set around an ancient 'bowl' barrow. From the top of the hill, there are wonderful views northwest to the Mendip Hills and southeast to the Isle of Wight.

The village of **Tollard Royal** stands in the heart of Cranborne Chase a couple of miles to the southeast. The community's royal connections date back to King John who had a small estate here and often hunted on the surrounding land which at that time was densely forested. A reminder of this once-great primeval forest is the fragmented belt of woodland known as the **Inner Chase** which runs along the downland ridge on both sides of Tollard Royal.

The name of King John is reflected in the village inn and in **King John's House**, an impressive part stone, part timber-framed residence dating from the 13th-century which was once a royal hunting lodge. The building's immaculate present condition is largely due to one General Pitt-Rivers, an early and highly enthusiastic English archeologist who inherited the estate in the late 19th-century and spent the last two decades of his life unearthing its many Bronze Age remains. The general founded a museum in the nearby village of Farnham to display his collection of historic discoveries; however, it was closed in the 1960s and its exhibits were transferred to Oxford and to Salisbury's South Wiltshire Museum which has a gallery named after him.

Tollard Royal's late-13th-century village church is dedicated, somewhat unusually, to St Peter Ad Vincula (St Peter in chains); it contains the tomb of General Pitt-Rivers and stands within a delightful churchyard a short distance from the village centre. The general was also responsible for laying out nearby Larmer Tree Gardens, the original 'larmer' tree being the place where King John met up with his hunting party.

From Tollard Royal, we retraced our steps down Zigzag Hill and continued northwestwards along the B3081 towards Shaftesbury. After a couple of miles, we made a short diversion to **Ashmore**, a charming village which lies just over the Dorset border to the west of the main road. At over 700 feet above sea-level, this is the highest village in Dorset; all the more incredible, then, that Ashmore should have a gigantic village pond, 40 yards in diameter and 16 feet deep in the middle. The village is recorded in the Domesday Book as *Aisemare*, the pond by the ash tree, and even in the most severe drought, this unlikely body of water is said never to have dried up. The inhabitants of the village celebrate its continuing presence in the *Filly Loo* ceremony which takes place each year around midsummer; while a band plays on a platform in the centre of the pond, teams of Morris dancers from all over the region dance around the edge.

On leaving Ashmore, we continued northwest along the B3081 for five miles before stopping in the lovely Dorset border town of **Shaftesbury**. Referred to as 'Shaston' in the novels of Thomas Hardy, the town is perhaps best known for its steep cobbled street, **Gold Hill**, which was featured in a famous 1980's television commercial for brown bread. Lined on one side with old cottages and on the other with an enormous mediaeval buttressed wall, this unique curved thoroughfare leads up to a 700 foot summit which provides some glorious views over Blackmoor Vale.

An abbey for nuns was founded in Shaftesbury by King Alfred around 888 AD, his daughter Aethelgifa being the first abbess. Some decades later, the fifteen year-old Anglo-Saxon king, Edward the Martyr, was buried here after being murdered in 978, an event which made Shaftesbury an important place of pilgrimage for many years. The abbey was finally dissolved in 1539 on the orders of Henry VIII; however, shortly before, the abbess is rumoured to have concealed the abbey's considerable treasure somewhere in the town. According to local legend, the only one to know its hiding place is the ghost of a monk who is sometimes seen walking on the site of the old abbey.

From Shaftesbury, we joined the A30 and drove east into Wiltshire for six miles before turning north to reach the village of **Ansty**. Our next destination was **Old Wardour**, a ruined 14th-century castle which is signposted from the village along a narrow lane. In 1643, the 61 year-old Lady Arundel and a garrison of fifty Royalist guards held the castle for six days against a 1300-strong Parliamentarian force. She is believed to have surrendered only after being offered acceptable terms; however, these were immediately disregarded by Cromwell's troops and the indomitable lady was thrown into the castle dungeons from where she is said to have escaped through a secret passage, probably a castle drain. To avenge the Parliamentarian treachery, her son returned to besiege the castle, an operation which eventually led to its destruction.

Wardour Castle

Present-day visitors to Wardour can view the remains of the old castle with its unique hexagonal courtyard and unusual grotto close by. The site stands within the grounds of the 'new' Wardour Castle, an 18th-century Palladian mansion which is now a girls' school and not open to the public. A exceptionally fine baroque chapel adjoins the school which has a striking interior and contains some impressive works of art.

A couple of miles further north, we made a point of stopping in the village of **Tisbury**, home of what is claimed to be the largest surviving tithe barn in England. Tithe barns were constructed to store 'tithes', one tenth of the local farm tenants' crops, which were payable to the owners of church lands. The barn at Tisbury stands on the mediaeval **Place Farm** and once belonged to the Abbess of Shaftesbury's estate. Much of the old farmyard remains, including its impressive 14th-century double gatehouse and nearby outbuildings. The massive 190 foot long barn was built of stone in the 15th-century and has thirteen pairs of storage bays. Its thatched roof covers a third-of-an-acre and its complex structure of timber posts and beams gives it an almost cathedral-like quality.

Elsewhere in Tisbury, the 13th-century village church of St John the Baptist has a splendid carved roof and a pulpit, pews and font-cover dating from the 17th-century. A tall spire stood on top of the church tower until it collapsed in 1762. The elegant Palladian-style Georgian country residence known as **Pyt House** lies two-and-a-half miles west of the village; this was the scene of a famous confrontation between angry farm workers and mounted soldiers during the agricultural protests of 1830. Open Wednesdays and Thursdays, 2.30pm to 5pm between May and September.

A number of interesting small communities lie on the northern side of the Nadder Valley to the northwest of Tisbury. The most westerly of these, **Chilmark**, is the site of the famous quarry from which the stone for Salisbury Cathedral, Wilton House and many other fine buildings in the area was taken. Stone was first quarried here by the Romans and several centuries of workings have left a network of deep tunnels and vaults which are now used by the Ministry of Defence for storing arms and ammunition.

Stone from Chilmark's quarry is much in evidence in the delightful villages of **Teffont Magna** and **Teffont Evias** a couple of miles further east. The settlements take their name from the Anglo-Saxon words *teo*, meaning boundary, and *funta*, meaning brook; the name for the stream which connects them, the Teff, has similar roots. In both villages, the old thatched cottages are connected to the outside world by a series of attractive small bridges over the stream.

Just to the north of Teffont Magna, and on the western side of the minor road which connects the village with the A303, we discovered **Farmer Giles Farmstead**, a 175-acre working livestock farm which is open to visitors. Attractions include a herd of 150 dairy cows, Shire horses, Highland cattle, Shetland ponies, sheep, goats, rabbits and a variety of domestic fowl, all of which can be seen at close quarters.

Visitors can try their hand and milking a Jersey cow or bottle-feeding a baby lamb, or enjoy a leisurely stroll around this beautiful stretch of Wiltshire farmland. There is also an interesting exhibition on the history of farming, a pond stocked with rainbow trout, and children's adventure area containing old tractors and several up-to-date pieces of playground equipment. Open daily, 10.30am to 6pm between late-March and early-November (also weekends during November and December). Admission charge payable.

Just on the other side of the A303 is **Chicklade**. When we were thinking about staying at **The Old Rectory** it was described to us by someone who had previously visited there as a place where you will experience the courtesy and charm of a gentler age; a time when life moved at a more leisurely pace. This was exactly what we found. It is situated in this beautifully unspoilt part of Wessex, where the borders of Wiltshire and Dorset meet with Somerset.

The Old Rectory   Chicklade   074789 226

It is as if time has passed by this beautiful area, with its rolling hills, quiet lanes and clear streams, and yet you are within easy motoring distance of such centres as Bath, Salisbury and Blandford. In addition there are many interesting gardens, such as Stourhead, as well as the stately homes of Longleat and Wilton. The Rectory is a fascinating house, full of period charm and character, and parts of the building date back to the 17th century. The gardens are beatiful, having been lovingly cared for and of course with the advantage of trees and shrubs that have matured over the years.

The accomodation offers spacious and comfortable bedrooms, furnished in a traditional style, each having hot and cold water, razor points and electric heaters. If you have young children, Mr and Mrs Ballard, who own The Old Rectory, will be delighted to babysit for you. You will take your meals ina lovely sunny room, decorated in soft pinks and greys which highlight the highly polished dark wood of the tables and chairs. The Old Rectory is licensed, so you will be able to enjoy a drink if you wish.

The George Hotel   Codford   0985 50270

Heading northwards once again, we joined the A303 for a short distance before turning northwest onto the minor road which runs parallel to the A36 Salisbury to Warminster road. This road follows the course of the upper Wylye river and passes through a series of charming small settlements. An Elizabethan merchant named Topp was responsible for building **Stockton House**, a handsome residence with mullioned windows and banded flint stonework; he also constructed Stockton's elegant almshouses which are set around three sides of a square courtyard a short distance away.

Next, we decided to have a look at the sister villages of **Codford St Mary** and **Codford St Peter**, so we turned north a short distance upstream from Stockton and crossed both the River Wylye and A36. The villages lie beneath the prehistoric remains of **Codford Circle**, an ancient hilltop meeting place which stands 617 feet up on Salisbury Plain. The church in Codford St Peter contains an exceptional Saxon stone carving which is said to date from the 9th-century. Thought to be part of a stone cross, it features a man holding a branch who is engaged in some kind of ritual dance. It is a surprisingly powerful piece and is widely regarded as one of Wiltshire's finest treasures.

We decided to break our journey in **Codford** and were fortunate enough to discover the impressive **George Hotel**, a first-rate establishment which stands in the heart of the village. Located on the edge of Salisbury Plain and within easy reach of the Marlborough Downs and the Nodden Valley, this charming hostelry is a marvellous place to stay. The restaurant here serves an extensive and varied menu which includes such mouthwatering dishes as deep-fried Camembert, homemade steak and

36

oyster pie, and chicken Kiev. There are also various bar snacks available ranging from wholesome sandwiches to substantial hot meals. The George also offers an imaginative vegetarian menu and has a well-deserved reputation for using fresh, local produce. Whatever your tastes, this is the ideal base for touring this lovely part of the country.

Prince Leopold   Upton Lovell   0985 50460

A mile or so further upstream at **Upton Lovell** we discovered the **Prince Leopold**, a lovely inn dating back to 1887 which stands on the banks of the River Wylye. It was named after Queen Victoria's youngest son who used to drink here when he lived in nearby Boyton. Today, it is a popular establishment run by Pamela and Graham Walden-Bradley which offers a wide selection of real ales and an extensive range of first-class bar meals; alternatively, you can enjoy an intimate dinner in the charming restaurant. There are also four lovely en suite guest rooms available and at the end of the evening, you will be glad you decided to stay. The Prince Leopold also has easy access to historic Bath, Salisbury, Longleat and Stonehenge providing you with ideas for the next day's touring.

Our continuing journey up the Wylye Valley led us to the old ecclesiastical centre of **Heytesbury**. During Norman times, the village church of St Peter and St Paul was a collegiate institution with its own dean and chapter of canons. Much of this fine cruciform building dates from the 13th-century, though like many of its rural counterparts throughout Wiltshire and Gloucestershire, the building was extensively 'restored' during the Victorian era. On this occasion, however, the refurbishment was carried out under the careful supervision of architect William Butterfield. The present-day church interior contains a number of interesting features, including some fine fan-vaulting and an intricate stone screen in the north transept. The almshouse known as the Hospital of St John was founded in Heytesbury by the Hungerford family during the 15th-century. The original structure burnt down in the mid-18th-century and was replaced by the Georgian building which can be seen today.

Angel Coaching Inn   Heytesbury 0985 40330

Heytesbury's ecclesiastical past is reflected in the name of its splendid pub, the **Angel Coaching Inn**. Standing in the heart of the old village, this delightful establishment is run by Sue Smith and Philip Roose-Francis. A true hostelry, it preserves the tradition of good food, fine ale and first-class accommodation. Sue is a Cordon Bleu chef and the restaurant food is both mouthwatering and beautifully presented, whilst Philip maintains equally high standards in the bars which serve excellent real ales and a quality wine list which includes some very rare vintages. The beautifully-appointed bedrooms all have en suite facilities and provide an atmosphere of great charm and comfort. This really is an enchanting place to stay and one not to be missed when visiting this lovely part of Wiltshire.

One of the strangest villages in Wiltshire lies within the Salisbury Plain military training area to the north of Heytesbury. The ghost-village of **Imber** remains permanently out-of-bounds to the public except on the one or two occasions each year when special permission to go there is granted by the Ministry of Defence. The inhabitants were evicted from their homes by the army in 1943 on the understanding that they would be allowed to return after the War. However, the MoD failed to keep its promise and the villagers remain in exile to this day. All that remains of their community is the shell of the parish church and a collection of decaying timber and brick-built cottages, many of which have been given concrete frontages to provide more realistic conditions for training soldiers in modern street fighting. A church service is held in the village each September in commemoration of the lost community.

On leaving Heytesbury, we drove northwest along the A36 for a mile before turning west onto the B3095. A nine-mile direct drive led us to the small town of **Mere**, a historic community which, thankfully, is now bypassed by the A303 trunk route. The town takes its name from one John Mere, a 14th-century merchant adventurer who founded a chantry in the church of St Michael's. The church dates back to the 11th-century and has a fine Perpendicular tower, one of the pinnacles of which has been hit by lightning three times this century, belying the old saying that lightning never strikes twice in the same place. Inside, there is some fine mediaeval glass, an octagonal font and a pair of monumental brasses believed to date from 1398 and 1426.

Mere

The Dorset dialect poet, William Barnes, lived adjacent to the church in the handsome 15th-century **Old Chantry**; he also ran his own school in a room above the **Old Market Hall** in the town square. The square is also the site of a Victorian clock tower which was gifted to the townspeople by the Prince of Wales in 1868. Among the other distinctive buildings in Mere are its two old coaching inns, the **Old Ship** with its 18th-century wrought-iron sign commemorating the family crest of John Mere, and the **Talbot** which claims to have been visited by Charles II following the Royalist defeat in the Battle of Worcester (he is said to have gone on to stay at Zeals House, a couple of miles further west). Magnificent views over Blackmoor Vale can be enjoyed from the top of nearby Castle Hill, the site of a now-demolished fortification built by Richard, Earl of Cornwall.

We left Mere along the Frome road, passing under the A303 a mile-or-so to the west of the town. A couple of miles further on, we turned west off the B3092 to reach **Stourton**, home of the famous **Stourhead House and Gardens**. The village itself is a neat community of estate cottages which lies at the bottom of a steep wooded valley (cars are normally left in the car park on the ridge above); it is especially pretty during the daffodil season, and again in early-summer. The main attraction here, however, is the beautiful country house and landscaped grounds which make up the famous Stourhead estate.

The house at Stourhead was built between 1722 and 1724 (the library and picture gallery were added a few years later) for a wealthy Bristol banker, Henry Hoare. It was designed in Palladian style by architect Colen Campbell and is one of the first examples of a Georgian country mansion. The interior contains a superb collection of works of art, including furniture by Chippendale the Younger, intricate woodcarving by Grinling Gibbons and a collection of paintings and sculpture by such artists as Angelica Kauffman and Michael Rysbrack.

Stourhead House and Gardens

However, it was the original owner's son, the second Henry Hoare, who made the biggest impression on the estate. Between 1741 and 1780, he designed and laid out one of the finest 18th-century gardens in Europe.

40

Using a wide range of classical and contemporary influences, he created a wonderful combination of carefully designed vistas and woodland walks. Special features include the 14th-century **High Cross** which was brought here from Bristol in 1765, a graceful stone bridge over the lake, a neo-Roman pantheon and an exquisite white-painted stone rotunda known as the **Temple of the Sun**.

The gardens also contain a magnificent range of rare trees and shrubs, including rhododendrons, azaleas and tulip trees, and are crisscrossed by a series of beautiful woodland walks and open pathways. In 1946, the Hoare family presented Stourhead to the National Trust who have continued the process of introducing unusual plant varieties. House open daily (except Thursdays and Fridays), 12 noon to 5.30pm between 1st April and 1st November; garden open daily, 8am to 7pm (or dusk if earlier), all year round. Admission charge payable (free to National Trust members).

On the northwestern edge of the estate, a 160 foot triangular redbrick folly stands at the top of the 790 foot Kingsettle Hill. **King Alfred's Tower** was built by Flitcroft in 1772 in commemoration of the great King of Wessex who is believed to have raised his standard against the Danes at this point in 878. Those climbing to the top are rewarded with a glorious view which takes in the three counties of Wiltshire, Dorset and Somerset. The tower lies three-and-a-half miles by road from Stourhead House and is open daily (except Mondays and Fridays), 2pm to 5.30pm between 1st April and 1st November. Admission charge payable (free to National Trust members). The Trust also owns **Whitesheet Hill**, the site of an Iron Age hill fort, which can be found on the Stourhead estate some distance northeast of the main gardens.

On leaving Stourhead, we rejoined the B3092 and headed north in the direction of Frome. After three miles, we reached the village of Maiden Bradley and turned east into a country lane to reach the ancient village of **Horningsham**. The village name is believed to mean 'bastard's farm' from the Early English words *horning*, meaning bastard, and *ham* meaning farm. Reference to the settlement is made in the Domesday Book of 1086, although evidence exists of earlier occupation by the Romans. Noteworthy buildings in the present-day village include St John the Baptist's church with its mediaeval tower, the 18th-century Bath Arms inn, a row of 14th- to 16th-century thatched almshouses, and the historic Old Meeting Place which was built in 1568 as a place of worship by Presbyterian masons who were brought down from Scotland to work at Longleat House.

Top quality farmhouse accommodation can be found at Horningsham's **Mill Farm**, a delightful establishment in a wonderful tranquil location.

Run by John and Vera Crossman, this beautiful Georgian mill has been providing first-class bed and breakfast accommodation for more than thirty years. To the front, there is a truly picturesque mill lake with resident swans, ducks and geese which is part of the Longleat Estate. Set in a perfect picture-postcard location and built on several different levels, the converted Mill House offers attractively furnished guest rooms with superb views. The house combines the old Butcher's and Baker's farms which, together with Mill Farm, supported the self-sufficient village of Horningsham for over 250 years.

Mill Farm   Horningsham   0985 844333

One of England's most famous stately homes, **Longleat House**, lies a mile to the north of Horningsham. This magnificent Elizabethan mansion was designed by Robert Smythson for Sir John Thynne, an ancestor of the present-day owner, the Marquess of Bath. Built to a largely symmetrical design, the imposing three-storey building was begun in 1568 and was still under construction at the time of Thynne's death in 1580. Over the centuries, the house has been furnished with some superb furniture and works of art, including tapestries, velvet and leather work, and paintings by Titian and Reynolds. Other noteworthy features include the state coach, the Victorian kitchen, the family's official robes and the waistcoat worn by Charles I at the time of this execution.

One of Longleat's most notorious inhabitants is the ghostly Green Lady who is said to wander the top-floor corridor. She is believed to be the spirit of Louisa Carteret whose husband, Thomas Thynne (the second Viscount Weymouth) is alleged to have killed her lover in a duel. He then concealed the body in the cellar where it remained until it was accidentally discovered under the stone-flagged floor earlier this century.

The grounds of Longleat House were landscaped by Capability Brown and now contain one of the best-known safari parks in the country. The famous 'Lions of Longleat' are joined by a number of other exotic animals, including elephants, rhinos, zebras and white tigers. The park also features safari boat rides, a narrow gauge railway, children's amusement area, garden centre and maze, and can be very crowded on summer weekends. House open daily, all year round; safari park open daily, except during the winter months. Admission charge payable.

Longleat House

After spending some time at Longleat, we returned to the B3092 and continued northwards across the Somerset border. A couple of miles south of Frome, we turned west off the main road and went in search of the farmhouse accommodation which is offered by Mrs Clifford at Southfield Farm near the hamlet of **Rodden**.

Enjoying an idyllic location on the banks of the River Frome just three miles from Longleat House, **Southfield Farm** is a superb touring base which provides absolutely first-class accommodation and service. Mrs Clifford is an accomplished hostess who welcomes families into her lovely home, a converted farmhouse built in 1350 which boasts its own 40 foot wishing well. All six guest rooms are en suite and furnished to the highest standards. After a refreshing night's rest, you will find yourself spoilt for choice at the breakfast table, with a selection including yoghurt, free range eggs, ham, cheese, fruit and more besides. Open from April to September, a stay here is sure to leave you with fond memories of a peaceful break away from it all.

Next, we wanted to have a look at the village of **Nunney**, and having crossed the River Frome, we diverted westwards along the A361 for a couple of miles, before turning north to reach this ancient mediaeval settlement. Nunney's focus is its picturesque ruined castle; this was begun in 1373 by Sir John de la Mare on his return from the wars in France and is thought to be modelled on the Bastille. The structure is made up of four solidly-built towers which stand on an island formed by a stream on one side and a wide ten-foot-deep moat on the other. The castle came under Parliamentarian artillery fire during the English Civil War despite having a garrison of only one officer, eight men and a number of civilian refugees. After two days, the building was damaged beyond repair and the gallant Royalists surrendered.

Southfield Farm   *Rodden*   *0373 462348*

One of the thirty-pound cannonballs which helped to demolish the castle walls is on view in Nunney's 13th-century All Saints' Church. This much-altered building also contains an interesting model of the castle in its original condition, as well as a number of tombs to the de la Mare family, including a stone effigy of Sir John. Nunney's old Market Place, which was granted a trading licence by the Crown in 1260, is also worth a visit.

Visitors to Nunney should also make a point of calling in at the charming **Bridge House**, an absolutely delightful Grade II listed house which is situated alongside Nunney Brook in the centre of this ancient mediaeval settlement. Your hostess Christine Edgely welcomes you with a smile into her enchanting home with its outstanding views of the surrounding countryside. She has a number of comfortable and attractively decorated en suite guest rooms available, whilst downstairs there is a lovely intimate restaurant where diners can savour a variety of mouthwatering dishes ranging from the traditional to the more creative, accompanied by a bottle from carefully selected wine list. Take time to

44

browse in Christine's lovely antique and bric-a-brac shop before exploring the castle or venturing out to some of the many other local places of interest.

The Bridge House   Nunney   0373 836329

Those keen to find an exceptional place to stay on the beautiful eastern fringe of the Mendip Hills should make the trip to **Chelynch** near **Doulting**, five miles further west along the A361. You would have to go a long way to beat the farmhouse accommodation at **Hurlingpot Farm**, an attractive working dairy farm which lies somewhat hidden in the heart of this delightful settlement. The home of Jean Keevil, her wonderful Grade II listed Jacobean farmhouse is set in a Tudor walled garden containing beautiful flowers and a 150 year-old monkey puzzle tree. Inside, there are three elegantly furnished en suite guest rooms which offer every modern facility. The lovely country-style kitchen has a warm, bright atmosphere and provides the perfect setting for the superb breakfasts Jean serves each morning.

Hurlingpot Farmhouse   Chelynch   0749 880256

Retracing our steps towards Frome, we joined the town's southern bypass before turning southeast onto the A362. Our next port of call was **Warminster**, a historic wool and coaching town with three old inns and some handsome 18th- and 19th-century buildings. The organ in the 14th-century minster church was originally intended for Salisbury cathedral; similarly, Warminster's famous school, which was founded in 1707, contains a doorway which was designed by Christopher Wren and was originally installed at Longleat House. Two miles to the west, the 800 foot **Cley Hill** forms part of the ancient Ridgeway which once ran from South Devon to the Wash.

On leaving Warminster, we drove northwards along the A350 to the small market town of **Westbury** with its fine Georgian houses, impressive town hall and pleasant little market place. However, Westbury's best-known feature lies a couple of miles to the east of the town on the side of the 755 foot-high Westbury Hill. Here, Wiltshire's oldest and most famous **White Horse** can be found which was carved into the chalk hillside in the 18th-century. (An earlier figure is believed to have been carved here to commemorate King Alfred's defeat of the Danes in 878.) The head of the White Horse stands just below the ramparts of **Bratton Castle**, a spectacular Iron Age hill fort which covers 25 acres and can be reached via Bratton village. Those climbing to the top will be rewarded with outstanding views over the surrounding countryside and farmland.

Two miles to the east of Bratton, the village of **Edington** possesses a 14th-century church of almost cathedral-like proportions. During a rebellion against Henry VI's corrupt government in 1450, the Bishop of Salisbury was dragged from here and stoned to death on top of nearby Golden Ham Hill. Today, Edington is a peaceful place full of unspoilt rural charm and from here we set off northwards along the country lanes into the area covered in our next chapter.

CHAPTER THREE

Trowbridge to Chippenham

Great Chalfield Manor

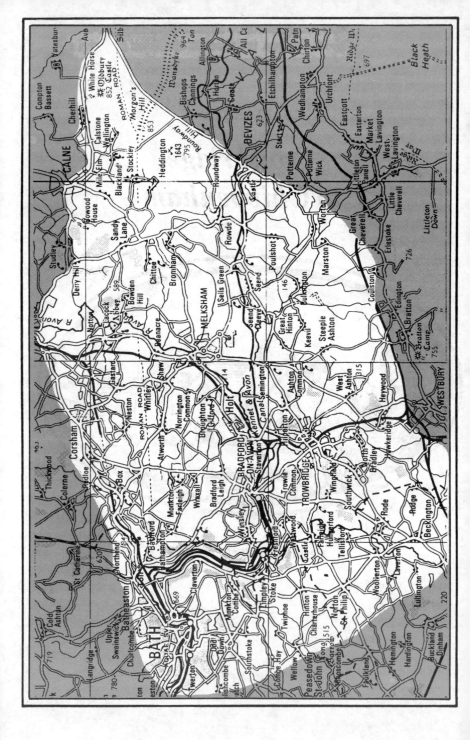

CHAPTER THREE

Index

75 High Street B&B, Corsham, Wiltshire

Arnolds Hill Guest House, Wingfield, Nr Trowbridge

Ashton Hill Farm Accomodation, Trowbridge, Wiltshire

Audrey's Tea Room, Corsham, Wiltshire

Bridge Cottage B&B, Bathford, Bath

Brookfield House B&B, Vaggs Hill, Trowbridge

Cheney Cottage B&B, Ditteridge, Wiltshire

Church Farm B&B, Steeple Ashton, Nr Trowbridge

Fern Cottage B&B, Forest, Melksham

Frane Lea Park Self-Catering, Forest, Melksham

King John's Hunting Lodge Tea Rooms, Lacock, Nr Chippenham

Lock Inn Cottage Tea Gardens, 48 Frome Road, Bradford-on-Avon

Magnolia Lodge B&B, 46 Wingfield Road, Trowbridge

Midway Cottage B&B, Farleigh Wick, Nr Bradford-on-Avon

Piccadilly Caravan Site, Lacock, Chippenham

Pickwick Lodge Farm B&B, Corsham, Wiltshire

The Stone Barn B&B, Atworth, Wiltshire

Thurlestone Lodge B&B, Corsham, Wiltshire

Trudy Oatley Interior Design, Cherhill, Wiltshire

Wick Farm Fishing, Caravan Park and B&B, Lacock, Chippenham

Woodlands B&B, Iford Hill, Nr Bradford-on-Avon

Woolley Grange Hotel and Restaurant, Woolley Green, Bradford-
    on-Avon

The Woolpack Inn, Beckington, Nr Bath

CHAPTER THREE

Trowbridge
To Chippenham

The first stop on our tour around the western area of central Wiltshire was the attractive village of **Steeple Ashton**. Set within tranquil country lanes four miles to the southeast of Trowbridge, the most striking feature in the village is its 15th-century parish church of St Mary the Virgin which, curiously enough, has no steeple (the original 93 foot spire was destroyed by lightning in 1670 and was never rebuilt). As well as some fine lierne vaulting and part-mediaeval stained-glass window lights, this impressive Perpendicular structure contains the renowned **Samuel Hey Library** which numbers among its catalogue the early-15th-century *Book of Hours*, an illustrated Latin prayer book containing recommended worship for every hour of the day.

Steeple Ashton

51

Other noteworthy features in Steeple Ashton include the Norman village cross with its four sundials, and the long main street with its unusual number of delightful old buildings, many of which are half-timbered and feature attractive red herringbone brickwork.

Church Farm   Steeple Ashton   0380 870518

First-rate farmhouse accommodation is also available here at **Church Farm**, a working farm which is situated adjacent to Steeple Ashton's famous church. The truly unique farmhouse is largely constructed of soft red bricks set within a timber frame and has parts dating back to the 16th-century. Inside, the bedrooms and reception rooms all have a marvellous quaint atmosphere yet have been tastefully updated to provide all the modern comforts. Mrs Cottle provides the warmest of welcomes including tea and farmhouse cake on arrival. Guests should make a point of finding the charming thatched summer house where they can relax and enjoy the sounds of the English countryside.

Next, we headed westwards along the country lanes and after a couple of miles, found ourselves in Steeple Ashton's sister village of **West Ashton**. This pleasant community is home to another excellent bed and breakfast establishment, **Ashton Hill Farm**, a lovely place to stay which can be found just off the Melksham to Westbury road. Sheena Awdry is your friendly welcoming hostess who goes out of her way to make you feel at home on her family's 400-acre working arable and beef farm. She is an excellent cook and will readily prepare a tasty farmhouse tea given prior notice. Enjoying a peaceful location on the banks of the River Biss, this is an ideal location for touring the Cotswolds, the West Country and Wiltshire. Children are welcome and guests are free to take a look around the farm, but check before you set off or you may meet up with Eric and Ernie, the pedigree bulls!

On leaving West Ashton, we joined the A350 for a short distance before turning northwest onto the A363 and then, after half-a-mile, west onto the minor road which passes through the village of North Bradley en route to Southwick. Here, we turned southwest onto the A361 and made a short detour over the Somerset border to visit **Beckington**, an attractive village with some fine attractions for visitors: a mediaeval castle, a 13th-century abbey, a church with a Norman tower and some lovely old gabled houses.

Ashton Hill Farm   West Ashton   0225 760359

In the heart of the village, we also discovered the locally-renowned **Woolpack Inn**, a superb 16th-century hostelry which has been sympathetically restored to provide every modern comfort in an atmosphere of mellow antiquity. The atmosphere in the bars and restaurant is cosy and welcoming. The food, too, is a sheer delight; the extensive menu offers excellent value for money and features such superb dishes as local game and fresh fish from Brixham. In fine weather, you can also eat outside in the high-walled, creeper-clad patio garden. The Woolpack's ten en suite guest rooms are beautifully furnished and provide first-class accommodation in keeping with the age and character of the building.

On leaving Beckington, we joined the main A36 Salisbury to Bath road for a mile-and-a-half before turning northwest onto the B3110 to reach the historic village of **Norton St Philip**. Much of the settlement's history seems to centre around the George, a wonderful old inn built in the 15th-century by nearby Hinton Priory as a house of hospitality. This exceptional timber-framed building has oriel windows, a gallery to the rear, an unusual archway, and an overhanging first floor which was once used a cloth warehouse. The rebellious Duke of Monmouth made his headquarters here before the Battle of Sedgemoor in 1685, and according to legend, nine local men implicated in the ill-fated uprising were imprisoned here after the battle (in what is now the Dungeon Bar), before being burnt at the stake in a nearby orchard. Some years earlier in 1668, there is a record of Samuel Pepys and his wife having dined at the George whilst on their way to Bath.

The village church of St Philip was rebuilt in the 17th-century and is believed to contain the grave of the Siamese-twin sisters who were born in the nearby hamlet of Foxcote. Their tombstone is now lost but is said to have been carved with a likeness of the girls who had 'two bodies upward and one stomach.'

The Woolpack Inn   Beckington   0373 831244

From Norton St Philip, we drove back towards the Wiltshire border along the A366 Trowbridge road. Our next stop was **Farleigh Hungerford**, site of the once-impressive Farleigh Castle which was built in the late 14th-century by Sir Thomas Hungerford, the first Speaker of the House of Commons. Sir Thomas had acquired the old manor house on the site and is said to have started to fortify the building without having first obtained permission from the Crown, a potentially serious offence which could have led to his disgrace. However, the Hungerfords were a powerful family who at one time owned land all the way to Salisbury and so were able to survive the king's displeasure.

In the 16th-century, however, one member of the Hungerford family did succeed in upsetting royal sensibilities by locking up his wife for four years in one of the castle towers. He was eventually executed by Henry VII for 'treason and unnatural vice'. In the early 18th-century, the castle changed hands; however, the new owners saw the edifice more as a quarry than a place to live and removed most of the walls to build a new Gothic-style house on the opposite side of the village.

Nevertheless, an impressive shell of towers and perimeter walls survived which was brought under the ownership of English Heritage earlier this century. The castle chapel of St Leonard's also remains intact; this contains an impressive 15th-century mural of St George, some striking stained glass, and a number of interesting tombs, including that

54

of the first Sir Thomas Hungerford. Open daily, 9.30am (2pm Sundays) to 6.30pm (4pm in winter), all year round. Admission charge payable.

A minor road to the north of Farleigh Hungerford led us to the village of **Westwood**, site of the National Trust-owned **Westwood Manor**. This charming stone-built manor house was constructed in the 15th-century and then remodelled in the late 16th-century. Its attractive landscaped grounds contain an interesting display of modern topiary, and inside there are a number of impressive period features including some fine Jacobean plasterwork. Open Sundays, Tuesdays and Wednesdays, 2pm to 5pm between 1st April and end-September. Admission charge payable (free to National Trust members).

Iford Manor

Another interesting country house, **Iford Manor**, lies just to the west of Westwood. Although this handsome Tudor residence is not open to the public, its gardens are. Indeed, visitors come from all over the world to enjoy the grounds which were laid out in Italian style by the landscape architect Harold Peto prior to the First World War. The design is said to have been inspired by Edwin Lutyens and Gertrude Jekyll, and makes imaginative use of its idyllic setting beside the River Frome. Behind the house, the land rises sharply in a series of delightful terraces, and there are a number of pools, summerhouses and classical buildings which give the entire garden a wonderful romantic feel. Open Wednesdays, Sundays and Bank Holiday Mondays between May and July. Admission charge payable.

Those wishing to stay in the vicinity of Westwood or Iford Manors should make a point of finding **Woodlands** at nearby **Iford**. Woodlands is a lovely house set in a superb, totally secluded setting on the edge of this peaceful hamlet. Home to Dorothy and Ken Farrell, it provides the perfect place for visitors to stay and enjoy the tranquil beauty of the surrounding countryside. Dorothy offers a warm welcome to all her guests. Her beautifully-appointed guest rooms all have lovely views over the impressive three-quarter acre garden. Guests are only a 200-yard walk from Iford Gardens, and many other famous gardens and beauty spots also lie within easy reach. A comfortable overnight stay here is assured, so for a quiet time away from the stresses of everyday life, Woodlands offers the perfect combination of a lovely home, a delightful garden and a completely relaxed setting. *Iford Hill   0225 862703*

Did you know....

When Box Tunnel was built in 1841, it was the longest railway tunnel in the world?

see page 67

From Iford, we joined the B3109 and drove southwards for a mile to reach **Wingfield**, an attractive small community which stands near the junction of the A366. This ancient village boasts is mentioned in the Domesday Book and boasts a fine 13th-century church.

Wingfield is also the location of **Arnolds Hill House**, a renowned country guesthouse which is situated on the edge of the village. This impressive residence was designed with the help of the great architect Edward Lutyens; he succeeded in creating a building with an air of tranquil Edwardian grandeur which is set within extensive landscaped grounds containing a swimming pool and a splendid sun terrace. The guest bedrooms are comfortable and enjoy wonderful views over the surrounding Wiltshire countryside. Proprietors Marjorie and Derek Dore extend a warm welcome to non-smoking guests in the elegant surroundings of their beautiful home.

A short journey along the B3109 to the south of Wingfield village led us to **Vaggs Hill**, home of the first-class place to stay, **Brookfield House**.

Tastefully converted from an ancient barn, this handsome building is the charming home of Duncan and Julia Parry, two fine hosts who provide accommodation in several spacious, beautifully furnished en suite guest rooms, all of which are equipped with excellent modern facilities. Downstairs, the residents' lounge, conservatory and dining room are of an equally high standard. The attractive garden offers panoramic views, and good local fishing and countryside walks are also available nearby. As a touring base for Bath, the Cotswolds and Salisbury Plain, Brookfield House really is beyond compare.

Arnolds Hill House   Wingfield   0225 752025

A two-mile journey along the A366 to the east of Wingfield led us into the heart of the lovely old town of **Trowbridge**. Now the county town of Wiltshire, the roots of Trowbridge go back beyond the Domesday Book. The modern town grew up around the Norman castle which belonged to the de Bohun family, the curved walls of which are indicated by the course of present-day Fore Street.

Brookfield House   Vaggs Hill   0373 830615

For centuries, Trowbridge was an important weaving centre and by 1830, as many as nineteen mills were sited in the town. An unusual number of handsome stone-built townhouses can be seen in the present-day centre, most of which date from this period of prosperity.

The remodelled parish Church of St James was founded in 1483 by a wealthy cloth-maker on the site of its 12th-century predecessor (it was altered once again during the 19th-century). It contains some lavish decorations and is crowned by one of the finest parish church spires in the county. The churchyard contains the grave of Thomas Helliber, a local weaver who allegedly led a rebellion against the introduction of cloth-making machinery; despite claiming his innocence, he was hanged in 1803 on the morning of his nineteenth birthday. The tomb of George Crabbe, one of the former church rectors, can be found in the chancel; an acknowledged poet, he was responsible for writing the work on which Benjamin Britten based his opera, *Peter Grimes*.

Another of Trowbridge's famous sons was Sir Isaac Pitman, the creator of the famous shorthand system, who was born in a now-demolished house in Nash Yard; Pitman Avenue, and a plaque and bust in the town hall commemorate his links with the town. An interesting collection of historic artefacts and locally-found relics are on display at the **Trowbridge Museum** in the civic hall. Items on show include a special collection of educational toys and children's games dating from the 18th-century. Open Tuesdays and Saturdays, 9.30am to 12.30pm, all year round.

Did you know....

There is a full list of Tourist Information Centres?

on page 323

Magnolia Lodge   Trowbridge   0225 763093

On the western side of Trowbridge David and Christine Harris, two charming hosts, run the first-rate bed and breakfast establishment, **Magnolia Lodge**. David is a former professional horticulturalist and his vast knowledge of plants is reflected in the many rare and exotic shrubs which can be found in the garden. The house itself is an elegant late-

Victorian town villa with a bright welcoming atmosphere and a number of spacious bedrooms which are all appointed to a high modern standard. David and Christine provide their guests with warm hospitality and a first-rate Wiltshire breakfast. Given prior notice, they can also provide delicious evening meals which are served in the pleasant airy surroundings of the dining room.

Before moving on to Bradford-on-Avon, we decided to have a look at **Melksham**, a busy market town which is located five miles along the A361 and A350 to the northeast of Trowbridge. William the Conqueror is said to have granted the village of Melksham to his knight Britric Aluric, an event which is recollected in the name of the present-day Aloeric School. Like Trowbridge, Melksham was an important weaving centre and the large number of substantial 17th- and 18th-century merchants' houses around Canon Square stand as a testimony to this prosperous time.

Frane Lea Park   Forest   0225 707778

Early in the 19th-century, Melksham attempted to become a spa town following the discovery of a chalybeate spring and indeed a pump room was built which can still be seen on the Devizes road. However, competition from the more fashionable Bath Spa soon stifled its ambitions and by 1822 the project was abandoned. The destiny of the town turned out to lie with manufacturing and in 1819, a branch of the Wiltshire and Berkshire Canal was opened to link the town's many industrial concerns with the outside world. Although much changed, the town still retains its industrial feel.

In the 13th- and 14th-centuries, the once densely forested countryside around Melksham was an important royal hunting area and indeed, the area to the northeast of the town is still known as **Melksham Forest**. Over the years, the forest has largely been cleared of trees, first for agricultural

59

use and then, as Melksham's cloth-weaving industry continued to expand, for house building.

Today, the Forest is home to **Frane Lea Park**, a first-rate holiday park offering excellent self-catering accommodation. The park is situated within the landscaped grounds of a former farmhouse in Church Lane; it is a modern purpose-built development of seven single-storey cottages which is owned and immaculately maintained by Mr and Mrs Frane. The attractive luxury cottages vary in size and can accommodate either two, four or six persons. All are furnished and appointed to a very high standard with fully-equipped fitted kitchens, colour televisions and private gardens.

After returning to the centre of Melksham, we joined the A365 Box road and drove northwest for a couple of miles to reach the pleasant community of **Atworth**. The village church of St Michael dates from the early-19th-century, with the exception of its saddleback tower which survives from an earlier rebuilding in the 15th-century.

The Stone Barn   Atworth   0225 706410

Atworth is also the location of a delightful place to stay, the **Stone Barn** at **Manor Farm**. Situated just three miles from Bradford-upon-Avon, this Grade II listed building has undergone extensive renovation and now provides first-class accommodation either on a bed and breakfast or self-catering basis. The rooms are all decorated and equipped to the highest standards with beautifully coordinated furnishings throughout. From the spacious breakfast room guests look out onto their own private garden, a real summer sun trap, and if they can tear themselves away, there are many interesting places within easy reach, such as historic Bath, the Kennet and Avon Canal, and slightly further afield, Stonehenge and Longleat.

The narrow country lanes to the south of Atworth led us to the National Trust-owned **Great Chalfield Manor**, a superb Tudor manor house which lies three miles due west of Melksham. Begun in 1480, this delightful moated residence was built by Thomas Tropenell who also was responsible for constructing the bell tower and spire on the nearby 13th-century parish church. The house is approached through an arched gateway and across a polished stone courtyard which is overlooked by oriel windows. Inside, the many noteworthy features include an original Tudor screen, a impressive great hall and a dining room which contains a portrait of Tropenell. Great Chalfield Manor is lived in by the descendants of Major R Fuller who carried out substantial restoration work earlier this century. Open for guided tours on Tuesdays, Wednesdays and Thursdays between 1st April and end-October. Admission charge payable (free to National Trust members).

Great Chalfield Manor

Another National Trust-owned property lies a mile or so to the south of Great Chalfield in the village of **Holt**. Known as **The Courts**, this was where local weavers came to settle their disputes until the end of the 18th-century. The present-day building was constructed in neo-Gothic style around 1800 though it has an elegant decorated façade dating from around a century earlier. Regrettably, it is not open to the public; visitors are however welcome to tour the magnificent seven-acre garden, half of which is arranged in formal style with a lily pond, herbaceous borders and dividing yew hedges, and the rest being a wild garden with an arboretum. Open daily (except Saturdays), 2pm to 5pm between 1st April and 1st November. Admission charge payable (free to National Trust members).

Holt itself consists of a series of handsome 17th- and 18th-century houses set around a village green. The village was once a popular spa and indeed the old well can still be seen in the grounds of a local factory.

From Holt, we drove westwards along the B3107 to reach the historic town of **Bradford-on-Avon**. A settlement existed on this important riverside site long before the days of the Domesday Book; indeed, the town's oldest building, the Saxon church of St Lawrence, is believed to have been built by St Aldhelm around 700 AD. Once part of a monastery which was largely destroyed by the Danes, the building 'disappeared' for over a thousand years, during which time the townspeople used it as a school, a charnel house for storing the bones of the dead, and a residential dwelling.

Bradford-on-Avon

In 1858, a clergyman looking down from the hill above the town detected the cruciform shape of a church; further investigations on the site revealed two carved angels, a discovery which precipitated the removal of the surrounding buildings and led to the uncovering of the Saxon gem which can be seen today. Only 38 feet long and with a chancel arch only three feet wide, it is one of the smallest churches in the country.

Bradford-on-Avon also boasts an attractive Norman church which was extensively restored in the last century. Inside, it contains a number of interesting memorials including that of Lieutenant-General Henry Shrapnel, an army officer who in 1785 invented the shrapnel shell.

One of the town's most distinctive features is its unique nine-arched bridge over the River Avon. Originally constructed in the 13th-century for packhorse traffic, it was extensively rebuilt in the 17th-century. The small, domed building towards the southern end of the bridge is a former chapel which was converted for use as the town gaol. John Wesley is said to have spent an uncomfortable night here; however, the two cells were more often required to house local drunks which led to the building being referred to as the 'Blind House'.

Another of Bradford's extraordinary buildings dates from the period when the town was under the administration of the nuns of Shaftesbury Abbey. By the 14th-century, the increased output from the surrounding farms had created a problem in storing the 'tithes', one tenth of the annual farm produce. To solve this, a tithe barn 164 feet long and 33 feet wide was constructed near the river which had fourteen bays, four projecting porches and a roof consisting of 30,000 stone tiles weighing an estimated 100 tons. Today, this magnificent stone building houses an interesting agricultural museum which contains a unique collection of antique farm implements and machinery.

Lock Inn Cottage   Bradford-on-Avon 0225 868068

During the 16th- and 17th-centuries, Bradford-on-Avon stood at the heart of one of Britain's great sheep farming areas. As a result, the town became a major centre of the textile industry and attracted skilled weavers from all over Europe (the town is even said to have given the Bradford in Yorkshire its name). Despite protests from local self-employed cloth-workers, by the early 1800s there were thirty water-powered cloth-mills operating in the town. Within 100 years, however, all had been forced to close as the industry transferred to the industrialised North.

Bradford-on-Avon's prosperity was also partly due to its position on the important Kennet-Avon east-west waterway. A bridge over this famous canal is the unusual location of the **Lock Inn Cottage**, a unique canal-side café which is also a specialist gift shop and an efficient bike-hire service. Dick and Jane Barrow's surprising family home is filled with artefacts which are hand-painted in the characteristic rose and castle designs which have traditionally adorned British narrowboats. Bikes can also be hired here (by the hour, half-day or full-day) for journeys through the surrounding lanes or along the towpath to a Saxon church and mediaeval tithe barn. Dick and Jane's thriving canal-side tearoom offers a mouthwatering range of drinks, hot savouries, cream teas and ice creams which can be enjoyed inside, by the canal or taken-away.

The period of prosperity during the 16th- and 17th-centuries left a legacy of handsome old stone buildings in Bradford-on-Avon, the most notable of which is **The Hall**, a fine early-Jacobean residence which was built by John Hall in 1610 (the grounds may be visited by appointment). Other interesting structures in the town include **The Shambles**, a unique early shopping precinct, the **Priory** and **Westbury House**, all of which are worth a visit.

Woolley Grange Hotel   Woolley Green   0225 864705

We decided to look for a place to stay in Bradford-on-Avon and were fortunate enough to find the **Woolley Grange Hotel and Restaurant** at **Woolley Green**. Situated just off the B3105 one mile northeast of the town centre, this splendid Jacobean manor house was constructed of mellow bath stone in the early 17th-century by the Randolph family. It stands within fourteen acres of beautiful landscaped grounds with wonderful southerly views of Salisbury Plain and the White Horse at Westbury. What makes this fine country house hotel so exceptional, however, is that it actively welcomes (and makes excellent provision for) children of all ages. A further noteworthy characteristic is its superb food, prepared in distinctive country house style from produce grown in the Victorian walled garden or brought by local suppliers. Recommended.

From Woolley Green, we joined the B3105 and drove west for a mile before turning northwest onto the A363 Bath road. Excellent bed and breakfast accommodation can be found at the aptly-named **Midway Cottage** in **Farleigh Wick**, an attractive hamlet which stands on the A363 midway between Bradford-on-Avon and the A4 at Bathford. (It also lies approximately midway between Trowbridge and Bath.) This lovely restored Victorian cottage is owned by Mrs Jayne Prole who provides her guests with comfortable accommodation and a truly splendid English breakfast. She has three letting bedrooms available, all equipped with en suite facilities, colour televisions, telephones and tea/coffee making facilities. One bedroom is situated on the ground floor, and with only two small steps, is suitable for the less mobile. Midway Cottage is English Tourist Board two-crown commended, but is unsuitable for smokers.

Midway Cottage   Farleigh Wick   0225 863372

To reach our next destination, **Monkton Farleigh**, we turned northeast off the A363 and within a mile, found ourselves at the lovely old village church of St Peter's. The building dates from around 1200 and contains some fine Norman features, including the inner door and archway in the north porch. Much of the detail carries the familiar zigzag moulding which is characteristic of the period. The sturdy tower was built a little later in the 13th-century to a saddleback design. Inside, there is an attractive Elizabethan carved pulpit and some fine pre-Reformation carving in the choir stalls.

We also came across a first-rate place to stay in Monkton Farleigh, **Fern Cottage**, an English Tourist Board commended bed and breakfast establishment which is owned and run by Christopher and Jenny Valentine. (For accurate directions, telephone the Valentines on 0225 859412.) Their charming stone-built residence dates from around 1680 and retains many of its original 17th-century features. Inside, it has been carefully and elegantly modernised and now offers a high standard of comfort in truly relaxed and tranquil surroundings. Christopher and Jenny are terrific hosts who offer their guests the warmest of welcomes and one of the best English breakfasts in Wiltshire.

Fern Cottage   Monkton Farleigh   0225 859412

From Monkton Farleigh, we continued northwest along the small country lanes until we found ourselves in **Bathford**, a pleasant village which lies within three miles of the centre of Bath and just across the Avon border.

In Ashley Road, we discovered a delightful bed and breakfast establishment, **Bridge Cottage**. This charming cottage is the home of Ros and Terry Bright, two fine hosts who offer their guests en suite accommodation appointed to a high standard. They also serve a first-class breakfast in the guests' private dining room. Through the arches there is a lovely three-tier patio garden filled with tubs of flowers and lawns. There are wonderful views across the valley from the cottage, and from Bathford you can follow a beautiful country and canal walk across the meadows to Bath, an enchanting experience which takes approximately one hour.

Bridge Cottage   Bathford   0225 852399

The straggling community of **Box** lies on the A4 midway between Bath and Chippenham, three miles to the east of Bathford. The village has been inhabited since Roman times and building remains from this period are dotted throughout the surrounding area. High quality Bath stone is still quarried nearby; the village is perhaps best known, however, for being at the western end of Brunel's remarkable feat of civil engineering, **Box Tunnel**. The 1.8 mile-long tunnel took five years to build and when completed in 1841, it was the longest railway tunnel in the world. The west portal can be seen from a viewing point on the A4 where, in 1987, a plaque was erected to commemorate the completion of a major cleaning and restoration programme. According to local legend, the sun shines through the entire length of the tunnel on one occasion each year – sunrise on April 9th, Brunel's birthday.

Cheney Cottage   Ditteridge   0225 742346

For those keen to stay in Box, first-rate accommodation is offered at **Cheney Cottage**. This attractive residence is a picturesque neo-Elizabethan thatched house, nestling in four acres of beautiful gardens with outstanding views across the Box valley. Its peaceful location belies the fact that it lies only six miles from historic Bath, making it an ideal base from which to tour the magnificent local countryside and explore the historic sites of the area. The cottage provides double, twin and single rooms, all with washbasins and tea/coffee making facilities. Breakfast menus range from full English to the lighter continental, with special diets catered for by prior arrangement; packed lunches can also be supplied on request.

On leaving Box, we continued eastwards along the A4 for three miles before turning southeast onto the B3353 to reach the delightful small market town of **Corsham**. A settlement existed here before the days of the Romans and over the centuries, it grew to become a significant weaving and cloth-making centre. The old town High Street is filled with mellow cream-coloured Bath-stone buildings, many of which date from the 17th- and 18th-centuries.

Visitors to this ancient and picturesque town will find a lovely place to stay at **75 High Street**, a charming Grade II listed mid-18th-century house owned and run by Pat Rodger. Pat has been welcoming guests into her delightful home for over five years and has a knack for making them feel completely at home. Situated in the centre of Corsham, Pat's house overlooks the 16th-century Flemish weavers' cottages, giving visitors the feeling of having stepped back in time. The peace and tranquillity of this town is all pervasive, and you can't help but awake refreshed, relaxed and ready for the superb breakfast Pat prepares, wherever possible, using fresh Wiltshire produce. (Telephone on 0249 713366)

Some of the most striking buildings in Corsham are the pedimented **Hungerford Almshouses** which were built in 1668 by the local lady of the manor, Dame Margaret Hungerford. The old warden's house, with its elegant bell tower and magnificent carved porch, is especially fine. Adjoining the almshouses is an old schoolhouse which still retains its 17th-century classroom layout, original seating and schoolmaster's pulpit-style desk.

At the other end of the High Street there is a row of gabled Flemish-style weavers' cottages which are particularly characteristic of the period. The nearby St Bartholomew's Church was built in the 12th-century on the site of an earlier Saxon chapel. It was added to on a number of occasions, then extensively restored in 1874; however, it still retains a number of interesting period features, both inside and out.

Before visiting Corsham's most famous attraction, Corsham Court, we decided to have a bite to eat in the centre of town. Corsham High Street is lined with buildings of great architectural interest. At No. 55 we discovered one that dates back to 1906 is now a spacious tearoom, **Audrey's**. It is situated just 100 yards along the road from Corsham Court and is open every day for morning coffee, lunch and afternoon tea. We found Audrey's to be very good value; everything is home-cooked and the menu includes such imaginative dishes as 'bacon hotpot'. This was a new dish to us and we found it delicious and very filling. The menu is changed regularly, but a good homemade soup is always available, along with a range of appetising dishes to tempt the palate. Lunch costs approximately £4.50 per head and tea around £2.00, value which is certainly hard to beat. (Telephone on 0249 714931)

Corsham Court

Saxon monarchs visited the old royal manor at **Corsham Court** long before the Norman invasion. However, the present Elizabethan mansion with its imposing pedimented gateway was built in 1582 by 'Customer' Smythe, a high-ranking Collector of Customs in Queen Elizabeth I's London treasury. Additions to the building were made by Nash during the Georgian era, and the surrounding grounds were laid out by the famous 18th-century landscape gardener, Capability Brown, with later work being completed by Humphrey Repton. The gardens contain an unusual Gothic-style bathhouse and a large number of semi-tame peacocks which sometimes wander out of the grounds and strut off down the High Street.

Today, Corsham Court is owned by the Methuen family who originally acquired it to accommodate their outstanding collection of 16th- and 17th-century paintings and furniture. The collection has been built up over the years and is now on view to the public. House and gardens open daily (except Mondays and Fridays), 2pm to 4pm (6pm June to September), all year round (closed mid-December to mid-January). Admission charge payable.

Thurlestone Lodge   Corsham   0249 713397

Corsham offers a number of first-rate places to stay. Among them, we discovered the excellent bed and breakfast establishment, **Thurlestone Lodge**, which is run by Mrs Ogilvie-Robb at 13 Prospect. Thurlestone Lodge is an impressive mid-Victorian villa set in its own well laid out gardens. The proprietor, Mrs Ogilvie-Robb, shares her elegant home with her many guests, providing them with a tranquil relaxing place to stay. The guest lounge and public rooms are beautifully furnished and the en suite bedrooms enjoy lovely views. An interesting feature of the house is the set of emblems of the British Isles carved into the stone uprights of the windows: a rose for England, daffodil for Wales, thistle for Scotland and shamrock for Ireland.

Those preferring farmhouse accommodation on the edge of Corsham should try **Pickwick Lodge Farm**. The name appealed to us when we first visited the area so we went to call on Mrs Stafford, who owns the house with her husband, to see what sort of accommodation she had to offer. This warm-hearted lady will certainly ensure that anyone who stays with her is well catered for. The accommodation is comprised of two letting rooms which are both warm and comfortably furnished. Children are very welcome and arrangements can be made for baby sitting if you have young ones and would like to take the opportunity of going out to one of the nearby villages for an evening meal. Mrs Stafford told us that the White Horse pub at Biddestone and The White Hart at Ford have excellent food. She herself only provides bed and breakfast. Although we state 'only', this is hardly the word to describe the super freshly cooked breakfasts that she serves to her guests in the pleasant dining room.

Pickwick Lodge Farm   Corsham   0249 712207

Pickwick Lodge has quite a history; part of it is early 16th-century and the remainder 17th-century. It was once a shepherd's cottage with two rooms upstairs and two rooms downstairs, but additions and extensions have been made over the centuries without sacrificing any of its charm. Pickwick Lodge Farm provides an ideal base for exploring Corsham and the many other places of interest in the surrounding district.

The network of minor country roads to the east of Corsham led us to exquisite National Trust-owned village of **Lacock**. Preserved as only an estate village can be, the buildings in Lacock are all said to be 18th-century or older. A stroll around the square of streets reveals a wonderful assortment of delightful mellow stone buildings, including the famous Red Lion Hotel in the High Street.

Now Grade 1 listed, the **Red Lion** is a handsome three-storey redbrick former coaching inn which is run by Kevin and Debbie Keeling, two

71

charming and highly experienced hosts who take great pride in providing the finest food, ales and accomodation. On the first floor, there is an elegant Victorian breakfast room with attractive window seats and an unusual gilded mirror. Here, an Egon Ronay-recommended menu is served which includes the seasonal house specialities, fresh local game, game pie, salmon, and a choice of wonderful puddings. Kevin and Debbie also serve an excellent range of top quality bar meals, a first-class wine list and a selection of fine ales, including the famous Wadworth 6X. They also have four delightful guest bedrooms available, each with its own ensuite facilities and unique character.

The Red Lion Hotel   Lacock   0249 730456

Another hostelry in Lacock worth a mention is The George, one of the oldest continuously licensed premises in the country. Lacock also possesses an exceptional 15th-century church, St Cyriac's, which contains a superb fan-vaulted chapel, some fine stained glass, the tomb of Sir William Sharington, and a memorial brass of Robert Baynard and his wife surrounded by their fifteen kneeling children.

The entire village once belonged to the estate of **Lacock Abbey**. This outstanding abbey and country mansion dates from 1232 when it was founded by Ela, Countess of Salisbury. Following the death of her father, Ela was married to Richard the Lionheart's stepbrother, William Longsword, and bore him several children. He, too, died shortly after returning from battle, and in her grief, she founded Lacock Abbey and continued to live on for another 35 years. The original cloisters, chapter house, sacristy and kitchens of the Augustinian nunnery still survive to this day.

However, much of the remainder of the present-day building dates from the mid-16th-century when the abbey was acquired by Sir William Sharington following the Dissolution of the Monasteries in 1539. He constructed an impressive country house around the abbey's core, which

Lacock Abbey

he left intact (with the exception of the chapel which was replaced by stables). He also built the elegant octagonal tower which overlooks the nearby River Avon.

The house remained in the Sharington family for a relatively short time, for in 1574, heiress Olive Sharington leapt from the roof into the arms of her lover, John Talbot, on hearing that permission for their marriage had been denied. Saved by her billowing undergarments and Talbot's heroic action, Olive was eventually given the go-ahead to wed her badly flattened suitor. The house then remained in the Talbot family until it was ceded to the National Trust in 1958. Open daily (except Tuesdays), 1pm to 5.30pm between 1st April and 1st November. Admission charge payable (free to National Trust members).

Perhaps the most eminent member of the Talbot family was the photographic pioneer, William Henry Fox Talbot, who carried out most of his experiments at Lacock in the 1830s. Indeed, one of the earliest photographs ever produced shows a detail of one of the abbey's latticed oriel windows. The **Fox Talbot Museum** celebrates his many discoveries and is housed in the 16th-century tithe barn, a Grade I listed building which is situated near the abbey gates. Open daily, 11am to 5.30pm between 1st March and 1st November. Admission charge payable (free to National Trust members).

King John's Hunting Lodge   Lacock   0249 730313

Visitors who come to Lacock to view its beautiful buildings, the magnificent Abbey and the Fox Talbot Museum should also make a point of calling in at **King John's Hunting Lodge Tearooms** in Church Street. The Hunting Lodge dates back to the 13th-century and, in fact, predates the Abbey. It is also said to contain as many as six very friendly ghosts. Over the last decade, Robert and Jane Woods have built up an international reputation for serving the most delicious homemade scones and cakes, and the finest specially-blended teas. They also have two superb letting

74

rooms available, one a family room with a four-poster and the other a mediaeval suite which overlooks the beautiful orchard tea gardens.

Wick Farm   Lacock   0249 730244

Marvellous farmhouse bed and breakfast accommodation can be found near Lacock at **Wick Farm**, a 15th-century manor farm which once belonged to Lacock Abbey and is now the charming home of Susan and Philip King. An absolute picture with Virginia creeper and winter jasmine climbing the walls, Wick Farm offers superb accommodation in its comfortably furnished guest rooms; it also offers one of the finest farmhouse breakfasts in the county. Wick Farm is also a coarse fishing enthusiast's paradise, with all types of fish available, including carp, chub and tench. The farm is also certified with the Camping and Caravanning Club as a 'Hideaway Site'. There are five delightful pitches and, with the ancient village and abbey of Lacock lying just down the road, an abundance of beautiful walks through the surrounding countryside.

Piccadilly Caravan Site   Lacock   0249 730260

Alternatively, those with touring caravans should make a point of finding the **Piccadilly Caravan Site** in Folly Lane. Lying only half-a-mile from the centre of Lacock, this is a real haven for both caravanners and campers. Set in two-and-a-half acres of secluded grounds in the rolling Wiltshire countryside, the site provides level ground for up to forty pitches. Excellent amenities are provided, including a shower and toilet block with hot and cold water, an Elsan disposal point, laundry room and children's play area; electric hook-ups are available for a small extra charge, gas cylinders and refills are available on site, and newspapers and milk can be delivered by arrangement. As well as being conveniently situated Lacock, the Piccadilly Caravan Site is located within easy reach of the magnificent city of Bath, Castle Combe and many other picturesque Cotswold villages, making it an ideal base for touring this beautiful part of Britain.

From Lacock, we continued eastwards along the country roads to the charming community of **Sandy Lane**. The village contains an assortment of traditional cottages, the imposing George Inn, and one of the few thatched churches in England. We then turned north onto the A342 Chippenham road and after a couple of miles reached Derry Hill, the entrance point to the splendid **Bowood House**.

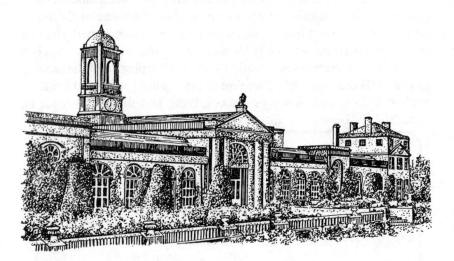

Bowood House

Concealed within the remains of Chippenham Forest, this elegantly proportioned country mansion has undergone a series of alterations since it was completely rebuilt in 1754. Designed in part by Robert Adam, the house includes an impressive library and a laboratory where Joseph

Priestley first identified oxygen in 1774. Much of the building is now used to display an extensive art collection; the orangery is now a delightful picture gallery, and there are also fine displays of sculpture, watercolours, costumes and a collection of Indian relics which was accumulated by the present owner's great-grandfather when he served as the Viceroy of India between 1888-94.

The grounds of Bowood House cover an area of over 1000 acres and were laid out by Capability Brown; they include a magnificent landscaped lake with an Italianate cascade, over 150 species of well-labelled trees, and some pleasant woodland walks which are particularly spectacular during the rhododendron season. The house and grounds are open daily, 11am to 6pm between mid-May and mid-June, and there is also a restaurant, shop and children's adventure play area. Admission charge payable.

On leaving Bowood, we joined the A4 and drove eastwards for two miles towards **Calne**. Standing at a busy road junction in the sheltered valley of the River Marden, this is a once-thriving weaving town which later became known as a meat-curing centre (for many decades, a Harris Bacon factory was located here). Calne also features some fine old almshouses in Kingsbury Street, an imposing 12th- to 15th-century parish church, and an impressive coaching inn, the Lansdowne Arms, which was built in the 18th-century on the site of an earlier inn, the old brewhouse of which can still be seen in the yard.

The pleasant village of **Cherhill** lies three miles further east along the A4. Today, this is a peaceful village with a hidden 14th- to 15th-century church and an excellent inn, the Black Horse, which is the only such establishment to survive from the days when this was an important staging post on the busy London-Bristol coaching route. The character of the village was very different in the 18th-century when an infamous band of robbers known as the Cherhill Gang used to surprise passing travellers. Their intrusion was particularly startling in view of the fact that, before attacking, the gang were said to remove all their clothes to avoid being recognised.

At the **Manor House** in Cherhill, Trudy Oatley combines her successful interior design business with providing first-rate bed and breakfast accommodation. The present house dates back to the 15th-century; however, the site has been occupied since ancient times and indeed, a fine Roman mosaic was discovered in the ruins of a villa which once stood adjacent to the present-day building. Trudy's flare for design, colour and arrangement is much in evidence throughout the house. The old manor has been beautifully and sympathetically restored, and provides accommodation and furnishings of a very high standard. Guests can

77

make use of the outdoor swimming pool and tennis courts, or stroll round the gardens working up an appetite for the wonderful food which Trudy provides. With its beautiful views both inside and out, the Manor House is truly a delightful place to stay.

Trudy Oatley   *Cherhill*   *0249 817085*

Cherhill Down, the chalk ridge to the south of the village, is the site of a famous White Horse which was cut in the hillside by Dr Christopher Alsop in 1790. The nearby **Lansdowne Monument** dates from 1845 and was built on the instructions of the Third Marquess of Lansdowne to commemorate his ancestor, Sir William Petty. This exposed hilltop is also the site of the ancient Iron Age earthwork, **Oldbury Castle**. Now owned by the National Trust, this 190-acre hill fort enjoys magnificent views of the Marlborough Downs and the Vale of Pewsey, the areas covered in our next chapter.

CHAPTER FOUR

East Wiltshire

Devizes Castle

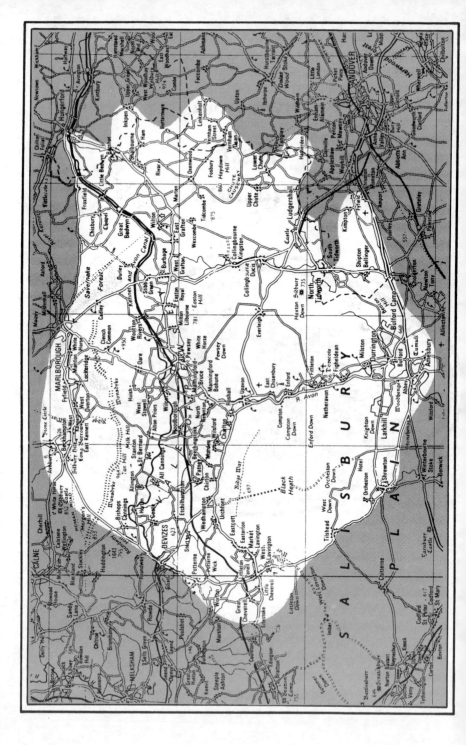

Index

The Bell Caravan and Camping Park, Lydeway, Wiltshire
Braybrooke Pottery, Upavon, Wiltshire
Dye House B&B, Dye House Lane, Devizes
Eastcott Manor B&B, Easterton, Nr Devizes
Kingstones Farm B&B, Cadley, Nr Marlborough
Lamb Inn and B&B, The Parade, Marlborough
Longwater B&B, Erlestoke, Nr Devizes
Mayfield Cottage B&B,West Grafton, Nr Marlborough
Pinecroft B&B, Potterne Road, Devizes
The Rose and Crown Inn, 108 High Street, Worton
The Savernake Forest Hotel and Restaurant, Savernake, Burbage
Sunrise Farm B&B, Manton, Marlborough
The Taffrail B&B, Lockeridge, Marlborough
Totteridge Farm B&B, Milton Lilbourne, Pewsey
Wheatsheaf Inn and B&B, West Lavington, Nr Devizes
Woodbridge Inn, B&B, Restaurant, Caravan and Camping, North
    Newnton, Nr Pewsey

Devizes Cross

East Wiltshire

We crossed into the eastern section of central Wiltshire near **Avebury**, an ancient settlement which stands at the centre of one of the most important Megalithic monuments in Europe. The village stands on a 28-acre site which is completely surrounded by a ring of standing (or *sarsen*) stones almost a mile in circumference; this in turn is surrounded by a ditch and a raised bank which enclose almost 100 standing stones dating from around 2300 BC. These are thought to have been erected by the Beaker people, immigrants from continental Europe who brought with them sophisticated pottery-making skills (some exceptional pieces have been found in the graves of their dead chieftains).

Avebury Stones

The standing stones come in two basic shapes: the tall narrow ones are believed to represent the male form and the broad diamond-shaped ones the female form, characteristics which led archeologists to conclude that the site was probably used for the observance of fertility rituals. Megaliths weighing as much as forty tons were dragged from the Marlborough Downs and erected in three circles. Sadly, only 27 of the stones in the central area remain, the rest having been removed over the centuries only to be broken down and used as building materials; the positions of the missing stones have, however, been marked by a series of modern concrete piers.

Alexander Keiller Museum

Avebury Stone Circle was extensively excavated by Alexander Keiller during the 1930s and a museum baring his name is located just outside the earthwork perimeter near the part-Saxon, part-Norman village church of St James. The museum is administered by English Heritage and houses a fascinating collection of artefacts which were discovered at Avebury and at **Windmill Hill**, a Neolithic hill fort (and later Bronze Age burial ground) which lies a mile-and-a-half to the northwest. Open daily 9.30am (2pm on winter Sundays) to 6.30pm (4pm in winter), all year round. Another attraction in the village is the Wiltshire Folk Life Society's exhibition of rural crafts which is situated in an enormous thatched barn. As well as containing a unique collection of historic farm implements, the **Great Barn** hosts regular demonstrations of lesser-known rural skills.

Avebury also possesses an elegant Elizabethan manor house, **Avebury Manor**, which was built on the site of a 12th-century priory and is now under the ownership of the National Trust. It has been much-altered over the centuries, particularly during the reign of Queen Anne and then in the Edwardian era, when major alterations were carried out by Colonel Jenner. Inside, there are some fine plasterwork ceilings and an interesting collection of antique furniture and porcelain. The manor grounds are partly laid out as a formal garden and contain a wonderful old dovecote, mediaeval walls and some splendid topiary. Open daily (except Mondays and Thursdays), 11am to 5.30pm between 1st April and end-October. Admission charge payable (free to National Trust members).

The Great Barn, Avebury

The largest manmade prehistoric mound in Europe can be found on the northern side of the A4 one mile south of Avebury. The huge flat-topped cone of **Silbury Hill** stands 130 feet high and covers an area of five acres. Its purpose, however, remains a mystery. Recent excavations have yielded up little about the mound except that it is thought to have been constructed in four stages between around 2145 BC and 95 BC. According to local legend, the structure contains a huge gold statue which was hidden here by the Devil while on his way to Devizes; another theory suggests that it was created as a burial place for King Sil and his horse.

Whatever its origins, the green cone of Silbury Hill has an uncanny presence which seems to dominate the surrounding landscape. Because of problems with erosion, however, members of the public are no longer permitted to climb to the top.

From Silbury Hill, we joined the A361 and drove southwest towards Devizes. Near the hamlet of Shepards Shore, approximately midway between Avebury and Devizes, the road crosses the ridge which carries the ancient **Wansdyke** path. This spectacular earthwork is thought to have been constructed in the late 6th-century by the Britons as a defence against the Saxons, and then strengthened two centuries later by the west Saxons as a defence against the Vikings. Consisting of a single raised bank and ditch, it once stretched for over fifty miles from the Berkshire border to northern Somerset. The twelve-mile eastern section from Savernake Forest to Morgan's Hill, near Calne provides one of the most spectacular archeological walks in England. (An excellent view of the Wansdyke can be enjoyed from the top of **Tan Hill** above the village of All Cannings.)

Avebury Manor

A mile-and-a-half further south, we reached the old ecclesiastical community of **Bishops Cannings**, so-called because the Bishop of Salisbury once owned a manor here. Probably as a consequence, the parish church is somewhat oversized and bears a striking resemblance to Salisbury Cathedral with a tall tapering spire and some fine stone carving.

The church organ was donated in 1809 by Captain Cook's navigator, William Bayley, who was born locally, and there is also an unusual meditation seat inscribed with some cautionary words in Latin on the subject of sin and death.

According to local legend, the term *Wiltshire Moonraker* has its origins in Bishops Cannings. During the 16th-century, a government excise patrol discovered two local men combing a village pond with a rake on the night of a full moon. When asked what they were doing, they villagers pointed to the moon's reflection replied that they were trying to scrape the thick yellow cheese from the surface. Convinced that they had lost their senses, the excisemen roared with laughter and rode off into the night, leaving the local men to get on with their task of retrieving their cache of contraband liquor from the bottom of the pond.

Devizes Castle

A hollow in the Downs one mile to the west of Bishops Cannings was the scene of a bloody battle during the English Civil War. On 13th July 1643, the Royalist forces under Prince Rupert's brother, Maurice, defeated the Parliamentarian forces at **Roundway Down**. Local legend has it that each year on the anniversary of the battle, the cries of the dead can be heard emanating from a long-lost burial ditch beside the battlefield. One mile further south, a stroll to the beech trees on top of **Roundway Hill** provides some spectacular views over the surrounding downland landscape.

87

Returning to the car, we continued southwestwards along the A361 into the centre of **Devizes**. By the standards of most other settlements in the locality, Devizes is a relatively modern town having been founded by the William the Conqueror's nephew, Bishop Osmund, in 1080. He was responsible for building a timber castle between the lands of two manors, a position which gave the town its name (it comes from the Latin *ad divisas*, meaning 'at the boundaries'). After the original wooden structure burnt down, Roger, Bishop of Sarum, built a stone castle in 1138 which remained in place until it was compulsorily dismantled following the English Civil War. (The castle which can be seen today dates from the 19th-century and is not open to visitors.)

St. John's Church, Devizes

Bishop Roger also built two fine churches in Devizes: St Mary's in New Park Street and St John's near the site of the old castle. The latter was built around 1130 and features a Norman tower and several original arches with characteristic zigzag carving. The churchyard containing some interesting tombs and is surrounded by a number of lovely old buildings including a 17th-century sexton's house. Beyond the church, Long Street is lined with elegant Georgian dwellings; it also contains the Wiltshire Archeological and Natural History Society's award-winning **Devizes Museum** with its superb collection of artefacts from such archeological sites as Avebury and Stonehenge.

Many of the finest buildings in Devizes are situated in and around the old market place; these include the town hall, the corn exchange and the handsome 16th-century coaching inn, the Bear Hotel. The market place is also the site of an unusual market cross, one panel of which is inscribed with the sobering story of Ruth Pierce, a market stall-holder who, in 1753, was accused of swindling her customers. On announcing to the assembled throng, 'May I be struck dead if I am lying', she dropped down dead on the spot.

A good place to stay in the centre of Devizes can be found within a few yards of the Market Place on the A360 Potterne Road. Here, we discovered **Pinecroft**, an excellent bed and breakfast establishment which is run by May and Philip Linton. Pinecroft is a spacious part-Georgian, part-Edwardian residence standing in a huge, delightfully-planted garden. The guest rooms are large and equipped with colour televisions and beverage making facilities. The Lintons also offer a first-rate mountain-bike hire service.

The Kennet and Avon Canal passes along the northern edge of Devizes. Designed in the early 19th-century by John Rennie, this impressive feat of civil engineering once linked London with Bristol. At that time, **Devizes Wharf** was a flourishing commercial centre through which most of the town's goods passed. Today, the wharf is a more genteel place, though in recent years it has undergone something of a rejuvenation; several of the old warehouses have now been renovated and are occupied by such concerns as the local tourist information office, the Wharf Theatre and the Canal Interpretation Centre with its fascinating exhibition on the background and history of the canal.

Pinecroft   *Devizes*   *0380 721433*

We would recommend a walk along the towpath to the west of Devizes to have a look at the famous **Caen Hill** flight of canal locks. Further west, the land falls 200 feet into a shallow valley within the space of two miles, an incline which created significant engineering difficulties for Rennie.

He solved the problem by constructing a giant staircase of sixteen locks, so tightly-spaced that they scarcely seem a narrowboat-length apart. In total, a series of twenty-nine double-gated locks were needed to traverse the valley, a sequence through which the hardest working barges took half-a-day to pass. The lock gates are currently undergoing an extensive programme of restoration and it is hoped that this stretch of canal will become navigable again by the mid-1990s. An excellent view of the lock staircase can be obtained from a white-painted bridge which spans the canal a few hundred yards along the gravel towpath.

Dye House   *Devizes*   *0380 722030*

Those looking for a wonderfully tranquil place to stay within easy reach of the canal should try **Dye House** in Dye House Lane. The house lies a short walk from the Kennet and Avon Canal and is so-called because it was once the site of a silk dying mill. Victoria Heaton-Renshaw provides outstanding hospitality at her spacious Victorian home which is set within two-and-a-half acres of beautifully cultivated gardens.

The Rose and Crown   *Worton*   *0380 724202*

In the centre of Devizes, we joined the A360 Amesbury road and drove southwards towards the heart of Salisbury Plain. Our next stop was the lovely old village of **Potterne**, home of a unique exhibition of antique fire engines and fire-fighting equipment which is administered by the Wiltshire Fire Service. The village itself contains some noteworthy buildings, including a 13th-century church with a Saxon font and the 500 year-old **Porch House**, a black-and-white timbered structure which in its lifetime has served as a priest's home, an alehouse, a bakery and an army billet.

Kennet and Avon Canal

In Potterne, we turned west into the country lanes to reach the charming twin communities of **Worton** and **Marston**. Worton's Christ Church is situated within an attractive treed churchyard and is unusual in this part of Wiltshire for not having a tower or spire.

Worton also possesses a splendid old country inn, the **Rose and Crown**. A genuine 'hidden place', this delightful village pub is tucked away on the old Melksham to Salisbury road and is well worth making the effort to find. The Saunders are friendly hosts who have turned the Rose and Crown into a popular watering hole for visitors and locals alike. Its popularity is readily understood when you sample their fine draught beers or taste their mouthwatering meals; the menu includes such house specialities as 'Worton beef and kidney pie', or 'pork in cider with Bramley apples'. The bar is full of historic artefacts and photographs,

91

including one of a real-life local giant, whilst in a separate building there is a full length skittle alley where customers can complete their evening's entertainment.

Worton's sister village, Marston, is situated a mile to the southwest and after passing through this pleasant community, we continued southwards towards the B3098 and the old Saxon settlement of **Erlestoke**. This village was much altered in the late 18th-century when a new manor house was built and the surrounding land 'emparked' by the London-based landscape architect, William Eames. About a century later, the old village church was replaced by the Gothic Perpendicular-style building which can be seen today. Today, Erlestoke provides a good sheltered base for exploring Salisbury Plain; it also offers a first-rate bed and breakfast establishment, **Longwater**.

Situated 300 yards north of the village centre, Longwater is a superb modern farmhouse which is licensed and ETB three crown commended. Mrs Pam Hampton offers luxurious en suite bedrooms, marvellous hospitality, delicious breakfasts and, by arrangement, evening meals.

From Erlestoke, we headed east along the B3098, and after crossing the A360, came to the long sprawling village of **Market Lavington**. Once the scene of a busy sheep and corn market, the community still retains its mercantile character and has a surprisingly good selection of shops and services.

Longwater   Erlestoke   0380 830095

One mile northeast of Market Lavington, the B3098 took us to the delightful hamlet of **Eastcott** where found **Eastcott Manor**, a splendid black-and-white half-timbered country residence which in the late 18th-century was the home of the rumbustious Squire Wroughton. Today, the house is known more for its peace and tranquillity and for its easy access to the spectacular countryside of the northern Salisbury Plain. The building is the home of Janet Firth and her husband, Major Malcolm Firth,

92

who offer first-rate overnight accommodation in charming historic surroundings. Janet, a trained cook, takes great pride in providing her guests with delicious meals which she prepares from the finest local produce.

Eastcott Manor   Easterton   0380 813313

The attractive settlement of **Urchfont** lies a further mile to the northeast. As well as possessing an exceptionally fine (and much-altered) 13th-century parish church, the village contains an elegant William and Mary manor house which once belonged to William Pitt and has since been converted to an educational institution. Look out also for the picturesque village duck pond.

Did you know....

The village of Wootton Rivers has a clock built from old prams, bicycles and farm implements, and is known locally as the Jack Spratt?

see page 104

Bell Caravan Park   Lydeway   0380 840230

Excellent facilities for campers and touring caravans are provided near Urchfont at the **Bell Caravan and Camping Park** at **Lydeway**. Situated on the Andover road, this attractive park offers thirty fully-equipped pitches in a secluded location at the foot of the Marlborough Downs. The park is set in the grounds of the former Old Bell coaching inn and is ideal for touring the surrounding area. With full washing facilities, showers, a heated outdoor swimming pool, take-away service, off-licence, shop, games room and more besides, guests have everything they could wish for. The site's four-key English Tourist Board rating indicates the standards that can be expected.

From Urchfont, we retraced our steps along the B3098 before turning south onto the A360 to reach the lovely old community of **West Lavington**. The village church, which dates from the late-12th-century, stands alongside an attractive wisteria-covered manor house. In the mid-16th-century, the local lords of the manor, the Dauntsey family, were responsible for founding West Lavington's famous school. They also constructed the handsome almshouses to the northeast of the church which were subsequently rebuilt in brick during the 1830s. Whilst here, we took the opportunity of calling in at the locally-renowned village pub, the Wheatsheaf Inn.

The Wheatsheaf is a superb establishment where you will find fine ales, first-class food and well-appointed accommodation. Lesley and Barry Curran are lovely, relaxed hosts who have developed a well-deserved reputation in the area for their excellent restaurant food; there is an extensive menu and homemade puddings are a house speciality. Recent refurbishment has not detracted from the inn's traditional character, with its exposed beams, welcoming log fires and lovely snug bar. Barry serves a variety of cask-conditioned beers as well as a good selection of wines. For those wishing to stay, there are ten very comfortable en suite guest rooms available, and the breakfasts here are rumoured to be amongst the finest in the county.

Wheatsheaf Inn   West Lavington   0380 813392

The A360 to the south of West Lavington took us across the central area of Salisbury Plain. Along this stretch, much of the land on either side is owned by the Ministry of Defence; indeed some 92,000 acres make up the **Salisbury Plain Training Area**, 30,000 acres of which are regularly used either for live firing or as impact areas. Public access, therefore, is severely restricted. However, the MoD do make the effort to open up most of the prohibited areas on certain specified days each year. There are believed to be 17,000 archeological sites within the military training area, many of which are under the protection of special management agreements. The area also contains nine Sites of Special Scientific Interest (SSSIs) and a rich variety wild flora and fauna; in addition, over three-and-a-half million trees have been planted here since the army took over in 1897.

Our route across Salisbury Plain took us through Tilshead and Shrewton, before passing along the northern perimeter of Stonehenge (the background details of which are included in chapter one). Our next destination was the ancient monastic town of **Amesbury**. According to Mallory, Queen Guinevere withdrew to a priory here on hearing of King Arthur's death (when she herself died, her body was taken back to Glastonbury by Sir Lancelot to be buried beside the king). A more verifiable account records Queen Elfrida as having the founded the abbey around 979 in reparation for her part in the murder of her son-in-law, Edward the Martyr, at Corfe Castle. Almost two centuries later, the abbey was rebuilt by Henry II in a cruciform shape with a large central tower. Sadly, none of the original buildings remain above ground except for the old church of St Mary which was founded by the Saxons and remodelled during the Norman era. The present-day abbey buildings were completed in 1840 and are not open to the public.

Today, Amesbury is a pleasant town which is set in a bend of the Wiltshire Avon. The river is spanned by the graceful five-arched Palladian-style Queensbury Bridge which connects the town with **West Amesbury**, site of the prehistoric earthworks, Vespasian's Camp, and the 17th-century West Amesbury House. A little further west, two lines of 100 year-old beech trees beside the A303 Amesbury bypass are said to represent the ranks of English and French ships at the Battle of the Nile.

We finally headed north out of Amesbury along the A345 Marlborough road and after approximately one mile, came to ancient site of **Woodhenge**. This is one of the earliest historic monuments in Britain to have been discovered by aerial photography, its six concentric rings of post holes having been spotted as cropmarks by Squadron-Leader Insall in 1925. The site is believed to date from around 2000 BC and once consisted of a series of timber uprights (now indicated by concrete posts) which, like nearby Stonehenge, were positioned to predict the sun's path across the sky on Midsummer's Day.

The one-and-a-half-acre site was extensively excavated between

Amesbury

1926 and 1928 and a number of Neolithic artefacts were discovered, including flint scrapers, arrow heads and two ceremonial chalk axes. Perhaps the most striking find, however, was discovered in the centre of the circle: the skeleton of a three year-old child with a fractured skull who was possibly the victim of a ritual sacrifice. The whole area is surrounded by a circular ditch some 220 feet in diameter, and is bordered to the northeast by another Neolithic structure, **Durrington Walls**. This once-spectacular earthwork enclosed an 80 foot ditch and is now virtually bisected by the Amesbury to Marlborough road. The two sites probably formed a single religious observatory which, for some unexplained reason, was moved to Stonehenge towards the end of the Neolithic period around 1800 BC.

For some distance to the north of Amesbury, the landscape is somewhat marred by the uniform rows of military housing. However, we chose to follow the minor road northwards along the eastern bank of the Upper Avon, a route which passes through some pleasant riverside settlements. Our next stop was the village of **Upavon**, an ancient Saxon river town which stands at the junction of the A345 and A342. This was the birthplace of Henry 'Orator' Hunt who became the Member of Parliament for Preston in 1830.

Braybrooke Pottery   Upavon   0980 630466

This is also where we discovered the renowned **Braybrooke Pottery**, an absolute gem of a hidden place. The proprietor, Sally Lewis, is a potter with a considerable reputation who designs all her own work, including specially commissioned commemorative pieces. On most days, visitors can watch Sally at work and admire her enviable artistic skills. A wide choice of beautiful pottery pieces are available to purchase, each of which is individually designed and handcrafted to make a very special gift at a surprisingly reasonable price. Braybrooke Pottery is also a well-known name at British craft exhibitions.

From Upavon, we joined the A342 and drove westwards for four miles before turning north to reach the ancient settlement of **Marden**. The 12th-century pinnacled church is thought to have one of the oldest doors in the country; the lock is known to be at least 300 years old, and the timber perhaps as old as the church itself. It is surrounded by an elaborately carved Norman doorway and inside, there is a fine chancel arch and an unusual ceiling in the nave. The village also possesses an imposing 18th-century manor house, Marden Manor, and a mill which was mentioned in the Domesday Book.

Across the river to the northeast of Marden is a 35-acre oval site which is believed to have been the largest Neolithic henge in Britain. Dating from around 1900 BC, it features entrances on its northern and eastern sides, and once contained an enormous earthwork mound, **Hatfield Barrow**, which stood 50 feet high and 200 feet wide at the base.

The minor roads to the east of Marden led us back towards the A345 via the village of **North Newton**. Here, we stopped to call in at the delightful Woodbridge Inn.

Mr Lou Vertessy and his family have made the **Woodbridge Inn** into a very inviting, attractive hostelry. Winners of the *Best Catering Pub of the Year Award*, he has successfully created an atmosphere of cosy informality where customers can enjoy mid-morning coffee, a pint of fine ale, a tasty bar snack or a delicious meal. The cosy intimate restaurant offers a superb menu which combines traditional English favourites with mouthwatering Mexican, far eastern and Cajun dishes. Beautiful en suite accommodation is also available here, as well as a number of pitches in the lovely secluded caravan and camping park which adjoins the inn. With good fishing, four petanque (French boules) pistes, a children's play area and an attractive beer garden, the Woodbridge provides just about everything the visitor could wish for.

Woodbridge Inn   North Newnton   0980 630266

Having rejoined the A345, we drove northeastwards to the lovely old town of **Pewsey**. Once under the ownership of King Alfred the Great, a statue of this 9th-century king of Wessex stands overlooking the River Avon at the crossroads in the centre of town. The main church is built on Saxon sarsen stones and has a 15th-century tower and an altar rail made from timbers belonging to the *San Josef*, a ship captured by Nelson in 1797. The streets contain an assortment of Georgian houses and thatched cottages and are the venue for a famous West Country carnival which takes place each year in September.

Totteridge Farm   Milton Lilbourne   0672 62402

The long rambling village of **Milton Lilbourne** lies just to the south of the B3087 one-and-a-half miles east of Pewsey. This pleasant community with its high pavements, fine cottages and handsome village church is a place of outstanding architectural and natural beauty. It also provides a good base for walks onto Milton Hill and to the Giant's Grave Neolithic long barrow.

Milton Lilbourne is also the location of a first-rate farmhouse bed and breakfast establishment, **Totteridge Farm**. A real haven for nature and animal lovers, this working farm combines a wonderful mixture of livestock and arable farming with an abundance of wildlife. There is a 100 year-old badger set on the farm's land, and rabbits, foxes, owls and many other birds and animals are all common sights here. Your charming hostess, Patricia Wells, provides very comfortable accommodation for non-smokers in her part-16th-century farmhouse home, all the guest rooms of which enjoy beautiful views over the Vale of Pewsey. A delightful place to stay, Totteridge Farm provides an excellent base for exploring the many lovely walks which crisscross the surrounding landscape.

After returning to the centre of Pewsey, we rejoined the A345 and continued northwards towards Marlborough. After half-a-mile or so, we came to the Kennet and Avon Canal and stopped to have a look at the old wharf, canal house and warehouse which together go to make up **Pewsey Wharf**. Half-a-mile further on, we turned west off the A345 to reach the famous white horse at **Alton Barnes**. According to local legend, the contractor who was commissioned to carve the figure on the side of Milk Hill ran off with his £20 advance payment. Notwithstanding, work on this, the largest white horse in Wiltshire, was completed in 1812 and today, it is visible from Old Sarum over twenty miles away to the south.

A good view of the horse can be had from the wonderful old **Barge Inn** in **Honeystreet**, a short distance to the south. The inn once contained a bakery and general store which served communities throughout the area. Alton Barnes itself possesses a tiny church with a Saxon shell and a timber roof dating from the 15th-century. In 1830, a mob protesting about the introduction of agricultural machinery stormed the rectory and manor house beside the church, injuring one of the rector's colleagues and causing the militia to be called out from Marlborough and Devizes.

The road northwards out of Alton Barnes climbs up the slope of Walker's Hill. Just below the summit on the northern side, a path from the road leads to the New Stone Age encampment of **Knap Hill**; another path provides a short but fairly demanding climb to a long barrow known as **Adam's Grave** from which there are fine views in all directions.

We continued our journey northeastwards and after approximately two miles turned northwest off the Marlborough road to reach the twin settlements of **East** and **West Kennet**. A pleasant half-mile stroll to the west of the villages crosses the River Kennet and leads to the top of a gentle rise on which is sited the **West Kennet Long Barrow**, the largest sectioned burial chamber in the country. This 4500 year-old tomb is over 330 feet long, 80 feet wide and 10 feet high and is approached by way of a semicircular forecourt. The narrow entrance is guarded by number of colossal standing stones through which it is just possible to squeeze. Inside, the five burial chambers were found to contain the remains of forty-or-so people, including at least a dozen children; these were discovered in 1956 when the structure was excavated. The barrow is thought to have served as a tomb for around 1000 years, carbon dating having fixed a date of 2570 BC on the oldest remains, whilst the final sealing of the tomb, dated by pottery fragments, is believed to have been carried out around 1600 BC.

At East Kennet, one mile further east, there is a smaller and as yet unexcavated barrow which is covered in tall trees; then at **Overton Hill**, near the village of West Overton, there is another large monument known as **The Sanctuary**. This stands at the southeastern end of **West Kennet Avenue**, the standing-stone-lined pathway which connects with the main megalithic circles at Avebury. The Sanctuary dates from the early Bronze Age and is believed to have been built as a replacement for an earlier structure which consisted of six concentric circles of timber posts. Concrete blocks have been erected to mark the missing standing stones and concrete posts to mark their timber equivalents, so that the whole pattern of the monument can be discerned.

Overton Hill is also the starting point of the **Ridgeway** long distance footpath which runs for 85 miles through the North Wessex Downs to the Chiltern Hills. Although a little steep at first, the first four miles offers a dramatic walk to the top of the 892 foot **Hackpen Hill**, followed by a gentler stroll through a downland landscape littered with sarsen stones and Bronze Age round barrows. A short diversion from the Ridgeway leads to **Fyfield Down**, the section of the Marlborough Downs which is believed to have been a source of the great stones used to build Stonehenge. The area is now a nature reserve and walkers should keep to the marked footpaths. The spectacular **Devil's Den** long barrow lies within the reserve in a shallow hollow known as Flatford Bottom. Satan is said to appear here at midnight and attempt to pull down the stones with a team of white oxen.

The Taffrail   Lockeridge   0672 86266

On returning to the car, we crossed back onto the southern bank of the River Kennet and drove eastwards to **Lockeridge**, a pleasant village with a good pub (the Who'da Thought It), a school, a shop, a number of attractive old houses, but curiously, no church.

A quiet corner of Lockeridge is the location of a first-class bed and breakfast establishment, **The Taffrail**. The owners of this impressive modern detached house, Julie and Les Spencer, are a truly cosmopolitan couple. Julie, the charming hostess, hails from California, and she and Les have travelled the world together. Their home is splendidly appointed; there is a two-thirds size snooker table in the guest lounge, and also a

101

swimming pool in the terraced garden. The three bedrooms, which share the bathroom and WC, are well furnished with small American and Japanese touches adding to the establishment's unique character. Guests are assured of a warm welcome at Les and Julie's lovely home, an exceptional place which makes a refreshing change from more traditional bed and breakfast accommodation.

Don't forget....

To tell people that you read about them in The Hidden Places

Sunrise Farm   *Manton*   *0672 512878*

Those preferring farmhouse-style accommodation should drive a mile-or-so further east to **Sunrise Farm**, a modern detached bungalow which is tucked away on the hillside behind the ancient village of **Manton**. Here, Mrs Couzens provides excellent accommodation at her charming country home. She has one double and two twin rooms available, both furnished to three crown English Tourist Board standard, and there is also a half-size snooker table and hot drinks facilities in the guest lounge. The south-facing conservatory adjoining the breakfast room provides a blaze of colour throughout the summer and is a favourite with guests for that last cup of coffee at breakfast time.

A mile-and-a-half further downstream, we arrived in the historic market town of **Marlborough**. The town is thought to have inherited its name from *Maerl's Barrow*, an ancient barrow which is now contained within the grounds of the famous Marlborough College public school. Many centuries later, the Normans built a castle on the site and a number of English kings are known to have come here to hunt in nearby Savernake Forest. In the 17th-century, the castle was rebuilt as a house by Inigo Jones' pupil, John Webb, and became a regular haunt of Samuel Pepys. Then around 1700, it was converted into the Castle Inn and became one of the most popular stopping places on the busy coaching route between London and Bristol. Finally, it was incorporated into Marlborough College when the school was founded in 1843.

The best way to explore Marlborough is on foot (look out for the first-class leaflet, *Marlborough, A Guided Walk*, which is available from the information office at St Peter's Church). Despite having experienced three damaging fires in the late-17th-century, the town possesses one of the most beautiful (and widest) old high streets in the country. Amongst the buildings which can be seen here are two Perpendicular churches, some handsome Tudor houses, and a number of Georgian shops with colonnades. A narrow passageway behind St Mary's Church leads to the Green, once the site of a Saxon settlement and the place where Sheep Fairs were held until 1893. Each year in October, a 'Mop Fair' is held in commemoration of the old hiring market, the annual custom where tradespeople looking for work would stand in the marketplace carrying a tool of their trade.

The Lamb Inn   Marlborough   0672 512668

Our walk around Marlborough led us to the Parade, Marlborough's former main thoroughfare which once formed part of the busy London–Bristol coaching route. This is where we discovered the **Lamb Inn**, a delightful former coaching inn which was built here in the 17th-century to cater for passing travellers. Today, landlord Viv Scott serves an excellent pint of Wadworth's ale and a varied range of bar meals; he also has a number of charming en suite letting bedrooms available.

From Marlborough, we drove southeastwards along the A338 Burbage road and after two miles, stopped in the village of **Cadley** to call in at the marvellous bed and breakfast establishment run by Hugh and Charlotte Renwick. **Kingstones Farm** stands in a magnificent position beside Savernake Forest, the only ancient forest in England left in private hands. With its orange-red brickwork, wisteria- and Virginia creeper-covered walls and old walled garden, this truly is an enchanting and quintessentially English place to stay.

103

To the east of the A338 lies the magnificent **Savernake Forest**. A royal hunting ground since pre-Norman times, the 2000 acres which survive today are leased by the Marquess of Ailesbury to the Forestry Commission, making this the only forest in England not to be owned by the Crown. Once under the stewardship of Sir John Seymour, it was here that Henry VIII is said to have met his daughter, Jane. The present-day forest is a legacy from the great 18th-century landscaper, Capability Brown. He laid out the four-mile Grand Avenue which runs in a straight line southeastwards from a crenelated toll house on the A4. He also created a circus about halfway along from which eight forest walks radiate in line with the points of the compass. Savernake contains some massive oaks, beeches and Spanish chestnuts and has been designated a Site of Special Scientific Interest for its wide variety of flora and fauna.

Kingstones Farm   Cadley   0672 512039

For a luxurious break away from it all, the **Savernake Forest Hotel and Restaurant** has everything you could wish for. Situated on the edge of Savernake Forest, this magnificent Victorian country house hotel provides first-class accommodation in tranquil and unspoilt surroundings. The hotel is run by actor Richard Johnson who recently starred in the *Camomile Lawn* and is world famous for his interpretation of Anthony in Shakespeare's *Anthony and Cleopatra*. The Savernake Forest is an outstanding hotel; there are sixteen beautifully furnished en suite bedrooms and a top class restaurant where an imaginative and varied menu is served, along with an extensive list of carefully-selected wines. Whether for a romantic weekend away or a holiday stopover, a stay here will leave you refreshed, relaxed and eager to return.

Two miles to the west of the A346, the village of **Wootton Rivers** has a highly unusual church clock. It was built by a local man in 1911 from old prams, bicycles, farm implements and pieces of mechanical scrap for the villagers who wanted to mark the coronation of George V. Known as the Jack Spratt clock, it has 24 different chimes and a clock face bearing letters instead of numbers.

After making our way to Burbage, we turned east onto the A338 Hungerford road, then within a mile turned south to reach the charming community of **West Grafton**.

Savernake Forest Hotel   Burbage   0672 811081

Visitors to this pretty village will find superb accommodation at **Mayfield**, the delightful home of Chris and Angie Orssich. Their charming thatched house dates from the 15th-century and was originally a Wiltshire 'A'-frame longhouse. The timbered brickwork dates from Elizabethan times and inside, the beautifully furnished rooms are full of character with sloping ceilings and little nooks and crannies. Guests soon feel at home in this family house which is full of life and atmosphere; the focal point is the homely farmhouse kitchen where a ready supply of wine, peanuts and cakes is always available. Set in eight acres, the extensive grounds incorporate a heated swimming pool, a Victorian fruit cage and an all-weather tennis court. A wonderful base for exploring the lovely Kingdom of Wessex, Mayfield comes highly recommended.

Returning to the A338, we drove east for another mile before turning north into the country lanes towards **Crofton**. Our next destination was the old engine house which stands at the highest point on the Kennet and Avon Canal. This handsome Georgian building contains some of the oldest and largest working beam engines in the world, one of which dates from 1812. At one time, these were capable of pumping water into the canal at a rate of eleven tons a minute. The working engines are demonstrated by the Kennet and Avon Canal Trust on a number of set days during the summer months.

The tomb of Sir John Seymour, the father Henry VIII's third wife, Jane Seymour, can be found in the chancel of the 11th-century Church of St Mary the Virgin in **Great Bedwyn**, two miles to the northeast. A

Victorian lamp standard on a traffic island in the centre of The Square marks the centre of this sizable village. A walk along Church Street to the south of here leads to **Lloyds' Stone Museum**, an exhibition dedicated to the skills of the stonemason. The museum is run by the seventh generation of a family of stonemasons which can be traced back over 200 years. Items on show include a stone aeroplane with an eleven-foot wingspan, a number of brightly-coloured tombstones, and a well-presented display on the history and secret skills of stone-carving.

Mayfield   *West Grafton*   *0929 480216*

Two miles further northwest, the road running parallel to the Kennet and Avon Canal brought us to back onto the A4 near **Froxfield**, an attractive village of brick and flint buildings which includes a 17th-century development of almshouses known as the Somerset Hospital. This consists of a chapel and fifty dwellings set around a quadrangle which is entered through an impressive early-19th-century archway. A minor road to the north of Froxfield led us to Littlecote House, the mysterious Tudor mansion which was to be our first stop in chapter five.

CHAPTER FIVE

Marlborough to the River Thames

The Great Western Railway Museum

107

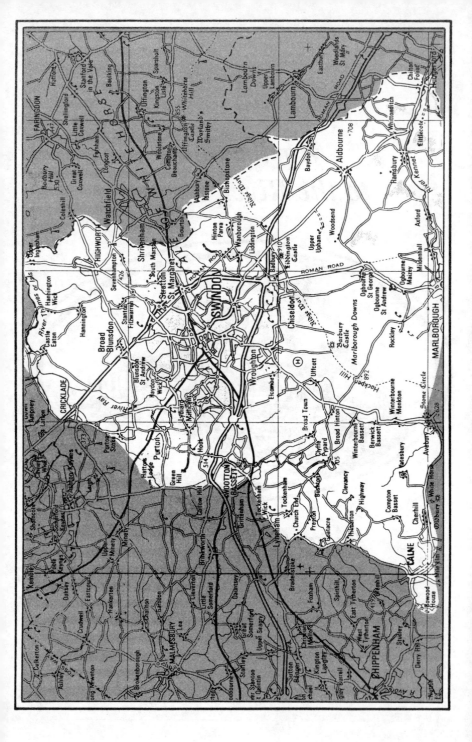

Index

Cross Keys Inn and Restaurant, High Street, Wootton Bassett
Crown and Anchor Pub, 1 Crowood Lane, Ramsbury
Emms Coffee Shop, 147 High Street, Wootton Bassett
Laurel Cottage Guest House, Southend, Ogbourne St George
New Inn Pub, Restaurant and B&B, Winterbourne Monkton
The Old Crown Pub and B&B, Ogbourne St George, Wiltshire
Parklands Hotel and Restaurant, Ogbourne St George
The Red Lion Pub, The Street, Castle Eaton, Wiltshire
The Rose and Crown Pub, Ashbury, Nr Swindon
School House Hotel and Restaurant, Hook, Nr Swindon
The White Hart Hotel, Inn and Restaurant, High Street, Cricklade

Lydiard Monument

Marlborough To The River Thames

From the A4 at Froxfield, we turned north into a minor country road to reach **Littlecote House**, our first port of call in northeast Wiltshire. This gabled Tudor country mansion was built between 1490 and 1520 on the site of a 13th-century manor and hamlet. Some of the earliest visitors to the house were Henry VIII and Jane Seymour whose entwined initials appear in a stained-glass window in the Great Hall, evidence that some of their early encounters took place here.

The most notorious occupant of the Littlecote, however, was 'Wild Darrell', the master of the house who was responsible for building the magnificent 110 foot-long Long Gallery. According to legend, he was also responsible for making one of the resident ladies-in-waiting pregnant, then after she had given birth, for taking the baby and throwing it onto a fire. The house is said to be haunted both by the spirit of a screaming infant and by the ghost of its mother who wanders the corridors looking for her lost child.

In 1589, the house was acquired by Sir John Popham who went on to become the Lord Chief Justice. An original set of the finger stocks he used to restrain offenders appearing before him can be seen in the Great Hall. During the English Civil War, his grandson, Alexander Popham, was a Roundhead colonel who commanded a force known as the Littlecote Garrison. A fine collection of Parliamentarian uniforms and arms from this period are on display in the Great Hall.

Littlecote House stands in a wonderful position on the banks of the River Kennet. The site has been occupied since Roman times, and indeed around 170 AD, a Roman villa was built here to which an elaborate floor mosaic was added around 360 AD. This was unearthed in the 18th-century, although to prevent its destruction, it was reburied *in situ* where it lay undiscovered until 1977. The three-acre villa site has now been thoroughly excavated and forms one of Littlecote's main attractions. Others include a Puritan chapel, steam railway, children's adventure playground and regular demonstrations of mediaeval jousting and falconry.

Open daily, 10am to 6pm between March and end-September. Admission charge payable.

The road to the northeast of Littlecote crosses the Kennet half-a-mile south of **Chilton Foliat**; this pleasant community contains a 13th-century flint-and-stone church, some lovely old timbered cottages and a number of handsome Georgian residential buildings. Our next stop, **Ramsbury**, was situated a mile-or-so from the B4192 Hungerford to Swindon road, three miles further west. Once an important ecclesiastical centre, the residence of the Bishops of Wiltshire was located here between 909 and 1058; the parish church was built in the 13th-century on the foundations of a much-earlier Saxon building.

Present-day Ramsbury contains a number of attractive Jacobean and Georgian buildings, many of which have gardens stretching down to the River Kennet. The oak tree in the square was planted by a building society in 1986 to replace a mature oak which they had used as a logo. The action in removing the old tree caused certain amount of controversy however, for according to village lore, it was thought to be the home of Maud Toogood, a legendary local witch.

Crown and Anchor   *Ramsbury*   *0672 20335*

Whilst in Ramsbury, we called in at the historic **Crown and Anchor** public house in Crowood Street. Once a private house, in 1778 this lovely old building was acquired by James Mors, a local gunsmith who augmented his income by selling beer; then around 1840, it was bought by a brewer, Richard Hazell, who turned it into an alehouse and gave it its present name. Old maps show a building on the site in the late 1600s and the original beams in the main lounge bar would appear to date from around that time. The large longitudinal beam was hand-carved by a craftsman who must have spent days fashioning the centre joint.

At one time, the old Victorian beer engines on display were connected to a cellar which collapsed around the turn of the century. The entrance

112

to this cellar was through a trap door which was situated at the entrance to what is now the dining room. The upper floor of the house is said to be haunted by an old woman who, it is claimed, once had an 'unpleasant experience' in the pub. What that experience was, no one knows, but she is supposed to appear at the top of the stairs at midnight when the moon is full, although the current proprietors, Kay and Paul Warner, admitted to never having seen her.

As well as a first-class pint of beer, you can enjoy a very good and reasonably priced meal at the Crown and Anchor. The menu is varied and you will leave the table feeling well fed. There are always delicious homemade daily specials too, including a choice for vegetarians. If you care for a glass of wine you will find that the house wine is more than palatable. Food is available at lunchtimes and in the evenings seven days a week, and there is a pleasant beer garden which can be enjoyed on warmer days. An attractive craft and coffee shop have also recently been added to this already pleasant watering hole.

Just outside Ramsbury, the River Kennet borders the grounds of the impressive **Ramsbury Manor**, a private house which was built in 1680 by Inigo Jones' son-in-law and pupil, John Webb.

We rejoined the B4192 to the north of Ramsbury, and after two miles arrived in the picturesque village of **Aldbourne**. Set 700 feet up in the Marlborough Downs, this attractive community has all the ingredients of a model English village: there's a charming village green with a duck pond and weathered stone cross, a 15th-century parish church containing a superbly-carved alabaster tomb of a priest, a 16th-century court house, and a square surrounded by ancient cottages and Georgian houses. In the 17th- and 18th-centuries, Aldbourne was renowned for its bell founding, millinery and cloth-weaving; today, it is a more tranquil place which is a regular winner of the best-kept village in Wiltshire award.

From Aldbourne, we headed due west along a minor road which took us into the heart of the Marlborough Downs. Our destination was the largest and most northerly of the three villages known as the Ogbournes, **Ogbourne St George**, an ancient settlement which lies just to the west of the main A345 Marlborough to Swindon road. The village has Saxon roots and is mentioned in the Domesday Book. Its delightful 12th-century church stands just below the Ridgeway long-distance footpath which at this point makes a dramatic curve around the village, almost surrounding it on three sides.

Within a few yards of the church can be found the splendid traditional inn, the **Old Crown**. Run by Megan and Michael Shaw, the cosy and traditionally-furnished bars offer a fine selection of beers and first-class bar meals, including imaginative daily specials, all of which can be enjoyed to a background of appropriate music – there are no juke boxes here. The thirty-seater dining room features a seventy foot wishing well and provides an excellent á la carte menu which includes an extensive range of vegetarian dishes. For those wishing to stay, there is also a beautifully appointed en suite guest room.

The Old Crown   Ogbourne St George   0672 841445

A truly exceptional place to stay or dine out in Ogbourne St George is the **Parklands Hotel and Restaurant**. This impressive establishment can be found in the centre of the village, just west of the A345 Marlborough to Swindon road and within easy reach of Junction 15 on the M4. Owners Peter and Faith Rostron have built Parklands into a truly outstanding hotel; all guest bedrooms have en suite facilities, telephones, colour televisions and beverage making facilities. Peter is also a renowned chef with an exquisite cosmopolitan touch who takes great pride in providing a top class food and drink. For the adventurous at heart, bicycles can be hired at Parklands for making the delightful journey down the old railway line (now a wonderful hidden bike trail) to Marlborough and the Savernake Forest.

Parklands Hotel   Ogbourne St George   0672 841555

Alternatively, those looking for first-rate guesthouse accommodation in this sheltered part of the Marlborough Downs should make a point of finding **Laurel Cottage**, a delightful thatched 16th-century cottage which is tucked away in the part of Ogbourne St George known as **Southend**.

Lying in a fold of the Marlborough Downs, Laurel Cottage is fully modernised and yet still retains its wonderful traditional charm. Your welcoming hostess, Adrienne Francis, is a superb cook who is happy to cater for any special tastes; she also makes a point of offering tempting alternatives to the traditional English breakfast. The three guest rooms offer first-class facilities and the Ridgeway Suite adjoining the house provides luxury accommodation for two. Outside, the gardens are a positive delight and guests can enjoy their breakfast on the patio in fine weather. Walking, riding, touring and sight-seeing can all be catered for, making Laurel Cottage an ideal holiday location which provides everything guests could wish for.

Laurel Cottage   Southend   0672 841288

From Ogbourne St George, we drove northwards along the A345 Swindon road for three miles before pausing to look at the dramatic remains **Liddington Castle**. Lying to the east of the main road and just off the Ridgeway long-distance footpath, this impressive Iron Age hill fort occupies a seven-acre site on top of a 910 foot down. The structure consists of a series of wide ditches and earthwork defences, the northwestern ramparts of which provide some magnificent views over the Vale of the White Horse and the Cotswold Hills.

Nestling at the foot of the White Horse Downs and surrounded by breathtaking scenery, the picturesque village of **Ashbury** lies three miles further northeast and just across the Oxfordshire border. The Ridgeway, one of Europe's oldest routes, runs close by the village, linking the Vale of Pewsey with Streatly-on-Thames.

In the heart of the village we discovered the **Rose and Crown Hotel**, a delightful village inn which provides a marvellous touring base for exploring the surrounding countryside. The Rose and Crown has recently been refurbished to provide first-class accommodation in eleven well-equipped and attractively furnished guest rooms. Guests can sample the fine real ales in the comfortable surroundings of the two bars, or enjoy the first-class cuisine in the elegant restaurant in an atmosphere of friendly hospitality. During the summer months, customers can relax on the patio and gaze out on a landscape of thatched cottages to the soothing backdrop of chiming church bells.

The Rose and Crown   Ashbury   0793 710222

Retracing our steps, we crossed back onto the southern side the M4 before turning west along the B4005 Wroughton road. After passing through the village of Chiseldon, we then turned south onto a minor road which led us up to the site of another Iron Age stronghold, **Barbury Castle**, one of the most spectacular and widely-visited hill forts in southern England. This clearly-defined twelve-acre site is surrounded by a double line of earthwork ramparts which are breached to the east and west by narrow entrances.

The view over the surrounding downland landscape from the perimeter rim of the castle is breathtaking; an Iron Age field system can just be made out to the east, and further on, a pleasant stroll leads along the Ridgeway Path to Burderop Down. An open hillside half-a-mile to the north of Barbury Castle was the scene of a bloody battle between the Britons and the Saxons in the 6th-century. This ended in defeat for the Britons and established a Saxon kingdom of Wessex under King Ceawlin. In contrast, the whole area has recently been designated the **Barbury Castle Country Park**.

After returning to the B4005, we continued westwards to **Wroughton**, home of the highly-regarded **Science Museum** which is housed in a

116

number of refurbished aircraft hangers on Wroughton's disused airfield. Two of these buildings contain the national collection of civil and commercial aircraft, along with a display of historic space rockets, hovercraft, fire-fighting appliances and aero- and marine engines. Another contains a large collection of vintage buses, steam and motor lorries, cars, motorbikes and bicycles, and yet another, a collection of historic farm machinery and agricultural implements. The museum stages a number of specialist air shows and motor rallies throughout the year, and the nearby **Butser Ancient Farm Project** and **Clauts Wood Nature Reserve** are two further places of interest which are well worth a visit.

Wroughton Science Museum

From Wroughton, we drove southwards through the dramatic rolling landscape of the Marlborough Downs. Our next stop was **Winterbourne Monkton**, an attractive village which can be found on the A361 Devizes road, two miles north of Avebury. The tiny village church has an unusual shingled belfry which is supported on timbers sited within the church.

We decided to break our journey here and were fortunate enough to discover the **New Inn**, a lovely establishment run by Eric and Rachel Matthews. Inside, you will find a cosy, welcoming bar, an excellent restaurant and first-class en suite accommodation. The restaurant overlooks ancient water meadows and features a fine old fireplace with an original studded iron 'soot catcher' door. The varied menu includes steak, rainbow trout and 'chicken breast in thyme and port sauce'; we found it

117

competitively priced and there is also a children's menu available. To accompany your meal, choose a bottle from the extensive wine list which features some excellent Australian wines.

The New Inn   Winterbourne Monkton   06723240

On leaving Winterbourne Monkton, we retraced our steps northwards along the A361 for three miles before turning northwest onto the Wootton Basset road. Within half-a-mile of this junction, the road passes through **Broad Hinton**, a charming village with a noteworthy church containing a carved alabaster effigy of Francis Glanville, a royalist colonel who was killed at Bridgewater during the English Civil War (the colonel's original armour is on display nearby).

The Cross Keys Inn   Wooton Bassett   0793 855476

Five miles further on, we came to the delightful small town of **Wootton Bassett**. This bustling community contains a number of fine old buildings including the **Old Town Hall**, an unusual structure which was built on a series of tall stone piers. The open-sided ground-floor area once served as a covered market and today provides shelter for the old town stocks; the upper floor once contained the town chambers and now

118

houses an interesting museum of local history.

Among the excellent shops and businesses in Wootton Bassett's High Street is the locally-renowned **Cross Keys Inn**. Once a busy coaching inn, the Cross Keys is a lively traditionally-run inn which is now a Grade II listed building. The proprietors, Paul and Jean Thomas, have worked hard to preserve the inn's character and appeal. (In fact, Paul was awarded the Gold Medal by the British Institute of Innkeepers in May 1992.) Take a drink in the Penny Bar where every surface is covered with pennies, or sample the excellent food accompanied by a bottle from the extensive wine list. With evening entertainment ranging from darts, pool and live music to Karaoke and outdoor barbecues, this truly is an inn in the finest tradition.

Don't forget....

To tell people that you read about them in The Hidden Places

Emms Coffee Shop   Wooton Bassett   0796 854783

If, instead, you are looking for a truly exceptional restaurant where top class dishes are personally prepared by the proprietor, then you should make a point of finding **Emms Coffee Shop and Restaurant** a little further up Wootton Bassett High Street at No. 147. Accomplished chef Marilyn Pullen is always on hand to provide her customers with the very best in cuisine, wine and service. We started with wild duck and damson soup and ended with fresh greengage crumble. Delicious!

On leaving Wootton Bassett, we joined the minor road which carried us northwards over the M4 to the pleasant village of **Hook**. Here, we discovered the **School House Hotel and Restaurant**, an exceptional establishment which stands at the gateway to the Cotswolds just five minutes' drive from Swindon. Formerly a Victorian school, it is now a Grade II listed building run by a charming and experienced couple, Mr and Mrs Ramselaar. The restaurant with its beautiful Victorian surroundings, is renowned for its creative menus using locally produced fish and poultry. You can sample such delights as 'pot-roasted boneless quail with chicken liver and apricot filling', 'king prawns with seaweed and shrimp sauce', or you can choose from the imaginative vegetarian menu. The bedrooms are all en-suite and excellently equipped, with charming period furnishings and delightful views over the rural downs. This is a very special place and a visit here will indeed be memorable.

Continuing northwards, our next port of call was **Purton**, a long sprawling community with a fine Norman church. St Mary's is unique in England in that it possesses both a tower *and* a spire. According to local legend, this peculiar state of affairs came about when the two sisters who originally commissioned the church were unable to agree on its design; their answer was to build two towers. It turns out, however, that the structures were built 150 years apart: the central tower with its spire was constructed around 1325 and the western pinnacled tower around 1475.

School House Hotel   Hook   0793 851198

Although much altered during the 14th- and 15th-centuries, evidence of the church's Norman origins can be seen in much of its architectural detail. The building also contains some wonderful fragments of mediaeval stained-glass and a number of striking painted murals, including a 17th-century interpretation of the *Death Of The Virgin*.

A bend in the road a mile to the north of Purton is known as **Watkins' Corner** after a man who was hanged here for a murder which turned out to have been committed by his father. According to local folklore, a sudden squall blew up as Watkins swung from the gallows' rope, causing the hangman's horse to bolt. The startled animal then proceeded to throw its rider to the ground, a fall which broke the hangman's neck . To this day, this lonely place is said to be haunted by the spirit of unjustly condemned man.

From the east side of Purton, we drove southeastwards towards the famous country house at **Lydiard Millicent**. Now under the ownership of Thamesdown Borough Council, **Lydiard Mansion** was once the home of the St Johns. One 15th-century member of this distinguished

120

family was grandmother to the House of Tudor; having married the Duke of Somerset in 1440, she gave birth to Margaret Countess of Richmond who went on to became the mother of Henry VII.

The original part-mediaeval manor house was rebuilt in 1745 with a neoclassical pedimented façade and a splendid rococo interior. The building has recently been extensively restored and is now furnished with fine paintings and elegant Georgian furniture. The mansion is the central attraction in the 260-acre **Lydiard Park**, an attractive area of open lawns and woodland which incorporates a visitor centre with an exhibition on local natural history and a children's adventure play area with a life-size western fort.

Lydiard Mansion

The settlement of **Lydiard Tregoze** was founded in Saxon times and once stood alongside the old manor house. However, the 18th-century fashion for 'emparking' large country houses required a landscape free from 'unnecessary' buildings and so the village was allowed to decline. The only building of note to survive is the lovely little church of St Mary which is known for its exceptionally bright and colourful interior. Among its many remarkable features is the **Golden Cavalier**, a full-size gilded effigy of Edward St John who was killed in 1645 at the second Battle of Newbury. Other items of note are the early-17th-century pulpit, the St John family pew, a cabinet containing a brightly coloured triptych, and some striking 15th-century stained glass.

From here, we made our way westwards onto the A3102 which carried us straight into the heart of **Swindon**, Wiltshire's largest town. Before the Great Western Railway's main London to Bristol line was built in 1835, Swindon was a sleepy community whose principal activity was agriculture. A station was built here in that year, though it wasn't until some time later that the GWR's main engineer, Isambard Kingdom Brunel, made the decision which was to change the town beyond all recognition. According to legend, one day Brunel was walking along the Swindon stretch of line whilst wrestling with the question of where to locate the company's main railway workshops. Apparently, he found the problem so exasperating that he finally threw his half-finished sandwich into the air and shouted, 'wherever it lands, there shall I build'.

Great Western Railway Museum

Construction soon got underway and during the golden age of steam, Swindon locomotive works grew to become one of the largest railway workshops in the world. At one time, 12000 workers were employed on the 320-acre site which incorporated a model **Railway Village**, a development of 300 artisan's homes which were built in Bath stone extracted from Box Tunnel (see chapter three). Today, this unique example of Victorian town planning is open to the public as a living museum; one of its most interesting features is a railway foreman's house which dates from 1842 and is furnished in period style. Open daily, 10am to 1pm (not Sundays) and 2pm to 5pm, all year round.

The Faringdon Road site also contains the world famous **Railway Museum** which is located in a former workers' hostel or 'navvies' barracks'. This houses a fascinating collection of steam locomotives, signalling equipment, railway signs and other GWR railwayana, and includes a special room devoted to the life and achievements of Isambard Kingdom Brunel. Open daily, 10am (2pm Sundays) to 5pm, all year round.

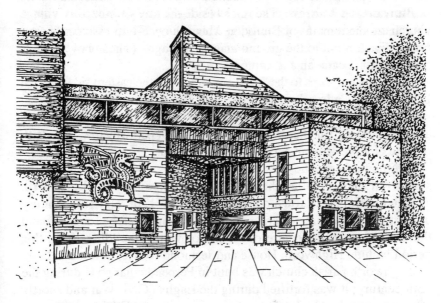

Wyvern Theatre

Present-day Swindon is a bustling commercial centre which at one time was the fastest growing town in Europe. Excellent shopping facilities are offered in Regent Street and the Brunel Centre, and the town is well catered for in the area of arts and entertainment. The Wyvern Theatre is a luxury 650-seat venue which stages everything from pop concerts to large-scale touring theatre and ballet productions, and both the Arts Centre and the Link Arts Studio have 200-seat auditoriums which provide a more intimate space for dance, drama and performance arts.

Swindon's renowned art gallery in Bath Road features work by such acclaimed modern artists as Ben Nicholson, Graham Sutherland and L S Lowry (open daily, 10am to 6pm (2pm to 5pm Sundays), all year round), and the town also contains a number of beautifully-kept parks and open spaces, including Queen's Park, Penhill Park and Faringdon Road Park, part of the GWR's original Railway Village development.

We left Swindon to the north along the A419 Cirencester road. This busy route follows the course of the **Ermine Way**, the great Roman road which linked the garrison towns of *Glevum* (Gloucester) and *Calleva* (Silchester) in Hampshire. The old road followed a virtually straight course for most of its sixty-mile length, a characteristic which is clearly demonstrated in the section which runs northwest from Swindon.

Three miles from the centre of Swindon, we turned west off the A419, and having passed the speedway stadium, came to the pleasant community of **Blunsdon St Andrew**. The ruins beside the tiny 13th-century village church are the remains of Blunsdon Abbey, a once-impressive monastic house which burnt to the ground many years ago. (The abbey grounds now contain a caravan and camping park.)

Retracing our steps to the A419, we crossed to the eastern side to reach Blunsdon St Andrew's sister village of **Broad Blunsdon**, an ancient settlement which lies just to the north of the B4019. The village possesses a fine Early English church which is linked by a pathway to **Castle Hill**, the site of a pre-Roman earthwork fortification.

A little further to the west, the B4019 climbs a 400 foot incline at the summit of which is sited the aptly-named community of **Highworth**. This delightful small town contains some fine 17th- and 18th-century domestic architecture, several examples of which can be found around the old square in the centre of town; noteworthy buildings from this period include Highworth House and Jesmond House, now a hotel.

Highworth parish church was built in Perpendicular style during the 15th-century; it was fortified during the English Civil War and shortly after, was attacked by Parliamentarian forces under Fairfax. A cannon ball which struck the building during the siege is on display inside. The church also contains a memorial to a Lieutenant Warneford who in 1915 was awarded the Victoria Cross for destroying the first enemy Zeppelin during World War I.

We would recommend walking to the top of the Highworth Hill; the views from here are spectacular and take in the three counties of Wiltshire, Gloucestershire and Oxfordshire. The land to the north of Highworth slopes gradually down into the valley of the River Thames, a gentle landscape which was to be our next destination.

After retracing our steps for a mile along the B4019, we turned north into a country road which led us through Hannington to the pleasant Thames-side community of **Castle Eaton**. The village possesses a small yet striking 13th-century church and an excellent pub, the **Red Lion**, with a garden stretching down to the riverbank.

For a taste of rural England at its very best, you need look no further than this famous hostelry. Standing at the highest navigable point on the upper reaches of the Isis, this, 'the first pub on the Thames', is a beautiful example of Jacobean redbrick architecture and is a Grade II listed building. It is run by David and Anne Lenthall, a very experienced couple who offer top class food and a fine selection of beers. Customers can play the ancient game of Petangue on the lovely lawn, or enjoy a meal in the charming Jacobean restaurant. With its excellent food, drink and atmosphere, a visit to the Red Lion is sure to be a memorable experience.

The Red Lion   Castle Eaton   0285 810280

From Castle Eaton, we crossed onto the northern bank of the Thames before continuing northwestwards through the country lanes to the charmingly-named community of **Marston Meysey**. This, the northernmost village in Wiltshire, has a long main street which is lined with handsome old houses and cottages. Just outside the village, we passed an unusual roundhouse, probably a former canal lock-keeper's cottage, and a bridge over the North Wiltshire branch of the Wiltshire & Berkshire Canal.

The road to the west of Marston Meysey passes briefly into Gloucestershire before returning to Wiltshire near the junction with the A419. The lovely old village of **Latton** lies a mile to the northwest of this junction. This pleasant community was originally part of an estate belonging to the Earl of St Germans, though in more recent times it has been brought under the ownership of the Cooperative Wholesale Society who use it for housing their agricultural workers, white collar staff and retired employees. Although relatively modest, the village possesses some delightful 17th-century Cotswold stone cottages, some rather more substantial Victorian houses, and a church founded in Norman times which was substantially rebuilt by the forthright Victorian architect, William Butterfield.

In the heyday of Britain's inland waterways, Latton stood at an important junction of the Wiltshire & Berkshire and Thames & Severn

125

canals. Latton Basin, the holding area where barges used to manoeuvre and wait, can still be made out in the old canal bed, and a footpath along the course of the canal to the northwest leads to the remains of a lock and a lock-keeper's roundhouse similar to the one at Marston Meysey. Looking somewhat out of place, the impressive old wharf owner's (or *wharfinger*'s) house with its imposing classical pediment can be seen from the A419 trunk road a little further to the southwest.

Church of St Peter and St Paul

Continuing in this direction, we soon arrived in **Cricklade**, an attractive small town which lies just to the west of the main road. The town has a long history stretching back beyond the days of the Roman occupation; a mint was located here during Saxon times, then several centuries later, the Normans were responsible for founding the town's main church which they dedicated to St Sampson, a Breton saint born in 465. The main building was constructed between the 12th- and 15th-centuries, and magnificent cathedral-like tower was added during the Tudor period by the Duke of Northumberland in 1553. The interior features some fine Norman details, some rare heraldic carvings and an unusual Elizabethan altar table; each September, St Sampson's is the principal venue for Cricklade's widely-renowned festival of music.

The smaller St Mary's Church can be found at the other end of the High Street near the remains of a 13th-century priory and hospital; the priory has now been converted into small residential dwellings. The town also possesses a famous school which was founded by a London goldsmith, Robert Jenner, in 1651. Those keen to find out more about Cricklade's long and eventful history should make a point of finding the town's interesting small museum which is situated opposite the clock tower in Calcutt Street (open Wednesdays 2pm to 4pm and Saturdays 10am to 12 noon).

Whilst in the centre of Cricklade, we took the opportunity of calling in for some refreshment at the excellent **White Hart Hotel**, an impressive former coaching inn which is run by a charming couple, Peter and Gillian Mortley. Once the meeting place of the local hunt, the townsfolk traditionally gathered here on Boxing Day to see the hunt off. (Although the hunt no longer meets, the tradition of meeting at the White Hart on Boxing Day continues.) An excellent pint of beer is served in the spacious bars, and there is also a beautifully appointed dining room where visitors can enjoy some of Gillian's mouthwatering and imaginative recipes. House specialities include game and fish, and all dishes are prepared using fresh locally-sourced produce wherever possible; customers can also choose from the extensive wine list. As well as providing excellent food and drink, the White Hart has fifteen attractively furnished and well-equipped guest bedrooms.

The White Hart Hotel   Cricklade   0793 750206

Those interested in industrial archeology should make a point of finding West Mill Wharf in West Mill Lane, a once-lively wharf which served the North Wiltshire branch of the Wiltshire & Berkshire Canal. Although now almost completely filled in, the site serves as a poignant reminder of the once-golden age of the narrowboat.

Cricklade is the only town in Wiltshire to lie on the River Thames (although at this point it could be better be described as a wide stream). At the northern end of the High Street, the river flows under a bridge, beyond which is a stile leading to a well-worn footpath. This leads to

North Meadow, an ancient water meadow which was designated a nature reserve in 1973. This exceptional area of meadowlands contains some rare plants and flowers which are a delight to behold in late-spring and summer (though please respect the nature reserve and on no account remove any of the plantlife). The path upstream leads to a footbridge, allowing the return journey to be made on the opposite bank of the River Thames.

From Cricklade, we drove westwards along the B4040 into the area covered in our next chapter.

CHAPTER SIX

North West Wiltshire

The Unicorn Gallery

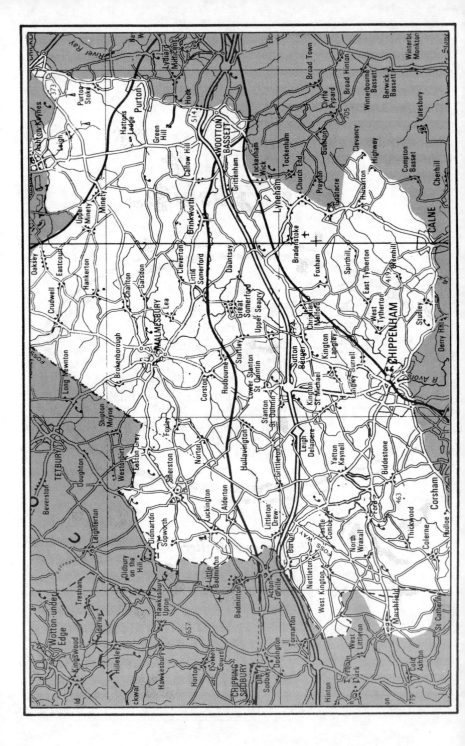

Index

Arches Farm B&B, Arches Lane, Malmesbury

The Bell Inn, Restaurant and Caravan Park, Yatton Keynell

Bremilam Guest House, Bremilham Road, Malmesbury

Big Thatch B&B, Ford, Nr Chippenham

The Coach House Guest House, Upper Wraxall, Nr Bath

Corner Cottage B&B, Ashton Keynes, Wiltshire

Fenwick's B&B, Lower Goatacre, Calne

'Finnygook' B&B, Kington Langley, Chippenham

Flisteridge Cottage B&B, Upper Minety, Malmesbury

Fosse Farmhouse Hotel, Nettleton, Nr Chippenham

Friday Street Farm B&B, Christian Malford, Chippenham

The Gates Tea Room and B&B, Castle Combe, Nr Chippenham

Manor Farm B&B, Corston, Nr Malmesbury

Manor Farm B&B, Sopworth, Nr Chippenham

The Nettleton Arms Pub, Nettleton, Chippenham

The Old Bell Hotel, Abbey Row, Malmesbury

Rattlebone Inn, Church Street, Sherston

The Smoking Dog Inn and Restaurant, 62 High Street, Malmesbury

Stanton Court B&B, Stanton St Quintin, Nr Malmesbury

Starfall Pottery, Sheldon, Nr Biddestone

The Unicorn Gallery Gift Shop, The Street, Castle Combe

West Crudwell B&B, Crudwell, Nr Malmesbury

The Whole Hog Inn, 8 Market Cross, Malmesbury

Widleys Farm B&B, Sherston, Malmesbury

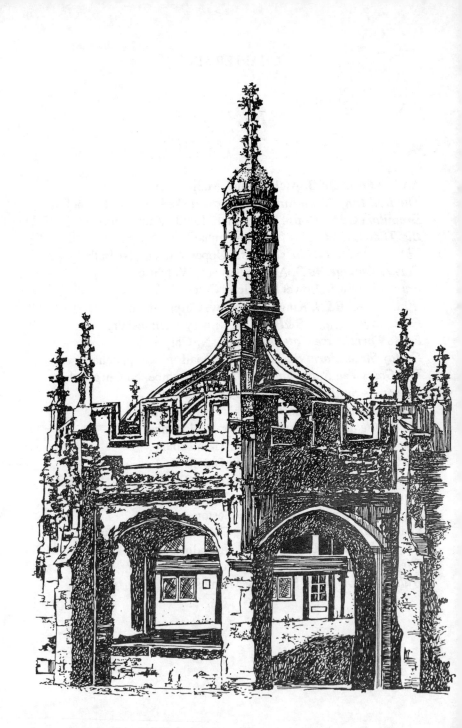

Malmesbury Market Cross

CHAPTER SIX

North West Wiltshire

For lovers of ancient English churches, the villages in the upper reaches of the Thames to the west of Cricklade contain a couple of gems. The first can be found just to the north of the B4040 Malmesbury road near the village of **Leigh**; now redundant, the church of All Saints lies a quarter-of-a-mile down a track from the Waterhay Bridge over the Thames. This lovely old building, which is also known as the **Old Chancel**, dates from the 12th-century and was later altered during the 14th- and 15th-centuries.

Holy Cross Church

A couple of miles to the northwest, the church of the **Holy Cross** stands on the edge of the sprawling village of **Ashton Keynes**. Also founded in the 12th-century, the church was extended in the 13th-century and extensively restored during the 1870s under the direction of William Butterfield, the architect of Keble College, Oxford. The farmyard adjoining the church is the site of a monastic house which was founded in Saxon times, and both the church and the monastery are surrounded by the remnants of a double moat from this period.

An ancient cross stands in the centre of the churchyard; this is one of Ashton Keynes' four 'preaching' crosses, all of which were damaged during the English Civil War (this one was restored as a war memorial in 1917). The churchyard also contains a number of table tombs belonging to the Richmond family, the local lords of the manor who lived at Cove House in the centre of the village. During the Civil War, the family's allegiances were seriously divided. Two sons chose to fight on opposing sides, and during a nighttime skirmish outside Ashton Keynes, one brother is reported to have unwittingly killed the other. When faced with the truth, the surviving brother was so full of remorse that he took off for America and subsequently founded a branch of the family there.

Corner Cottage   Ashton Keynes   0285 861454

Once a manor belonging to King Alfred's sister, Ashton Keynes is crisscrossed by hidden walkways which connect with the village inn and the ancient church. The village contains a number of fine old Cotswold-stone residences, including Brook House and Ashton Mill. At the Ashton Mill end of the village, the infant Thames runs beside the main street and each house is reached by way of an attractive small footbridge.

In Fore Street, we were fortunate enough to discover the first-rate bed and breakfast establishment, **Corner Cottage**, which is run by Rosina and Jim Wiltshire. Rosina and Jim have lived in Ashton Keynes for more than twenty years and have welcomed guests into their delightful Cotswold cottage for almost as long. Set in a lovely part of the village, Corner Cottage offers excellent accommodation for which the Wiltshires have been awarded an English Tourist Board two-crown rating. All guest

134

rooms have en suite facilities, making this is an ideal base for hikers and motorists to explore the outstanding Cotswold countryside.

The country lanes to the southwest of Ashton Keynes led us through the pleasant rolling countryside of northwest Wiltshire. Just outside the village of **Upper Minety**, we came to **Flisteridge Cottage**, a charming private residence which offers superb overnight accommodation. For a real taste of English heritage, a stay here is a must. This charming colour-washed cottage overlooks Flisteridge woods and is situated just outside Minety village, the professed home of the distinguished Quaker family, the Penns, after whom Pennsylvania was named. Fay Toop-Rose loves sharing her home with her guests. Her house is beautifully decorated and offers a friendly and homely atmosphere, with the additional bonus of a delightful English garden in which guests are welcome to relax. Flisteridge Cottage provides a truly lovely and peaceful base for touring the Cotswold countryside.

Flisteridge Cottage   Upper Minety   0666 860343

After passing over the B4040 near Minety village, we continued southwards through the country lanes, crossing the B4042 and then the M4 near Callow Hill. Our next stop was the peaceful hamlet of **Lower Goatacre**, a pleasant community which is situated just off the A3102, one mile south of the town and military airport at Lyneham. Here, we discovered **Fenwick's**, the small country house bed and breakfast establishment which is run by Margaret and Fen Fenwick.

Visitors to Fenwick's will find Margaret and Fen warm and welcoming hosts. Their non-smoking house provides high quality accommodation comprising one double room with en suite shower, and one double room with en suite bathroom and a single room adjoining (thus creating a family suite when required); all offer excellent facilities, including colour televisions. There is a choice of traditional English breakfast or a selection from Margaret's á la carte menu, either of which can be enjoyed

135

on the beautiful patio overlooking the garden. One of the finest ways guests can relax is to take tea, either on the terrace in summer, or in front of a blazing log fire in the drawing room in winter.

Fenwick's   Lower Goatacre   0249 76645

From Goatacre, we headed west into the country lanes, and after passing through the hamlet of Catcomb, continued southwest towards our next stopping place, the lovely old village of **Bremhill**. The village stands at the eastern end of **Maud Heath's Causeway**, a remarkable raised footpath which runs for four-and-a-half miles towards Chippenham. This surprising work of civil engineering was constructed in 1474 on the instructions of a local market trader, Maud Heath. Maud died owning property and land in Bremhill which not only provided funds for the building and upkeep of the causeway, but also for the construction of the village bridge.

Friday Street Farm   Christian Malford   0249 720146

A couple of miles to the northwest, the raised footpath runs over 64 brick and stone arches near the village of **Kellaways**. In 1698, a ball and pillar was erected here in memory of the market pedlar who never forgot

136

the many times she had to trudge, often wet through, with her basket of goods from Bremhill to Chippenham. A wonderful statue of Maud, her basket at her side, stands overlooking the flood plain at Wick Hill.

The attractive Anglo-Saxon village of **Christian Malford** lies a couple of miles to the north of Kellaways. This is where we found **Friday Street Farm**, an exceptional farmhouse bed and breakfast establishment run by Linda Di Claudio. The farmhouse is tucked away in the beautiful Wiltshire countryside at the edge of the village. It is a centuries old 'A'-frame longhouse, full of character and charm, with original beams and an open log fire. Linda offers excellent accommodation in this non-smoking establishment which comprises one single and two double rooms, all with colour televisions and beverage making facilities. After enjoying a wholesome Wiltshire breakfast, guests are encouraged to take a stroll around the working dairy farm; however, it is worth checking before you set off in case you should encounter Barnaby the bull grazing quietly in the paddock!

Finnygook   *Kington Langley*   *0249 750272*

On leaving Christian Malford, we joined the B4069 and drove southwestwards in the direction of Chippenham. After three miles, we noticed a sign to **Kington Langley**, a pleasant community which lies between the B4069 and the main A429 Chippenham to Cirencester road.

Here, we made a point of calling in at the charmingly-named **Finnygook**, a delightful private home which also offers excellent overnight accommodation. Visitors will find this perfect retreat in Days Lane. A lovely secluded house set in delightful gardens, its tranquillity belies the fact that it is situated only a few minutes away from the M4. Run by Ena Weston and her husband, a lovely friendly couple, Finnygook is a very relaxed and welcoming establishment offering spacious, well furnished accommodation. Ena is an excellent cook and is happy to cater for special tastes given prior notice. As a touring base Finnygook is ideal; Bath, Bristol, Longleat and Castle Combe are all close by, and a warm welcome awaits you on your return. All in all, this is a truly delightful place to stay.

A short journey southwards from Kington Langley led us into the centre of the charming old market town of **Chippenham**. This historic settlement was founded on the banks of the Bristol Avon around 600 AD by the Saxon King Cyppa from whom the town gets its name. Within 250 years it had become an important administrative and hunting centre in King Alfred's Wessex. At the heart of present-day Chippenham is the ancient market place which still hosts a flourishing weekly market every Friday.

Sheldon Manor

The streets of Chippenham contain number of fine old buildings, including the 15th-century twin-gabled town hall with its unusual wooden turret. The half-timbered Yelde Hall was used by the Bailiff and Burgesses of the *Chippenham Hundred* until 1841; having been extensively restored, the building was reopened as a museum of local history in 1963. The museum contains a number of interestingly arranged rooms, including one which has been refurbished as the old town lock up. Open Mondays to Saturdays, 10am to 12.30pm and 2pm to 4.30pm between mid-March and end-October. Admission free.

Of the four churches in Chippenham, St Andrew's is the oldest. It was founded during Saxon times, and although little from this period now remains, it contains some fine monuments from the 13th- and 15th-centuries. There is also an exquisite stained-glass window and several references to the Hungerford family, the local lords of the manor. St Paul's Church in Malmesbury Road was built in Gothic revival style by architect Giles Gilbert Scott in 1855.

Other noteworthy buildings in Chippenham include the handsome early-19th-century structure, Ivy House and the Grove, the home of a short-lived spa during the 18th-century. At Hardenhuish Hill (pronounced *Harnish*) on the edge of Chippenham, John Wood the Younger of Bath built the Georgian church of St Nicholas on the site of a ruined mediaeval church. Completed in 1779, it is noted for its elegant Venetian windows.

We left Chippenham along the A420 Bristol road, after a mile or so, turned south to reach the historic country house of **Sheldon Manor**. A manor has existed here since the late 12th-century when the lands of the old Chippenham Manor were divided into three (the lordship of the Chippenham Hundred was awarded to Sheldon). With parts of the present-day house, including the porch, dating from the late-13th-century, the building has been continuously occupied since 1424, the year the Hungerford family first acquired the estate. After remaining in their family for over 250 years, the house changed hands several times before being bought by the current owning family in 1917. Sheldon Manor is open to the public on Thursdays, Sundays and Bank Holiday Mondays; garden 12.30pm to 6pm, house 2pm to 6pm. Admission charge payable.

Starfall Pottery   *Sheldon*   *0249 713292*

Continuing westwards along the country lanes, we soon passed a sign to **Starveal Farm**, a delightful old farmhouse which has been converted into a working pottery. Situated between Biddestone Manor and Sheldon Manor, half-a-mile from the picturesque village of Biddestone, the **Starfall Pottery** provided us with an afternoon of great interest. In the studio, you can see the beautiful and skilled work of Gordon and Dorothy Whittle, two delightful people who are always pleased to see visitors. As

139

well as being able to admire their pottery making skills, you can also view a wide range of domestic stoneware and commemorative pottery for all occasions. We saw some very pretty wedding plates which had been specially commissioned, and also some charming christening mugs.

The skills of the Whittles made us very envious. Not only are they superbly clever with their hands, but they can also decorate the articles they have made with equal skill. As well as a display of pottery, there is a range of hand-woven and knitted items, including those from hand-spun, natural dyed wool. All the articles on display are for sale at very affordable prices, or if you wish to order a special item, then all you have to do is ask. In our experience, potters often seem to have a keen interest in herbs and the Whittles are no exception. They grow and sell a wide range of herb plants and are extremely knowledgeable on the subject. The Starfall Pottery is open every day from 9am until dusk, all year round.

A little further west, we came to **Biddestone**, an attractive community of stylish 17th- and 18th-century houses set around a village green with a large duck pond. Among the noteworthy buildings to be seen here is a handsome gabled farmhouse with a Georgian gazebo which can be found near the pond, and a grey stone manor house with a large walled garden which stands on the edge of the village.

The Bell Inn   Yatton Keynell   0249 782216

Keeping to the minor roads, we drove northwards from Biddestone across the A420 to our next destination, the historic village of **Yatton Keynell**. In the centre of the village is its one and only pub, the **Bell Inn**. Not just a public house, the Bell has caravan and camping facilities for people touring the area or visiting the motor racing circuit at nearby **Castle Combe**.

The Bell overlooks the centre of the village and faces the 15th-century church of St Margaret of Antioch. Part of the church was built as a shrine by local landowner Sir William Keynell who had it made to show God his gratitude for protecting him in battle and returning him safely to England from the Crusades.

The Bell was originally constructed as a farmhouse during the 15th-century and only became a coaching inn some years later because of its proximity to what was then the main road between Bristol, Chippenham and London (the Bell lies 97 miles from Hyde Park Corner). During renovation work, an unusual fertility stone was uncovered (evidently, this had not been in use for many years as the population of the village remains very small!). The interior is well preserved, with original oak-beamed ceilings and a 15th-century central fireplace. In winter, simulated log fires give off a surprisingly warm and cheering effect.

Landlords Don and Jan Milburn have been at the Bell for a number of years. When Don left the Royal Air Force he chose to join the licensed trade, something that was not new to him as his father had run a pub when Don was a lad. Jan has had many years experience working behind a bar and they both thoroughly enjoy the hectic pub life. One of Jan's hobbies is collecting owls and owl pictures, a large collection of which can be seen in the attractive lounge bar where there is also an interesting photograph of the village taken from a Hercules aircraft.

The aromas coming from the kitchen made us feel like having an early lunch. We only wanted something light so we chose cauliflower cheese served with a crispy roll and butter. Home-cooked and very tasty, the cauliflower was just right (in other words it didn't fall apart as we ate it). Pizzas, burgers, basket meals and omelettes, as well as the usual pub food, made up the rest of the menu. A choice of vegetarian and children's meals are also available.

Lunch over, Don came and sat with us and began telling us tales from the area's past. He also explained to us how the nearby hamlet of Tiddlywink got its unusual name: at the market in Chippenham, the cattle would mostly be sold in the afternoons. As it was not possible to transport them on foot after dark because a toll was charged in Yatton Keynell (the old toll board can be seen in the pub entrance), they were kept overnight at the small hamlet which got its name from the drovers who would stop off for a jug of ale and ended up drunk, or 'tiddly', and would then have to sleep off the effects, or 'wink'.

An inn over five centuries old should have a ghost and Don confirmed our suspicions. Although he has never seen one himself, his predecessor claims to have seen a young lady walk past him in the pub and straight through the far wall. Behind this wall, there is a spiral staircase which is no longer in use.

The Bell Inn is a friendly place where locals and visitors mix well and everybody is made to feel welcome. In summer there is a garden to enjoy with children's swings, a slide and a climbing frame. Badminton is only five miles away, the beautiful Bowood House eight miles, and of course Bath with its beautiful buildings and shops is only half-an-hour's drive.

From Yatton Keynell, it was only a short drive northwest to **Castle Combe,** featured on our front cover, and one of the loveliest villages in the whole of Wessex. Indeed in 1962, Castle Combe was named the prettiest village in England, one of the factors which led to it becoming a location for the film, *Doctor Doolittle*. Although this means the village is now well and truly on the tourist map, in the 15th- and 16th-centuries, it was a well-established cloth-weaving centre. Many of the present-day buildings date from this period of prosperity, including the Perpendicular St Andrew's Church with its fine fan vaulting, 13th-century font and memorial to Walter Dunstanville, the founder of the now-demolished castle from which the village takes its name.

Castle Combe

Castle Combe lies in a deep, tree-lined valley and visitors are encouraged to park their cars at the top of the hill and walk down through the narrow streets. Once there, one of the finest views of the old village can be had from the picturesque three-arched bridge over the By Brook (this is also a good place for spotting trout). Castle Combe also contains a number of other impressive buildings, including a covered 15th-century market cross, the site of a once-regular wool market, and a lovely 16th-

142

century manor house, now a hotel, which was much altered during the Victorian period.

Unicorn Gallery   Castle Combe   0249 782291

Visitors to Castle Combe's main street will delight when they discover the **Unicorn Gallery**, a veritable Pandora's Box where they can be sure to find a gift for that special occasion. The gallery's reputation has been built up and maintained by its owners, Jennifer and Brian Shepherd, and it has regular clientele of local customers who come to seek out that special anniversary, birthday or wedding present; it is also a focal point for any Christmas shopping trip. Visitors can browse at their leisure, taking in the exquisite collection of gifts and antiques, and friendly and helpful advice always on hand, if required. Prices range across the board and there is something to suit everyone's taste and pocket. On your way out, you may well be tempted to take a photograph of the beautiful 'typical English cottage garden' which adjoins the gallery.

The Gates   Castle Combe   0249 782111

On Castle Combe's old Market Place, we also discovered a delightful tearoom and bed and breakfast establishment, **The Gates**. The Gates is

143

a delightful establishment run by Hilary Baker and her cheerful staff whose attention to detail is renowned. Situated in the heart of this lovely Cotswold village, it was built in the 15th-century and was formerly a bordello. It is the perfect place to relax and enjoy a tasty lunch or to while away an hour or two over a cup of coffee and a piece of one of the mouthwatering cakes on offer. Hilary also provides bed and breakfast accommodation in two rooms, one family and one double, both of which have low-beamed ceilings and are full of character.

In marked contrast with the rest of Castle Combe, a popular motor racing circuit is located a mile or so to the east of the village.

Big Thatch   *Ford*   *0249 782107*

The attractive village of **Ford** lies a mile downstream from Castle Combe at the point where the By Brook crosses the A420 Chippenham to Bristol road. Hidden away just off the main road in the heart of this tiny village is a beautiful old English dwelling known as **Big Thatch**. Now owned by a charming lady, Patricia Townson, Big Thatch boasts some celebrity former owners, including actress Joanna Lumley and rock musician Peter Gabriel, from whom Patricia bought the cottage. Originally constructed over 800 years ago, the cottage in its present form dates back some 400 years. It is built of Cotswold stone in a traditional 'A' Frame structure and has a magnificent sweep of thatch. The beamed rooms are attractively furnished and decorated, and the delightful English gardens and sheltered rear cloisters add to its ever-present air of peace and tranquillity. It is really hard to imagine a lovelier cottage anywhere in Wiltshire.

At Ford, we joined the A420 and drove westwards for two miles before turning north to reach our next stopping place, the tiny hamlet of **Upper Wraxall**. This quiet rural backwater is one of several delightful communities which lie on the southwestern fringe of the Cotswold Hills; it is also the location of The Coach House, an impressive country

144

guesthouse which is set within eight acres of beautiful secluded grounds.

If you are looking for somewhere to stay that combines peaceful seclusion with easy access to places of interest, then the **Coach House** at Upper Wraxall is perfect. This tiny hamlet lies in beautiful Wiltshire countryside just off the A420 and provides a tranquil setting for this beautifully converted barn. David and Helga Venables are friendly and welcoming hosts whose former guests often return as friends. Their lovely stone-built house offers first-class accommodation. The interior is elegant and spacious and has three beautifully furnished en suite guest rooms which provide every modern comfort. Set in attractive landscaped grounds containing a full-sized croquet lawn and hard tennis court, the Coach House makes a perfect holiday hideaway.

The Coach House   Upper Wraxall   0225 891026

A mile or so to the west, and just over the Avon border, we made a short detour to visit the exceptional old coaching village of **Marshfield**. The village stands on a ridge which, in the 18th-century, formed part of the main London to Bristol coaching route. At almost a mile long, the High Street is one of the longest in the country; in its heyday, it contained over a dozen coaching inns, including the famous Catherine Wheel, one of only three survivors. Another of Marshfield's relics from the era of the stagecoach is an 18th-century road sign with the inscription, '103 miles to London, 12 miles and 1 furlong to Bristol'.

Marshfield was also an important wool trading and malting centre, and many of the large stone-built houses which line the main street were built on the proceeds of these activities. Despite them having been constructed in two almost continuous rows, the buildings still manage to create an atmosphere of elegance and charm. Indeed, much of the old part of the village, between the early-17th-century *Crispe* almshouses at one end of the High Street and the imposing parish church of St Mary at the other, is now a designated conversation area.

One of Marshfield's more eccentric businesses operated in the High Street until 1983. Bodman's grocery and drapery shop was opened by Mr Bodman Snr in 1860s, and when it passed to his son at the beginning of this century, Mr Bodman Jnr made so few alterations that the store gradually became a living museum. Young Mr Bodman refused to make any changes to the Edwardian fixtures and fittings, and if a long-standing item of stock took his fancy, he would often refuse to sell it. This situation persisted until his death at the age of ninety, after which the contents of the shop mostly fell into the hands museum curators and antique dealers.

Retracing out steps back across the Wiltshire border, we turned north into the country lanes before stopping for some refreshment in the charming Cotswold village of **Nettleton**. Here, we were lucky enough to find the **Nettleton Arms**, a traditional inn which also offers first-rate overnight accommodation.

The Nettleton Arms   Nettleton   0249 782783

For lovers of country pubs, a visit to the Nettleton Arms is a must. It has a well-deserved reputation for good food, fine beers (there is a guest cask-conditioned beer each week), and an excellent selection of wines. The landlords, Sheena and Chris Phizaklea, are charming hosts, and the wonderful culinary skill of Sandra House allows customers to savour such delicacies as stuffed local trout, pork Provencale and beef Wellington, as well as a tasty selection of vegetarian dishes, all at very affordable prices. For those wishing to stay there are four beautifully appointed rooms in the old coach house (two doubles, two singles), all with en suite facilities.

The nearby hamlet of **Nettleton Shrub** is the location of an exceptional country hotel and restaurant which goes under the unassuming name of **Fosse Farmhouse**. Located in the heart of the Beaufort Hunt on the historic Fosse Way, Fosse Farmhouse is a lovely Cotswold country house built in 1750 which is now a first-class hotel and restaurant. It is owned

146

and run by Caron Cooper, a chef of international repute who has built a substantial reputation in the area for outstanding food and stunning interior decoration. An orchard links the main house to the tea and breakfast rooms where guests can enjoy a light lunch or treat themselves to a luscious cream tea. In the evening, there are further temptations on the dinner menu, such as smoked duck breast with salad, followed by chicken with wild mushroom sauce. Before leaving, guests are advised to look around the outhouses which are filled with interesting relics from the past, as well as antiques, flowers, homemade jam and lovely country gifts, all of them for sale. Immediately opposite the farmhouse is the Castle Combe Golf and Country Club which guests are welcome to use.

Continuing northwards, we crossed the M4 near the village of Burton before turning northeast onto the B4040 Malmesbury road. The 15,000-acre **Badminton Estate** lies a mile or so to the east of this road. Famous for its annual three-day horse trials which take place each April, this has been the country seat of the Dukes of Beaufort since the 17th-century. **Badminton House**, an imposing Palladian-style mansion, contains an impressive art collection, including paintings from the Italian, English and Dutch schools and some exquisite wood-carving by master-carver Grinling Gibbons.

Fosse Farmhouse   Nettleton Shrub   0249 782286

Many of the buildings on the Badminton Estate, including the parish church of St Michael and All Angels which stands adjacent to the main house, were designed by architect Thomas Wright in a romantic castellated style. Examples of his architectural influence can also be seen in the two estate villages of **Little** and **Great Badminton**, the latter of which contains some substantial stone-built residences and a row of splendid 18th-century almshouses.

On one wet afternoon during the 1860s, guests to Badminton House are said to have come up with an idea for a novel new game. Having found

147

some crude children's rackets and corks studded with feathers, they decided to attempt a game of indoor tennis and proceeded to stretch a string across the hall as a net. That afternoon, the game of badminton was born. A few years later, one of the guests is believed to have taken a version of the game to the Indian subcontinent where the first formal rules were drawn up in Karachi in 1877.

Manor Farm   Sopworth   045423 8676

Returning to the B4040, we turned north near the village of Luckington to reach the lovely old community of **Sopworth**. Those looking for top quality farmhouse bed and breakfast accommodation should look out here for **Manor Farm**, a charming Jacobean country farmhouse which stands in a wonderful position overlooking the village.

The Rattlebone Inn   Sherston   0666 840871

This charming Jacobean country farmhouse is run by a lovely lady, Diana Barker, who was born here and has provided bed and breakfast accommodation for many years. Many of her guests return time and time again to enjoy her warm friendly hospitality and excellent cooking. All the guest rooms are en suite and have breathtaking views over the

148

surrounding countryside. The farm is actually part of the Badminton Estate, home of many spirited and finely-bred horses. Set in this idyllic location on the Gloucestershire-Wiltshire border, Manor Farm is a simply enchanting place to relax and get away from it all.

From Sopworth, it was only a short drive to **Sherston**, an attractive village lying beside the B4040, two miles to the east (the village is also known by its historic name, Sherston Magna). At the centre of this ancient settlement, we discovered the charmingly named **Rattlebone Inn and Restaurant**, a first-rate hostelry with a long and interesting history. In 1016, Edmund Ironside defeated Canute near here in the Battle of Sherston, then John Rattlebone, a local hero, sustained a mortal wound and expired, it is believed, on the site where the inn now stands.

Today, the Rattlebone Inn has a deserved reputation for fine cask-conditioned ales and excellent food, with such delicacies on the menu as smoked trout mousse, or deep-fried brie with redcurrant jelly, followed by the likes of mushroom and chestnut Stroganoff or lamb steak with Madeira, honey and tarragon. Customers can also enjoy playing traditional and modern pub games in the public bar, or wander out to the old stables for a game of skittles. Full of traditional atmosphere, this really is a fine example of a typical English inn.

Widleys Farm   *Sherston*   *0666 840213*

A delightful place to stay in this tranquil backwater can be found at **Widleys Farm**. Situated in the heart of the Wiltshire Cotswolds at **Sherston**, Widleys Farm is a 300-acre working arable and dairy farm. The 18th-century farmhouse is run by a lovely lady, Mary Hibbard, who provides three spacious family rooms all with washbasins, colour televisions and hot drinks facilities. Here, you can be sure of real countryside hospitality and Mary will readily provide a fabulous four-course dinner on request. The farmhouse is surrounded by beautiful gardens and stables, whilst among the farm buildings, there is an

149

impressive Cotswold stone tithe barn. With the famous Westonbirt Arboretum close by and Slimbridge Wildfowl Trust within easy reach, Widleys Farm makes a very comfortable touring base for the Cotswolds.

From here, we continued northeast along the B4040, and having passed through Sherston Magna's sister village of Sherston Parva, arrived in the fine old community of **Easton Grey**. Here, the Sherston branch of the River Avon is spanned by a 16th-century bridge consisting of five low stone arches. The village itself rises from the riverbank along a curved main street of densely-packed grey limestone houses, most with mullioned windows and steeply-pitched gabled roofs.

A manor house has looked down from the hill above Easton Grey since the 13th-century. The present-day mansion dates from the early-18th-century and has a classical façade with an elegant covered portico. The building stands within beautiful landscaped grounds which also contain a small church with a Norman tower and font and an interior which was extensively renovated during the 1830s. Once owned by his sister-in-law, the house was used a summer retreat by Herbert Asquith, Britain's prime minister from 1908-16, then in 1923, it was occupied by the Prince of Wales for the duration of the Duke of Beaufort's hunting season at Badminton.

Stanton Court   *Stanton St Quintin*   *0666 837210*

We decided to explore the country lanes to the south of Easton Grey, and after passing though the quiet hamlet of Norton, reemerged on the main A429 Chippenham to Cirencester road near junction 17 on the M4. The village of **Stanton St Quintin** lies a mile or so southwest of here. This attractive community possesses an exceptionally fine village church, St Giles, which dates from the 11th- to 15th-centuries and was much altered by the Victorians. Outside under the west window, there is an unusual 12th-century carved figure of the enthroned Christ with a dragon at his feet.

150

Superb bed and breakfast accommodation is also available at Stanton St Quintin's elegant former rectory, **Stanton Court**. Now the impressive country home of Anne Adams, Stanton Court lies just one mile northwest of junction 17 on the M4. (Mrs Adams also has connections with the **Whole Hog**, a first-class food, ale and wine house which stands on **Malmesbury**'s Market Cross.)

From here, we rejoined the A429 and drove north towards Malmesbury. After a couple of miles we found ourselves passing through **Corston**, a pleasant village which is the home of one of our favourite farmhouse bed and breakfast establishments, Manor Farm.

Manor Farm   *Corston*   *0666 822148*

Corston's **Manor Farm** is one of those delightful old farmhouses which is steeped in the age-old tradition of agriculture. Wiltshire still has a very strong farming community and nowadays, more and more of these wonderful farmhouses are opening their doors to welcome guests into their homes. We were invited to sample the hospitality which John and Ross Eavis extend to their guests. Situated beside the main Malmesbury to Chippenham road and surrounded by attractive open countryside, the farmhouse is set amongst 436 acres of farmland producing milk and cereals.

We found Ross busy pottering in the front garden when we arrived and were given a warm welcome. Once inside, we were offered a cup of tea. The house is full of character and guests have use of a shared lounge which has a lovely large stone fireplace. In winter, log fires are a treat for guests to enjoy and there is also a colour television for those wishing to curl up in front of the fire. In the dining room, we were delighted to find an old inglenook fireplace and a beautiful antique dining table on which guests are served their meals.

Ross told us all about her famous breakfast menu and warned that the traditional English breakfasts she serves are large enough to satisfy the hungriest of appetites. We were shown to our bedroom and noted how tastefully Ross has colour coordinated the curtains, covers and carpets. We were told that the lovely old beams in the room had originally come from ships which had been broken up in the Bristol Channel. The rooms were well furnished and very comfortable, and our room overlooked the beautiful Wiltshire countryside. Ross and John added to the lovely tranquil atmosphere of Manor Farm by making us feel very welcome throughout our stay.

Malmesbury Abbey

From Corston, it was only a short drive north to the old ecclesiastical centre of **Malmesbury**, a gem of a town which thankfully is bypassed by the main A429 Chippenham to Cirencester road. One of the finest attractions in this part of northwest Wiltshire, this historic settlement stands between two branches of the Bristol Avon around the site of a Saxon hill fort. A Benedictine abbey was founded here in the 7th-century by St Aldhelm, then in 880, Alfred the Great granted the town a charter and so created what is perhaps the oldest borough in England.

King Athelstan, Alfred's grandson and the first Saxon monarch to unite the whole of England, was buried in the abbey in 941, an event which was commemorated in the 15th-century when an impressive monument was erected on the site. Some years before, King Athelstan

152

granted 500 acres of land to the townspeople of Malmesbury who had helped him resist a Norse invasion. The area known as King's Heath still belongs to around 200 residents of the town who can trace their ancestry back to the men who fought for the Saxon king in the 10th-century.

One of the first attempts at human-powered flight was made from the abbey tower by a monk of Malmesbury early in the 11th-century. Brother Elmer (who is also known as Oliver) strapped a pair of homemade wings to his arms, and flapping wildly, flew for some 200 yards before returning to earth with a crash, breaking both of this legs and crippling himself for life. Despite this mishap, he lived on for another fifty years and is said to have predicted the Norman invasion following a sighting of Halley's comet. (Elmer's pioneering flight is commemorated in one of the present-day abbey's stained-glass windows.)

King Athelstan's Tomb

Following Henry VIII's Dissolution of the Monasteries in 1539, the abbey was sold to a wealthy local wool merchant, William Stumpe, for the sum of £1517 15s 2d. He proceeded to set up cloth-weaving workshops in several of the old abbey buildings; however, the great church, much of which is Romanesque, survived this indignity and was presented to the town as a new parish church in 1541. (The old parish church of St Paul's was already crumbling by then, although its main tower survived in the corner of the abbey churchyard to become the belfry of the new church.)

153

The remains of Malmesbury Abbey contain some of the finest Norman features in the south of England, most notably the south porch with its ornately carved arch depicting scenes from the Bible. Other noteworthy features are the 'watching loft', the 15th-century church screen and the ornate roof bosses in the nave. The building is also believed to have once possessed the oldest church organ in the country.

The base of the old town of Malmesbury is virtually surrounded by the two branches of the Avon. To reach the centre of town, it is necessary to cross one of six bridges and then climb up the steep slope leading to the Market Square. An elaborate covered Market Cross stands in the centre of the square; an unusual octagonal building, it has some fine faulting and was constructed in the late 15th-century to provide shelter for the market traders. A few steps from here we found the **Whole Hog**, a first-class food, ale and wine house which has connections with Stanton Court, the excellent bed and breakfast establishment we visited in the village of Stanton St Quintin.

Other noteworthy buildings near Malmesbury's Market Square are the **Old Stone House** with its handsome colonnade and grotesque gargoyles, the arched **Tolsey Gate** whose two cells once served as the town gaol, and the **Abbey House** which was constructed by William Stumpe to replace the old abbot's residence. A stroll down the High Street led us past some lovely old buildings, most of which are constructed of locally-quarried stone. At No. 62 we paused to call in at the **Smoking Dog**, a historic pub with a wonderful friendly atmosphere.

The Smoking Dog   Malmesbury   0666 825823

The Smoking Dog in Malmesbury is a hostelry with an air of old-fashioned affability. The Bath stone walls and old black beams reflect the town's Anglo-Saxon roots and create a wonderful mellow atmosphere. It is apparent that this is a popular pub as soon as you enter the busy
154

laughter-filled bars. The proprietor, Susan Robson, has a well-deserved reputation for serving excellent food, wine and cask-conditioned ales. The meals are reasonably priced and the portions healthy; the house specialities such as Old English eggnog pie and farmhouse chicken are particularly recommended. A visit to the Smoking Dog is sure to leave you relaxed and refreshed.

At the bottom the High Street, we found the impressive **St John's Almshouse**, a mainly 17th-century structure with a late-Norman arch, then back at the top of the town, we called in at the **Old Bell Hotel**, an ancient inn and former abbey guesthouse which is thought to incorporate parts of the old Saxon castle which was demolished in the early 13th-century.

The Old Bell Hotel   Malmesbury   0666 822344

The **Old Bell Hotel** is situated in the centre of town next to Malmesbury Abbey and is believed to be one of the oldest hostelries in England. Established by an early Abbot of Malmesbury, the Old Bell was mentioned in the Domesday Book and is now a Grade I listed building. Present-day visitors can feel the great sense of history as they walk through the door. A wonderful original fireplace remains in the reception hall and visitors can imagine being welcomed in the way King John's guests would have been received 750 years ago; at that time, large numbers of people came to Malmesbury to study in the Abbey's famous library.

Each of the present-day guest rooms has been individually designed to reflect a part of the building's fascinating history. All have their own style and character, with heavy beams and mullioned windows adding atmosphere to the elegance of the rooms. All bedrooms are centrally heated and have tea/coffee making facilities, colour televisions, telephones and private bathrooms. One suite, the Athelstan, is named after the Saxon King who, in 925 AD, made Malmesbury his capital.

155

Before dinner, visitors can enjoy a drink in the cocktail bar which, like the dining room, is Edwardian, having been added in 1908. The whole atmosphere is one of elegance and quiet grandeur in keeping with the hotel's history. The menu is imaginative and tempting, and the wine list extensive and well-chosen. (The monastery was well known for the vines which grew on Malmesbury's south-facing slopes, and in common with the present-day visitors to the Old Bell, the 13th-century monks would have appreciated a glass of fine claret from the cellar.) Like the Stonehouse Court Hotel mentioned in our next chapter, the Old Bell is a member of the Clipper Hotels Group. This small collection of first-class hotels offers a high standard of comfort, service and a great attention to detail.

Those looking for more secluded guesthouse accommodation in Malmesbury should make a point of finding **Bremilham House** in Bremilham Road. This handsome residence is a true Edwardian country villa built in the golden days before the First World War. Run by Sue and Peter Ball, the guesthouse has a friendly, relaxed atmosphere and first-class service is always provided with a smile. The accommodation comprises two double, one twin and one single room, all furnished to a very high standard. Sue is an excellent cook and her breakfasts are a real treat. The gardens are delightful and on fine days guests can enjoy their tea or coffee outdoors, or take the pleasant walk into Malmesbury.

Bremilham House   Malmesbury   0666 822680

Alternatively, first-rate farmhouse bed and breakfast accommodation is available on the southern outskirts of Malmesbury at **Arches Farm**. This traditional 17th-century farmhouse stands at the heart of a 250-acre working farm just to the south of Malmesbury. Run by a lovely lady, Ruby Webb, her light and airy house provides visitors with spacious and comfortable accommodation. The charming dining room, with its panelled and shuttered alcove windows, makes the perfect setting for the á la carte breakfasts which Ruby prepares for all her guests. The south-facing windows offer lovely views over rolling farmland and fill the house with light and warmth, enhancing the welcoming atmosphere.

A minor country road to the east of Malmesbury leads to **Garsdon**, a peaceful community whose village church is noted for containing the 'Stars and Stripes' monument. This unusual tomb belongs to Laurence Washington, a local lord of the manor who was buried here in 1640, many years before the Stars and Stripes became a symbol of America. Washington bought the manor from Richard Moody, a contemporary of Henry VIII who is reputed to have been given the estate as a reward for freeing the king from a deep mud-filled mire and helping him back onto his horse. Earlier this century, the Stars and Stripes monument was restored with the help of funds donated by a number of American benefactors including the Bishop of New York.

Arches Farm   Malmesbury   0666 822367

The narrow country lanes to the north of Garsdon led us through the villages of Hankerton and Eastcourt to our next destination, the sprawling settlement of **Oaksey**. The village possesses some fine 17th-century cottages and a small 13th-century church which contains a number of rare mediaeval paintings. The south wall was also features an unusual painting entitled *Christ of Trades* which shows Jesus surrounded by an array of hand tools, a vivid reminder to the congregation that moral salvation lies in hard labour. The local lord of the manor, Lord Oaksey, is perhaps better known as John Oaksey, the former jockey and TV racing commentator. The interesting remains of the Norman motte and bailey fortification known as **Norwood Castle** lie on private land near Dean Farm to the north of the village.

From Oaksey, we retraced our steps to Eastcourt before turning west towards our final destination in Wiltshire, the lovely old village of **Crudwell**.

An excellent base for exploring the Cotswolds can be found a short distance away in the ancient farming hamlet of **West Crudwell**. Here, Zandra Browning not only provides wonderful farmhouse bed and breakfast accommodation, but she also has two superbly-equipped four-bedroom holiday cottages available which, like the farmhouse, are beautifully appointed and decorated in striking contemporary style.

Jacks and Rabbit Cottage   Crudwell   0666 577205

From Crudwell, a minor country road led us westwards across the county border to the delightful small town of Tetbury, our first destination in Gloucestershire.

From Tetbury to the River Severn

Chavenage Manor

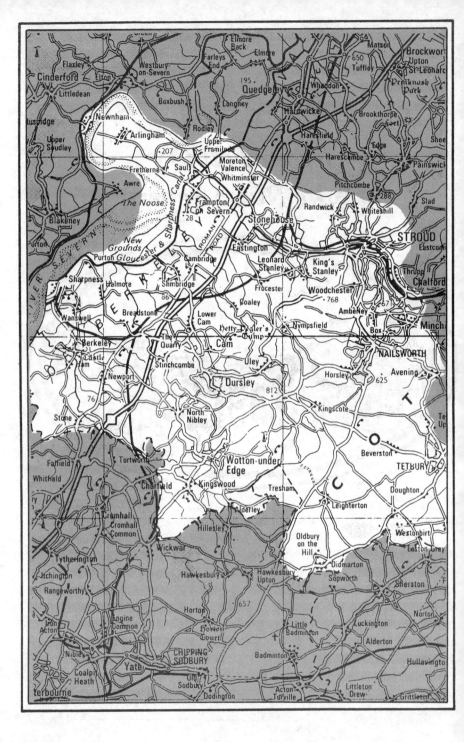

CHAPTER SEVEN

Index

The Berkeley Arms Hotel and Restaurant, Berkeley
The Bird in Hand Pub and B&B, Mary Brook Street, Berkeley
Gordon Guest House, 12 Silver Street, Tetbury
Mill's Café, 8 Withy's Yard, High Street, Stroud
The Old Forge Pub, Bristol Road, Whitminster
Ruskin Mill Crafts Centre, Old Bristol Road, Nailsworth
Stonehouse Court Hotel, Bristol Road, Stonehouse
Tavern Guest House, Willesley, Nr Tetbury
Westonbirt Arboretum, Tetbury, Gloucestershire

The Great Hall, Berkeley Castle

162

From Tetbury To The River Severn

We began our tour around minor roads of Gloucestershire in the delightful Elizabethan market town of **Tetbury**. Once an important centre for the wool trade, the now-restored 17th-century **Market House** can still be seen in the middle of the town. At one time, fleeces were weighed and sold amongst the stone pillars in the open colonnade. On Wednesdays, the building is filled with antique stalls and the exterior is surrounded by modern market stalls which sell an enormous variety of produce from fresh fruit and vegetables to handmade local crafts.

Don't forget....

To tell people that you read about them in The Hidden Places

Chipping Lane connects the Market House to **The Chipping** (an Old English word meaning *market*) via the famous **Chipping Steps**. This ancient stairway descends past a collection of charming stepped houses which together give a marvellous impression of the town's historic past.

Also worth visiting in Tetbury is **St Mary's Church**. Restored in 1781 at the height of town's wool-trading prosperity, the interior is now considered an 18th-century period piece. It features pews with unusually high backs, vast windows made from recycled mediaeval glass, and slender timber columns which conceal iron supports, an innovative building system at the time. Look out also for stone tablet with the wonderful inscription:

> *In a vault underneath*
> *lie several of the Saunderses,*
> *late of this parish; particulars*
> *the Last Day will disclose. Amen*

The interesting **Tetbury Police Bygones Museum** is housed in the original cells of the Old Court House and police station and can be found adjacent to the tourist information office in Long Street. Admission is free to this unusual exhibition of historic artefacts, uniforms and memorabilia from the annals of the Gloucestershire Constabulary. Open Monday to Saturday, 10am to 4.15pm, Easter to the end-October.

A point in the road outside the Crown Inn is the start-finish line of the Tetbury Woolsack races. Every year competitors run up and down nearby **Gumstool Hill**, one of the steepest in Gloucestershire. The name Gumstool derives from the 'ducking stools' which were used to inflict a damp and cruel torture on many an unfortunate inhabitant.

Gordon House   Tetbury   0666 503383

Those looking for top quality guesthouse accommodation in Tetbury should look out for **Gordon House** in Silver Street. This handsome Grade II listed residence is a fine example of an 18th-century merchant's house with a 19th-century frontage. Visitors receive a warm welcome from hosts Josie and Danny Drinkwater who provide good value and tasty home-cooked breakfasts; they are also happy to cater for vegetarian tastes. Weather permitting, guests can take coffee in the beautifully-kept walled garden, and indoors, there are two delightful dolls' houses on show. Indeed, Josie and Danny actually make one-twelfth scale reproduction 19th-century furniture and figures using pure silk, velvet and needlepoint for which exclusive commissions are undertaken. Gordon House is a non-smoking establishment.

The number of outsiders visiting Tetbury has increased in recent years due to the town's close proximity to the royal residence of **Highgrove House**, despite the fact that it is rarely open to the public.

On the western side of the B4014 one-and-a-half miles northwest of Tetbury, we visited **Chavenage House**, a fine Elizabethan mansion built of mellow grey Cotswold stone in the characteristic 'E' shape. The beautiful front aspect of Chavenage has remained virtually unchanged since Edward Stephens added the wings and porch to the former manor house in 1576. At that time, the Stephens family were exceedingly wealthy but over the years they grew less so and Chavenage became heavily mortgaged. Despite this, it has always remained in the family, the present owners, the Lowsley-Williams, being connected to the Stephens by marriage.

Chavenage House

Inside, there are some superb rooms containing rare 17th-century tapestries, period furniture, fine pictures and many relics of the Cromwellian era. In the main hall there is a contemporary screen which

165

forms a delightful minstrels' gallery, and there are also two tapestry rooms where Cromwell is believed to have been accommodated. (Curiously, despite its Cromwellian connections the house is said to be haunted by King Charles I.)

Separated from the house by a narrow passage is the family chapel. The chapel tower was built as a folly in the early 1700s and the rest of the building was attached to it some 100 years later. Look out for the amusing gargoyles incorporated into the masonry. Opening times are limited to 2pm to 5pm on Thursdays, Sundays and Bank Holiday Mondays between May and September. Admission charge payable.

From Chavenage, we headed south onto the A 4135 Tetbury to Dursley road to reach **Beverstone**, a model village which was built by Victorian estate-owner R S Holford, a noted connoisseur of the Renaissance period. Conceived by consultant architect Lewis Vulliamy, the housing in the village combines careful design with improved standards of accommodation. The terraced cottages, lodges and model farms are built of golden Cotswold limestone and are positioned along the road which runs directly through the village. A side road leads to **Beverstone Castle** which was occupied by Earl Godwin, the father of King Harold, around 1051. We carried on past its partly-inhabitable keep until we reached the mediaeval village church. This has a tower containing a marvellous, though damaged, pre-Conquest sculpture of the Resurrection which is worth making the effort to find.

From Beverstone, we headed south again, this time towards Holford's sister project, **Westonbirt House**. The 22-acre Westonbirt Gardens contain magnificent lawns, trees and stonework and are a product of the once-fashionable practice of *emparking*, the process by which all village buildings standing within sight of the main house (except, in this case, the church) would be removed and rebuilt a discreet distance away. In this way, Holford and his landscape architect accomplice, W S Gilpin, were able to guarantee uninterrupted views over the country estate.

Westonbirt House is now a celebrated girls' boarding school and is only open to the public twice a year. The Gardens are open in the afternoons of May 29th, August 7th and 28th each year under the National Gardens Scheme. Admission charge payable.

Adjacent to Westonbirt Gardens and just a short distance further along the B4067 lies the world-famous **Westonbirt Arboretum**. Now incorporated into a 600-acre Forestry Commission estate, this unique place was founded in 1829 by Robert Stayner Holford of Westonbirt House, an amateur enthusiast who had a great love of trees and began planting for his own pleasure. In due course his son, Sir George Holford, acquired his father's passion for trees and continued the work with even

166

greater zeal until 1926, when he died and was succeeded by his nephew, the fourth Earl of Morley. However, it was not until 1956 that Forest Enterprise acquired Westonbirt and opened it to the general public.

The grounds now contain some 18,000 listed specimens of trees and shrubs from all over the world, a collection which is considered to be one of the largest and most important in the world. Some plants are very rarely found in cultivation, others are extinct in the wild, their only sanctuary being collections such as this. Because Westonbirt Arboretum is primarily a research and conservation establishment there is always something going on at any time of the year. Perhaps the spring flowering shrubs in April and May and the autumn foliage colours in October are the most spectacular features of the Westonbirt, but whenever you come you will find the arboretum beautiful.

Westonbirt Arboretum   *Tetbury*   *0666 880220*

We were able to wander wherever we wished; however, for those who prefer a guided walk, there are several waymarked trails along selected sections of the seventeen miles of paths and glades. We bought a trail guide at the visitor centre which also contains an interesting and informative exhibition area, a video presentation and a country gift shop. There is also a cafeteria which opens from 10am to 5pm each day from Easter until mid-November. Picnic tables are also provided adjacent to the car park.

A good place to stay within easy reach of Westonbirt Arboretum is **Tavern House** in **Willesley**. This charming part 17th-century former coaching house is run as a first-rate guesthouse by a lovely couple, Tim and Janet Tremellen. The house enjoys a tranquil secluded setting opposite Silk Wood, a stretch of woodland which leads to the famous Arboretum, home of one of the largest collections of shrubs and trees in the world. Inside, visitors will find superb accommodation in the form of three doubles and one twin room; all are exquisitely furnished with antique furniture and are equipped with en suite bath- or shower-rooms

167

(most also have a bidet). The full English breakfast menu is varied and includes freshly-cooked fillet of kipper or haddock. In fine weather, meals can be served outside in the beautiful walled garden. Despite its secluded setting, Tavern House is situated within a thirty-minute drive of Bath and Bristol; it also lies only about three miles from Badminton, venue for the famous horse trials.

Tavern House   Willesley   0666 880444

From here we continued southwest on the A433 until we reached the charming village of **Didmarton**, site of the mediaeval church of St. Lawrence. Now disused but remaining open to visitors, this lovely little building stands bedside a towering Wellingtonia and, unlike most of its contemporaries which were remodelled by the Victorians, has remained unaltered since the 18th-century. Inside, there are antique box pews painted in Georgian green, an unusual three-storey pulpit, and at the rear of the church, a row of hat pegs set sixteen feet above the floor, evidence that the church was either populated by a congregation of giants or that there was once an upper gallery.

Set back from the church behind the Wellingtonia is a 17th-century manor house which has seen better days. On the other side of the road, look out for the semicircle of stones which marks the site of **St. Lawrence's Well**. According to village legend, St. Lawrence himself visited the spot in the 6th-century, and after blessing the well, he assured the local inhabitants that it would never run dry.

In the centre of Didmarton, look out for **Kingsmead House** which stands out from the rest because of its unusual octagonal gazebo which was strategically built on the highway to allow the owner to get an early glimpse of the coaches from Bath. In the garden, there is also an interesting Gothic hermit's house made from yew wood.

From Didmarton, we headed north along a minor country road until we reached the secluded village of **Leighterton**. Here, we stopped to take

168

a look at the church which is approached past a row of stone-built cottages and a pleasant-looking inn. This striking building has an ancient tower with a timber belfry and an oak spire and is surrounded by a churchyard containing characteristic dark-leafed yew trees.

From Leighterton, we headed west across a narrow strip of Avon and descended into a wooded vale near the Gloucestershire village of **Alderley**, another pleasant community with a castellated church and a handsome Elizabethan house which has been converted into a school. The gardens of **Alderley Grange** at Brackenbury contain some fine aromatic plants, herbs and old-fashioned roses. They are open under the National Gardens Scheme to individuals on June 9th and to groups of ten by appointment only during the whole of that month. Also of interest is the nearby **Alderley Trout Farm**.

A mile north of Alderley village, we made a point of stopping in **Wortley** to visit the site of a Roman villa which was discovered in 1981 when some local people were digging a hole for a fence post and unearthed a section of mosaic floor. Further excavation has taken place each year since then, and so far a bath house complex in two phases with over six rooms has been uncovered. Further Roman ruins have been discovered nearby, along with a 3rd-century paved courtyard and some enormous stone drain-blocks. A small museum on the site contains a selection of the many hundreds of historic items found here during excavations. Open 2pm to 5pm, mid-June to end-September.

One-and-a-half miles west of Wortley, we went out of our way to visit **Kingswood**, a compact village lying just off the B4060 which features a 15th-century gatehouse, one of the few remaining signs of the Cistercian **Kingswood Abbey** which was built by William de Berkeley in 1139.

Our next stop was the delightful small country town of **Wotton-under-Edge**. For centuries, the town was involved in the wool and silk trade and at one time contained as many as thirteen textile mills. Several 17th- and 18th-century town houses remain, the top floors of which were once used as weaving rooms. These are built in a mix of styles from traditional stone-built Cotswold to the half-timbered brick more characteristic of the Severn Vale. Also constructed around this time (1632) were the **Perry and Dawes Almshouses** which are set around a hidden cobbled quadrangle in Church Street. Look out also for **Tolsey House** on the corner of Market Street, an old brick building with a cone of Cotswold tiles which was once the toll house for the market.

Going further back into the past, Wotton-under-Edge has a 14th-century school and a fine 13th- to 15th-century church dedicated to **St Mary The Virgin**. Subsequently refurbished on the wealth of wool and cloth trade, the room above the porch once contained a collection of rare books which are now housed at Christ Church, Oxford. The church also has a noteworthy organ which was removed from St Martin-in-the-Fields in London and is said to have been played by Handel.

During the time **Isaac Pitman** (1813-97) was a schoolmaster in Wotton he owned a house in Orchard Street where he devised his world-renowned system of shorthand. Another interesting building in the town is the imposing gabled woollen mill which has a clock tower and a large pond and dates from around 1800. The present-day complex still operates as a textile factory, though the old buildings are open to visitors by appointment. These contain a number of interesting industrial relics including a wool stove and a circular kiln in which washed wool was dried.

For those with a special interest in the local history of the district, Wotton-under-Edge **Historical Society's Library and Museum** is situated adjacent to the main library in Ludgate Hill. This contains a fascinating collection of books, documents, maps, photographs and historic ephemera. Open Saturdays 10am to 12 noon; also Tuesdays (Easter to end-October), 2.30pm to 4.30pm. Admission free.

Two miles east of Wotton-under-Edge, we made a point of visiting **Ozleworth** for two reasons: firstly, the village Church of St Nicholas is one of the most noteworthy in Gloucestershire in that it stands within a circular churchyard, one of only two in England (the churchyard is thought to have been a holy place since pagan times). It also has an unusual six-sided Norman tower which is constructed in the middle of the church. Secondly, Ozleworth is the location of the National Trust-owned **Newark Park**, an impressive hunting lodge built close to a precipice by the Poyntz family in Elizabethan times. Major alterations were carried out by James Wyatt in 1790 to create a four-square castellated country house, and today, the house is undergoing a further course of renovation by the present tenant, R L Parsons, who is responsible for showing visitors around. Open 2pm to 5pm, Wednesdays and Thursdays during April, May, August and September. Admission charge payable (free to National Trust members).

There are some fine walks around Ozleworth including one which takes in **Midger Wood Nature Reserve** (managed by the Gloucestershire Trust for Nature Conservation) and on up to **Nan Tow's Tump**, a huge round barrow which, being nine feet high and some 100 feet in diameter, is one of the largest and most mystical Bronze Age barrows in the west of England. It is thought to contain the remains of Nan Tow, a local witch who was buried in an upright position.

From here we headed northeast along the B4058 towards **Owlpen Manor**. We discovered the house was unfortunately undergoing extensive

170

renovations and was to be closed for the whole year, so instead, we made a diversion north to visit **Nympsfield**, an attractive village which was formerly a coaching stop in the 18th-century. Marvellous views of the surrounding area can be enjoyed from the top of **Coaley Peak** where the Neolithic chambered **Nympsfield Long Barrow** can be found. Nympsfield Gardens are also worth a look, and for those interested in gliding, trial lessons and five-day holiday courses are offered by the locally-based **Bristol and Gloucestershire Gliding Club** (telephone 0453 860342).

On leaving Nympsfield, we joined the B4066 and came across **Woodchester Park Mansion**, an uncompleted Gothic country house which was designed by Benjamin Bucknall. This unfinished masterpiece is currently finding a new life as a centre for training stonemasons and building conservationists in traditional methods of construction. The site is open April to October on Bank Holiday weekends and the first weekend in every month. Admission charge payable. Unsuitable for children under twelve and dogs.

From here, we drove south to the delightful old cloth-making village of **Uley**. During the 17th- and 18th-centuries, Uley was a hive of economic activity, and as early as 1608, it was recorded that three local cloth-merchants earned a living from marketing the products of 29 local weavers, most of whom produced broadcloth.

Today, the village is a peaceful place which lies in the shadow of the massive **Uley Bury** Iron Age hill fort. Banked ditches mark the outer rim of this magnificent 32-acre construction which are mostly given over to the cultivation of arable crops and remain largely unexcavated. However in recent years, some evidence of the wealthy community who inhabited the fort in the first century BC has been unearthed. Items discovered include bronze, glass and shale jewellery, gold coins and iron ingots (a form of currency) which have been attributed to the Dobunni tribe within whose lands Uley Bury is situated.

About one mile north of the hill fort lies **Uley Tumulus** which is better known as **Hetty Pegler's Tump**, so-called after Hester Pegler, the wife of a landowner who lived nearby in the 17th-century. This 180 foot long Neolithic long barrow contains four burial chambers, the keys to which can be obtained from Crawley Hill Farm, half-a-mile to the south on the B4066. Each of the chambers is reached by creeping along a short low passage. When inside, the torchlight reveals that the walls and ceilings were constructed of huge stone slabs filled with dry-stone material. In the last century, as many as 38 skeletons were discovered within these shadowy vaults.

Back in the car, we drove west through **Dursley**, an undistinguished small town with an industrial feel. However, there are a couple of notable old buildings: the **Market House** dating from 1738 has overhanging upper floors supported by pillars and an interesting bell turret on the roof. It also contains a statue of Queen Anne and the coat of arms of the Estcourt family. The parish **Church of St James** was constructed in the 14th- and 15th-centuries and is also worth a look. William Shakespeare is rumoured to have spent some months staying with relatives at Dursley whilst laying low after being spotted poaching Thomas Lacy's deer at Charlecote. One legacy of his stay is the reference to a local bailiff in *Henry IV*.

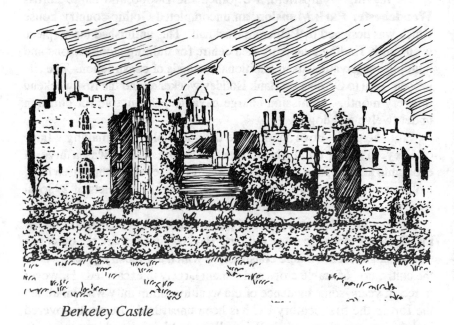

Berkeley Castle

From Dursley, we headed towards the village of **Cam**, one mile to the north. Its modern urban appearance disguises the fact that it dates from the 11th-century when its manor, known as Camma, formed part of the huge Berkeley estate. The village has been a cloth-making centre for centuries and today, **Cam Mill** continues the practice which began in 1522. Look out also for Hopton Manor School which was founded in 1730 making it one of the oldest primary schools in the country.

A short distance from Cam village, we came across the small, uniformly-shaped hill known as **Cam Long Down**. This strange, isolated peak is steeped in local mythology. It is said that the Devil, thinking the landscape too much God's country, decided to cart the Cotswolds away in barrow loads to dam the Severn. After loading up, he set out on his journey and met a cobbler laden with shoes. 'How far is it to the river?'

172

asked Satan. The cobbler showed him one of the shoes he was taking home to mend and replied, 'Do you see this sole? Well, I've worn it out walking from the Severn.' At this point, the Devil abandoned his task and tipped out his barrow, an act which is said to account for the unusual formation that can be seen today. Cam Long Down is also rumoured to be the site of King Arthur's final battle. Legend has it that he crossed the River Severn and confronted his enemies at an unknown place known as Camlann. Whatever its history, a strange mystical atmosphere persists here today.

From Cam we headed west along the B4060 to **Stinchcombe**, a charming village which stands beneath Stinchcombe Hill on the edge of the Vale of Berkeley. A couple of noteworthy buildings can be found in and around the village: **Melksham House** was built in the 17th-century and was home to the Tyndale family for over 300 years; **Piers Court**, built during the 18th-century, was once the home of Evelyn Waugh.

To the south of Stinchcombe lies **Stancombe Park**, a fine country residence rebuilt in 1880 on the site of a Roman villa whose original mosaic floor was removed and transported to Gloucester museum. The surrounding gardens are open to the public under the National Gardens Scheme for a limited number of days each year.

Before crossing the M5, we made a slight detour south along the B4060 to visit **North Nibley**, the place where William Tyndale was born in 1484. He is thought to be one of the first scholars to translate the Scriptures into English, and it is upon his work that the authorised version of the Bible was subsequently based. For his trouble, he was unfortunately strangled and burned at the stake at Vilvorde near Brussels in 1536.

The **Tyndale Monument** was later constructed to commemorate the life and work of this early pioneer. Built in 1866 by public subscription, the monument stands 111 feet high on top of a 700 foot escarpment and forms a prominent landmark on the route of the Cotswold Way. North Nibley is also noted for being the site of the last 'private' battle in England which took place in 1471 between the rival barons William Lord Berkeley and the Viscount De Lisle.

From North Nibley, we headed northwest along a minor country road which, after crossing the M5, led us to the peaceful little town of **Berkeley**. By now we were in need of a refreshment stop, and so before setting out to explore the town, we called in at the **Bird In Hand** in Mary Brook Street.

Dating from the 17th-century and containing original oak beams throughout, the Bird In Hand is a pub rich in character where customers come to enjoy an appetising bar meal or relax with a drink in front of a welcoming open log fire. Its location makes it an ideal touring base, being close to Slimbridge Wildfowl Trust and within easy walking distance of Berkeley Castle and the Jenner Museum. Run by Keith Wood, this charming establishment has recently been modernised and extended and now includes a skittle alley, a luxurious guest lounge and a lovely restaurant with an extensive á la carte menu. Twelve comfortable en suite bedrooms have also been available at the Bird In Hand since the spring of 1993, complementing the excellent facilities of this already first-rate establishment.

The Bird in Hand   *Berkeley*   *0453 511192*

Although most of the buildings in Berkeley date from Georgian times, the town is dominated by its imposing castle, said to be the oldest inhabited castle in England. Built between 1117 and 1153 on the site of a pre-Norman fort, it has remained in the Berkeley family for over 800 years.

It was here that in 1215, the barons of the west congregated before setting out to witness the sealing of the Magna Carta by King John at Runnymede. Perhaps the event for which **Berkeley Castle** is most notorious, however, is the gruesome murder of King Edward II in 1327. Having been usurped from the throne by his wife and her lover because of his ineffectual rule and ill-judged choice of friends, Edward was imprisoned for months at the castle before meeting a literally terrible end, supposedly 'with a hoot brooche put into the secret place posteriale'.

Subsequent monarchs appear to have received rather better hospitality when visiting Berkeley: Richard II was well-entertained here and Elizabeth I is known to have stayed on several occasions.

The castle has been magnificently preserved and sumptuously furnished over the centuries by the various lords and earls of Berkeley. Today, members of the public are welcome to walk around this former military stronghold which is entered by a bridge over a moat. Visitors can view the circular keep, the 14th-century great hall, the state apartments with

174

their fine tapestries and furniture, the mediaeval kitchens, the dungeons, and the actual cell where Edward II met his sticky end.

The castle is surrounded by a terraced Elizabethan garden which contains an example of an early bowling alley and a beautiful lily pond, formerly a swimming pool. Further afield, there is a free-flight butterfly house, gift shop, tearoom and a large well-populated deer park. Berkeley Castle is open April to September, daily except Mondays (though open Bank Holidays) and on Sunday afternoons only during October. Admission charge payable.

On leaving the castle, we spotted the famous **Berkeley Arms Hotel**. A focal point of the town, this imposing 16th-century coaching inn has an impressive coat of arms above its broad, arched entrance. Run by Chris and Annie Bryant, the hotel offers something for everyone. For a quiet dinner there is the Mallard and Claret Restaurant which offers fine food and an extensive wine list, or visitors can relax in the lounge atmosphere of the Boot and Bottle Bar with its good selection of bar meals. Morning coffee and afternoon teas are available each day, and in fine weather, guests can sit out in the courtyard and beer garden. The tastefully-decorated bedrooms all have en suite facilities and are equipped with colour televisions, mini-bar, hot drinks' facilities and direct-dial telephones.

Berkeley Arms Hotel   Berkeley   0453 810291

An easy walk around Berkeley led us to **St Mary's parish church** which has a Norman doorway and a detached tower built in 1783. Inside, there are memorials to several members of the Berkeley family and an impressive east window which has nine lights depicting scenes of Christ healing the sick. The churchyard contains the grave of pioneer immunologist Edward Jenner (1749-1823) who spent most of his life in the town.

175

The son of a local parson, Jenner became apprenticed to a surgeon in Chipping Sodbury in 1763 at the age of fourteen. Seven years later, he moved to London to become a student at St George's Hospital, studying under the great surgeon John Hunter. Some years after, he returned to Berkeley to practice as a country doctor and to continue his pioneering work in immunology.

While still an apprentice, Jenner had become aware of the link between cowpox and smallpox, noticing that one protected against infection from the other. His work over several decades resulted in his discovery of a vaccination against smallpox, a disease which is thought to have killed as many at 60 million people worldwide in the preceding century. Today, the disease has effectively been eradicated from the planet.

Jenner Museum

Jenner's former home in Church Lane is a splendid Georgian house known as **The Chantry**. A thatched rustic hut where he vaccinated the poor free of charge still stands in the grounds and was named by Jenner the **Temple of Vaccinia**. In the early 1980s, the building was purchased, thanks in part to a donation from the Japanese philanthropist Ryoichi Sasakawa, by a trust who converted it into **The Jenner Museum** and immunology conference centre. Open Tuesdays to Sundays between April and September. Small admission charge payable.

On leaving Berkeley, we made our way northeast onto the A38 Gloucester road. Our next point of call was **Slimbridge**, a long rambling village with a fine 13th-century church. (Look out for the large 18th-century windows which contain fragments of glass from the earlier mediaeval period.)

The main attraction in here, however, is the world famous **Slimbridge Wildfowl and Wetlands Centre** which was founded in 1946 by Sir Peter Scott, the artist and naturalist son of Antarctic explorer, Captain Robert Falcon Scott. The centre is now a sanctuary for many thousands of wildfowl, some of which remain here all year round and others which drop in on their annual migrations each spring and autumn. Up to 3000 birds can be in residence at any one time making Slimbridge the largest collection of wildfowl in the world. (The Trust have now established seven other centres in the UK which together are home to over 200 different species of wetland birds.)

Slimbridge's 73 acres of landscaped pens, lakes and paddocks stretch down to the River Severn and are open to visitors all year round. Numerous species of ducks, geese, swans and other wildfowl can be viewed at close quarters (there are observation towers and hides for viewing the shyer birds). The collection also includes many rare and exotic species including the largest flock of flamingos in captivity. There is also a tropical house which simulates rain forest conditions and contains a variety of brilliantly-plumaged water birds and hummingbirds.

Slimbridge is the headquarters of the **Wildfowl and Wetlands Trust** and provides an ideal day out for anyone with an interest in birds. The visitor centre includes indoor displays, a permanent exhibition area and a 100-seater cinema, as well as a restaurant and gift shop. Open daily (except 24 and 25 December), 9.30am to 5pm. Admission charge payable.

Our next stop was the delightful village of **Frampton-on-Severn** which lies just off the B4071, four miles north of Slimbridge. As we approached the village, we could see the dim and distant Welsh mountains in the background. Frampton-on-Severn is noted for having one of the largest village greens in England, the 22-acre Rosamund Green. It contains a cricket ground and three ponds, and was formed by draining the marshy ground outside the gates of Frampton Court in the 18th-century. The Bell Inn is conveniently sited on the green for enthusiasts of cricket and good beer.

Frampton Court is an outstanding example of Georgian country house. Now Grade I listed, it was built in Palladian style in the early-1730s by architect John Strachan. Inside, there is a wonderful collection of antique porcelain, fine furniture, and the paintings from which the best-selling book *Frampton Flora* was comprised in 1985.

The house is screened from the green by trees, but it is still possible to catch a glimpse of the huge Vanbrugh-inspired chimneys and the Gothic-style orangery designed by William Halfpenny. (The orangery has since been converted into holiday accommodation.) The grounds are inhabited by strutting peacocks and contain a reflecting ornamental canal and a unique octagonal tower which was built in the 17th-century as a dovecote. Frampton Court is the seat of the Clifford family and is open all year round by appointment only (telephone 0452 740267). Admission charge payable.

Black Swans, Slimbridge

On the other side of the green is the Clifford family's former home, **Frampton Manor**, which was built between the 12th- and 16th-centuries. The part timber-framed manor house is thought to be the birthplace of Jane Clifford, Henry II's 'Fair Rosamund' who bore him two children and lived in a house surrounded by a maze at Woodstock. Legend has it that Queen Eleanor found her way through the labyrinth to Rosamund's bower by following a thread of the king's cloak and once there, she forced her rival to drink poison. (Rosamund was subsequently buried at Godstow nunnery.) Frampton Manor has a lovely old walled garden and is open all year round to parties of ten or more by written appointment only. Admission charge payable.

178

On the southern edge of the village, the charming 14th-century **St Mary's church** is reached via a footpath across a low meadow. The church stands beside the Sharpness Canal which joins Gloucester to the Severn estuary. Look out for the canal keeper's house built in mock-Doric style. The sight of sea-going ships passing along the canal within a few yards of the church is an occasional eye-opener.

Next, we decided to explore the **Arlingham peninsula**. We retraced our steps and left Frampton-on-Severn in the direction from which we had approached.

The nine-mile long circumference of the Arlingham peninsula forms part of the **Severn Way** Shepperdine-Tewkesbury long distance walk. Along this stretch, the trail passes close to **Wick Court**, a 13th-century moated manor house which was extended three hundred years later, and the 200 foot **Barrow Hill**, which commands magnificent views of the Severn Bridge, the Forest of Dean, Gloucester and the Cotswolds.

The village of **Arlingham** dates from the Iron Age, its name being derived from the Old English word meaning 'village by the running water'. The land on which it is built originally belonged to the Berkeley hundreds, though it was subsequently acquired by St Augustine's Abbey in Bristol. One reason for this is that a place further to the west marks the point where St Augustine is thought to have crossed the Severn on his way to convert the Welsh tribes to Christianity thirteen centuries ago. From the riverbank, there are fine views across to Newnham and Westbury-on-Severn.

Nearby **St Augustine's Farm** was built on the site of a monastic house in the 16th-century, and indeed parts of the old building still survive today. However, the St Augustine's is now better-known as a fascinating open farm where visitors of all ages come to see a working 124-acre livestock farm in action. Activities include watching the cows being machine milked in a herringbone parlour, helping to feed the animals, following an interesting farm trail, and meeting the horses, sheep, goats, pigs, rabbits and other animals.

Owners Robert and Elaine Jewell and their staff promise a family day out with something for everyone, including a display of historic farm memorabilia, a children's playground, a picnic area, gift shop and refreshment area. St Augustine's Farm is open daily 11am to 5pm, end-March to end-October. Admission charge payable.

We decided to follow the river upstream as far as **Epney**, a village which is perhaps better-known on the Continent than it is in the UK. Each year, thousands of three year-old elvers (baby eels) are exported from here to the Netherlands and other parts of Europe to replenish the stocks in the canals.

From Epney, we turned east to reach the historic hamlet of **Moreton Valence**. Here, the ramparts of a 600 year-old castle which once belonged to the De Valence family can still be seen. The largely 15th-century church also remains. This features an earlier Norman doorway which incorporates a sculpture of the Archangel Michael thrusting a spear into a dragon's mouth.

In need of refreshment before continuing on to Stroud, we broke our journey in the pleasant village of **Whitminster**. Here, we called in at the **Old Forge** public house in Bristol Road, a delightful free house which is full of history and charm. Originally a 16th-century agricultural dwelling, its roof was removed in 1604 to allow another storey to be added and was then put back. Thus, for many years, the building doubled as a coaching inn and a farriers; indeed, the old forge is still visible, set into the wall. During recent renovations (during which only original 300 year-old Frampton bricks were used), a Tudor rose was found behind the plaster which is now on show at Stroud Museum. Inside, customers will find themselves tempted by an excellent bar meals menu which includes duck and trout. All dishes are prepared using fresh local produce and there is also a fine selection of real ales. All in all, the Old Forge is a lovely establishment which makes a perfect stopping off place.

The Old Forge   *Whitminster*   *0452 741306*

Just south of Whitminster, we joined the A419 Stroud road which crosses the M5 at junction 13. Within a mile-and-a-half of this junction, we came to the renowned **Stonehouse Court Hotel**, an impressive establishment which offers exceptional food, service and accommodation.

We first heard about **Stonehouse Court** when the hotel was recommended to us as an excellent place to stay when travelling north. Situated around a mile from the M5 motorway, it provides a very convenient place for an overnight stopover. A visit for just one night, however, will not do justice to this wonderful 17th-century Grade II listed

180

hotel which is set in six acres of parkland overlooking Stroud Water.

Stonehouse Court is somewhere to relax in true style and comfort. We found that just wandering around the beautifully kept gardens observing the abundance of rare shrubs and plants was totally therapeutic after a hectic time travelling; there is also the opportunity of some excellent fishing for those so inclined. (As we sat quietly admiring the gardens, we watched a helicopter come in to land on the hotel's landing pad and wondered what the 17th-century inhabitants of Stonehouse Court would make of today's world.)

Stonehouse Court   *Stonehouse*   *0453 825155*

On entering the hotel, guests are immediately struck by the style and warmth of the interior, with its mellow oak panelling, soft lighting and superb open stone fireplaces. The 37 guest bedrooms are all have en suite facilities and are furnished in a style more in keeping with a country house than a hotel. Each room has hospitality facilities, a colour television and telephone. The charming panelled dining rooms offer both table d'hôte and á la carte menus, complemented by an extensive and carefully selected wine list. As one might expect, standards are high. Lunch starts from 10.50am, and dinner from 5.50pm. We found the service excellent, and the staff throughout the hotel both efficient and friendly.

Using Stonehouse Court as a base, guests can visit the quiet villages of the Cotswolds, explore Berkeley Castle, delight in the Slimbridge Wildfowl Trust or travel the Severn Valley Railway with its regular steam train service, a must for railway enthusiasts. The city of Bath also lies within easy reach (when visiting this enchanting city, do take along the Somerset, Avon and Dorset edition of *Hidden Places* in which you will find a chapter devoted to 'Incomparable Bath').

Stonehouse Court is a member of the **Clipper Hotels Group**, a small group of first-class hotels which are located in Jersey, Dorset, Hampshire and Wiltshire. Details about the other fine hotels in the group, including the Old Bell at Malmesbury which we mentioned in chapter six, can be obtained at the reception desk.

The country lanes to the south of Stonehouse pass through some of the loveliest villages in the Severn Vale. The chapel in the centre of **Frocester** was built in 1680 using materials taken from the private chapel of nearby Frocester Court, the present owners of which will usually allow visitors to look round their 180 foot mediaeval tithe barn, one of the finest in the country.

Continuing eastwards, our next stop was the village of **Leonard Stanley**. Here, we found the remains of a 12th-century priory and a largely-intact Saxon chapel. The latter contains an early clock and mediaeval carvings, despite having been used as a barn for many centuries. Henry VIII and Anne Boleyn are reputed to have visited Leonard Stanley in 1535 when the village would have been at the height of its wool-trading prosperity.

A further mile to the east brought us to the larger community of **King's Stanley**, a village with historic roots going back to Roman and mediaeval times. The parish church is Norman in origin though was comprehensively remodelled by the Victorians in 1876. The village also boasts one of the earliest nonconformist places of worship, the Baptist church constructed in 1640. Another architectural first, **Stanley Mill**, can be found on the outskirts of the village. Built as England's first fireproof industrial building, a measure of its success is that it is still used for the manufacture of cloth to this day.

Heading east once again, we came to the village of **Selsley** which stands to one side of the B4066 Stroud to Dursley road. The village is associated with the Marling family, wealthy Stroud mill-owners who were responsible for building the local church. This is modelled on one Sir Samuel Marling spotted on his travels around Europe and features fine interior work by William Morris and Rossetti.

On the eastern side of the B4066, we visited the **Selsley Herb and Goat Farm** in Water Lane. Established in 1982 by Peter and Gillian Wimperis, this four-acre smallholding has been developed into a thriving enterprise. Here, visitors can learn how best to plant and cultivate herbs, whether in a wide herbaceous border or on a small urban patio. There is an attractive formal garden planted with 150 herb varieties, a traditional planted cartwheel, a herb ladder and a nursery selling a wide selection of herbs and aromatic plants.

Peter and Gillian also keep between ten and twelve goats and in spring and early summer, baby kids can often be seen (and sometimes bottle fed) by visitors. Goats' milk and soft cheese can be purchased at the farm shop, along with a wide range of items connected with herbs including chutneys, mustards, dried herbs and potpourri. Open daily, April 1st to end-September. Small admission charge.

From Selsley, we headed northeast and finally reached the old cloth-producing centre of **Stroud**, for centuries considered the capital of the Cotswold woollen industry. The town's geographical position on the River Frome at the point where five Cotswold valleys meet made it an ideal centre for the emerging cloth-manufacturing industry in the early 16th-century; the area's hill farms provided the raw material and its fast-flowing streams the power. By the 1820s, there were over 150 textile mills in the immediate locality and the area became famous for producing broadloom fabrics and 'Stroudwater scarlet', a thick, brightly-coloured cloth used for military uniforms. Today, only six mills remain including one specialising in green baize for snooker tables.

For a town with such a history, Stroud made an unexpectedly disappointing first impression. Its continual economic development has meant that few clothiers' houses and other old buildings can be found in the town centre. However, there are a number of interesting places which are best explored on foot. Before setting out, we decided to have a bite to eat and called in Mills Café at 8 Withy's Yard, just off the High Street.

Mill's Café   *Stroud*   *0453 752222*

Tucked away in a corner down a narrow 13th-century alley, **Mill's Café** is a European-style meeting place with a beautiful courtyard garden. Owned and run by John and Maggie Mills, the emphasis is on good wholesome food, freshly made from local produce including organic meat and vegetables. The café is renowned for its vast range of cakes, which are all baked on the premises, and for its delicious coffee, which is roasted and blended to a special house formula. Mill's Cafe is open Monday to Saturday from 8.30am to 6pm, and on Sunday mornings. It also offers a supper menu from 7pm to 11pm on Friday evenings for which early booking is advised.

183

Also situated in the High Street is the excellent **Inprint Bookshop**, which specialises in secondhand and antiquarian books, and Stroud's **Mediaeval Hall**, a carefully restored civic hall which is believed to be the oldest building in the town. Dating from the Middle Ages, it contains a well and some fine stonework. (Some of the ground floor area is now let as shops.) Perhaps the most famous part of Stroud, however, is **The Shambles**, the old commercial market which, together with the Tudor town hall built in 1597, forms a fascinating enclave which still plays host to a busy weekly market.

A short distance away in George Street, we found the **Stroud Subscription Rooms**. The building has a splendid classical façade featuring a *porte-cochére* with Tuscan columns and a balustraded balcony above, and also incorporates the George Room art gallery where regular exhibitions are mounted.

Cowle Museum, Stroud

Further afield, those interested in early industrial architecture should look for **Lodgemoor** and **Ebley Mills**. Similarly, **Rooksmoor Mills** on the Bath Road is a handsome 19th-century woollen mill which has been converted into a flourishing business offering a wide range of crafts and giftware.

Those interested in finding out more about the town's fascinating past should visit **Stroud District (Cowle) Museum** in Lansdown. Exhibits here include a twenty-foot dinosaur, fossils and information on

184

local archaeology and the history of the textile industry. Nearby **Lansdown Hall** features a display of local crafts and industrial artefacts. Both open Mondays to Saturdays, all year round. Admission free.

Situated near the Paganhill Maypole on the western edge of Stroud, we discovered the **Paganhill Arch**, a Cotswold stone memorial erected to commemorate the 1833 Emancipation Act which ended slavery in the British colonies. The memorial once marked the entrance to Henry Wyatt's estate on Farmhill.

It is also worth making a trip into the beautiful **Slad Valley** which stretches northwards from Stroud, a magical place which was immortalised by Laurie Lee in his autobiographical novel, *Cider With Rosie*. Such a trip could perhaps be combined with a visit to **Lypiat Hill Farm**, a working livestock farm where visitors of all ages are encouraged to observe the animals being cared for in a natural environment. The farm is situated a mile-and-a-half west of Stroud on the Bisley road and is open daily 10.30am to 4pm, 1st April to 30th October. Closed Mondays (except Bank Holidays).

We left Stroud on the A46 Bath road and soon found ourselves climbing upwards into the Cotswolds. After a couple of miles, we came to **Woodchester**, the location of a 26-acre Roman Villa, one of the largest archeological sites of its kind in Britain. Originally excavated in 1796, it is kept covered in earth, only allowing an inspection on one of the rare occasions it is exhumed.

Continuing south on the A46, we spotted a sign to **Amberley** and turned east off the main road; we then followed a minor country road onto a ridge 700 feet above the Woodchester Valley. Amberley has a surprising amount to offer the casual visitor. There is a 13th-century privately-owned castle, a church dating from 1837 which was once described by a former Bishop of Gloucester as 'the ugliest in Gloucestershire', the grave in the churchyard of *Beau Geste* author P C Wren, and Rose Cottage where writer Mrs Craik worked on her novel *John Halifax, Gentleman*. Amberley is also the home of the **Chalk Pits Museum** (open 11am to 5pm on Wednesdays to Sundays between June and October) and the **Fine Arts Centre** which holds exhibitions and offers courses in painting and photography. For those interesting in seeing the Cotswolds from the basket of a hot-air balloon, Cheryl Gillott offers expertly piloted flights from nearby Culver Hill (telephone 0453 873529).

One-and-a-half miles further east, the small Cotswold town of **Minchinhampton** stands perched on the hill between the Golden and Nailsworth Valleys. At one time, it was owned by the nuns of Caen and its market charter is said to date back to 1213. Following the Dissolution of the Monasteries, Henry VIII presented **Minchinhampton Manor** to the first Baron Windsor in a forced exchange for their existing family estate near Windsor, a piece of land which Henry had apparently had his eye on for some time.

In 1651, the manor was acquired by Samuel Sheppard and one his descendants, Edward Sheppard, built Gatcombe Park, the current residence of the Princess Royal. Another member of the Sheppard family, Philip, was responsible for constructing the Market House in the centre of Minchinhampton which was once used for wool trading, but now is more commonly used as a theatre. Visits by appointment only at weekends between 9am and 5.30pm.

Cotswold stone has long been quarried around Minchinhampton and at **Ball's Green**, freestone mines extend underground for over a mile. The material used for facing the inside of the Houses of Parliament was quarried here in the last century.

However, Minchinhampton is most widely known for the impressive ancient monuments which can be found on top of the nearby steep-sided plateau. **Minchinhampton** and **Rodborough Commons** are now under the ownership of the National Trust, the former having been donated in 1913 by Henry Ricardo so as to preserve one of the Cotswolds' last remaining commons. Together, they amount to almost 1000 acres of high woodland and open grassland which are rich in wild flora and fauna.

A number of important archeological sites can be found here including the remains of the Iron Age defences known as **Minchinhampton Bulwarks**, the Neolithic long barrow known as **Whitefield's Tump** from where the great methodist preacher George Whitefield is reported to have addressed a large audience in 1743, and the spot known as **Tom Long's Post** where six roads meet and where an notorious highwayman was hanged.

From Minchinhampton, we headed southwest to **Nailsworth**, a small commercial centre which, like many of its neighbours, was once an important clothiers' town. Despite its industrial feel, some fine Jacobean and Georgian merchants' houses can still be found in the centre. **Stokescroft**, a building known locally as 'the barracks', stands on Cossack Square. Originally constructed in the 17th-century, graffiti uncovered during restoration work in 1972 suggests that local troops were billeted here in 1812 and 1815. It was also used to house Russian prisoners during the Crimean War, an occurrence which explains the name of the square. Several former woollen mills have been updated and continue in their manufacturing role. Others, such as Egypt Mill, have been given a new life. Formerly a grain and logging mill, this popular family pub retains two working water wheels and takes its name from the preindustrial site where gypsy merchants and 'travelling people from Egypt' once camped.

Ruskin Mill　　　*Nailsworth*　　　*0453 83257*

Another interesting place to visit in Nailsworth is **Ruskin Mill**. Originally a 19th-century wool mill, this recently renovated structure is now a thriving craft centre, the concept of which was inspired by the work of William Morris, John Ruskin and Rudolph Steiner. A vibrant place, the emphasis is on traditional crafts. There is an exhibition gallery showing a variety of arts and crafts, plus a working water wheel and an exhibition showing flow forms as a new type of water treatment. Workshops covering such skills as cobbling, woodworking, glass staining and environmental water design are available by prior arrangement. After touring the mill, visitors can relax in the vegetarian café which is open from 11am to 4pm on Tuesday to Saturday, and from 3pm to 6pm on Sundays and Bank Holidays.

A climb up the 1 in 2.25 'Nailsworth Ladder' to the hamlets above the town is worth the effort. One of these, **Watledge**, is the place where *Supertramp* poet W H Davies (1871-1940) spent his declining years.

From Nailsworth, we travelled east along the B4014 for two-and-a-half miles to reach the ancient village of **Avening**. The village church dates from 1070 and contains a memorial to the Hon. Henry Bridge, an infamous 17th-century highwayman who in his youth was reported to have carried out 'deeds of lawlessness and robbery almost unsurpassed'.

On the Sunday nearest to 14th September each year, Avening celebrates '**Pig Face Sunday**'. This unusual festival originates from the time when wild boar roamed free throughout the area. One animal is said to have created so much havoc that when it was finally captured, it was 'hung from a sturdy oak before being roasted and eaten', a custom of which continues in an updated form to this day.

In Hampton Fields, just off the B4014 to the northeast of the village stands the **Avening Long Stone**, a massive prehistoric standing stone which is eight feet high and pierced with holes. According to local legend, it has been known to mysteriously move on Midsummer's Eve.

On leaving Avening, we took the minor road to the north which led us down into the valley formed by the River Frome. Perched above the Thames and Severn Canal on the northern side of the valley we found **Chalford**, our first stop in the next chapter.

CHAPTER EIGHT

The Cotswolds

Chastleton Manor, Moreton-in-Marsh

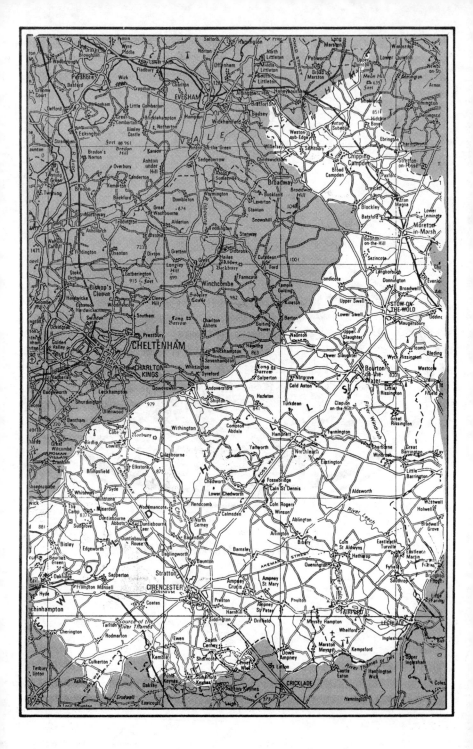

CHAPTER EIGHT

Index

Bank Villas Guest House, Northleach, Cheltenham
'Brymbo' B&B, Mickleton, Chipping Campden
Campden Needlecraft Centre, High Street, Chipping Campden
Colesbourne Inn, Colesbourne, Nr Cheltenham
Coombe Guest House, Rissington Road, Bourton-on-the-Water
Crown Inn and B&B, Cerney Wick, Nr Cirencester
Glebe Farm Holiday Cottages, Barnsley Road, Cirencester
The Lawns B&B, Station Road, Bourton-on-the-Water
Lower Farm Holiday Homes, Blockley, Moreton-in-Marsh
The Marshmallow Restaurant, High Street, Moreton-in-Marsh
Portland Guest House, Evenlode, Moreton-in-Marsh
Poulton Fields Riding Centre and Self Catering, Poulton,
     Cirencester
Rooftrees Guest House, Rissington Road, Bourton-on-the-Water
South Cerney Riding School, Cerney Wick, Gloucestershire
Townend Cottage Restaurant and B&B, High Street, Moreton-in-
     Marsh
Treetops B&B, London Road, Moreton-in-Marsh
Washbourne Court Hotel, Lower Slaughter, Nr Cheltenham
Westley Farm Cottages, Chalford, Gloucestershire

Cirencester

The
Cotswolds

The first stop in our journey through the central Cotswolds was **Chalford**, a unique community consisting of a maze of narrow lanes which sprawl over the steep northern slope of the Golden Valley three miles southeast of Stroud. This is centre of the area known as the 'Alpine Cotswolds', and at one time food and fuel had to be delivered up the steep gradient by donkey. Today, Chalford is best explored on foot, its tight thoroughfares being filled with interesting shops and pubs. Though not impressive architecturally, the church contains some interesting pieces of furniture made by craftsmen Peter Van Der Waals, Norman Jewson and W G Simmonds. The Round House, an unusual example of a former canal lengthman's house, stands opposite.

An easy walk from Chalford took us to the isolated settlements of **France Lynch**, **Avenis Green** and **Bournes Green**. Here, we discovered an imposing Victorian parish church dating from 1856 and a disused 17th-century Congregational church whose decaying churchyard contains the graves of several old Puritan families.

Westley Farm Cottages   Chalford   0285 760262

Just outside Chalford, we saw a sign to **Westley Farm Cottages**. If you are looking for somewhere to stay in the lovely Cotswold countryside

193

close to Cirencester, then Westley Farm is conveniently situated midway between Cirencester and Stroud. Set on the steep slopes of the beautiful Golden Valley, there are breathtaking views all around. This working family farm raises cattle, sheep, horses and domestic fowl. It also provides horse riding and pony trekking facilities and is crisscrossed by numerous well-maintained woodland paths and bridleways.

The farm's formerly-redundant stone outbuildings have been converted to provide four impressive self-catering cottages and two flats which each sleep from two to five. All well-equipped, the facilities include night storage heating, washing machines, telephones, televisions and open log fires, and there is also a farm shop. Whether on foot or on horseback, Westley Farm makes an ideal base for touring the beautiful Cotswold countryside.

From here, we headed north along the country lanes until we reached the historic village of **Bisley**. The village stands 780 feet above sea level is known by local people as 'Bisley-God-Help-Us' because of the winter winds which sweep across the exposed hillside. The gabled Cotswold houses stand huddled together against the elements, and when approached from the southwest, they appear to form a semicircular amphitheatre. In its time, the village has also been known as 'Beggarly Bisley' because of the hardship the inhabitants suffered during the decline of the local textile industry which was brought on by the Industrial Revolution.

Bisley's fine All Saints' Church dates from the 13th-century and was restored during the early 19th-century by Thomas Keble, the brother of poet and theologian John Keble after whom Keble College, Oxford was named. Thomas Keble was responsible for restoring the seven wells of Bisley which are set in an arc below the church. In 1863, he also founded the annual custom of 'dressing the wells' on Ascension Day, an event which continues to be witnessed by hundreds of spectators to this day. A decaying ornamental construction in the churchyard known as the 'Poor Souls' Light' dates from the 13th-century and was used to hold candles lit for the souls languishing in purgatory. It is thought to be the only outdoor structure of its type in the country.

Perhaps the village's main claim to fame however, is the legend of the '**Bisley Boy**'. In the days of its wool-based prosperity, Bisley possessed a royal manor, **Over Court**, where the young Princess Elizabeth (who went on to become Queen Elizabeth I) stayed on a number of occasions. Rumour has it that during one of these visits, the ten year-old princess caught the plague and, to the horror of her hosts, actually died. Fearing the wrath of her father Henry VIII, they hurriedly looked for a substitute and were fortunate enough to find a local child with red hair and remarkably similar physical characteristics. Similar, that is, except for

194

Fairford

one thing. Elizabeth's stand-in was a local lad called John Neville. Perhaps this would explain the Virgin Queen's reluctance to marry, her problem with hair loss and her 'heart that beats like a man's'?

Before leaving Bisley, we had a look at the 17th-century Bear Inn at the top of George Street, the frontage of which is supported by a row of external stone columns. We then drove southwest, back towards the valley of the River Frome and the Thames-Severn Canal. Before reaching the A419, we turned east in **Frampton Mansell**, a pleasant village with some photogenic old buildings including the impressive Crown Inn and a manor farm which was built in the time of Charles II. The village church dates from a more recent period than its Norman appearance would suggest.

At **Sapperton**, a short distance to the east, the Thames-Severn Canal disappears into the two-mile long **Sapperton Tunnel** which, on its completion in 1798, was the longest in England's inland waterway system. Closed in 1911, the tunnel has a Gothic western portal at Daneway and a classical eastern portal at Coates, the latter having been restored as part of the plan to reopen the canal in the not-too-distant future. There are also interesting pubs at either end: the 18th-century Daneway Inn to the west and the Tunnel House at Coates to the east. These used to be the haunts of the bargees and professional *leggers*, the freelance artisans who used to 'walk' the narrowboats through the tunnel by lying on their backs and pushing against the walls and ceiling with their legs.

The village of Sapperton itself contains a number of fine old buildings, some dating from the 17th-century and others built in sympathetic style during a short-lived renaissance which was ended by the outbreak of the First World War. It was during this fifteen-year period that Ernest and Sidney Barnsley and Ernest Gimson founded a group of local artist-craftspeople known as the **Sapperton Group**. This had close links with William Morris and was centred around **Daneway House**, a nearby manor dating from the 14th- and 17th-centuries. The house containing the group's furniture workshops and showrooms can still be viewed (by appointment only) at any reasonable time between March and October. Small admission charge payable. The three group founders also designed and built distinctive houses for themselves in the village.

From Daneway House, we continued northeast towards **Daglingworth** and the **Duntisbournes**, five delightful settlements which are sited along the exquisite valley of the River Dunt, or Duntbrook. Just to the east, the A417 diverts the speeding traffic along the undeviating course of the former Roman highway, Ermin Street. However, this charming little valley gives the impression of lying a million miles from the pressures of modern civilisation. The three-mile journey upstream took us through three villages, two hamlets and four fords in the river.

The church in **Daglingworth** contains a number of wonderfully-preserved Anglo-Saxon sculptures which are highly regarded for their simple artistry. The village also contains a handsome, if somewhat exposed, Georgian house, a large Victorian former-rectory, and a number of characteristic Cotswold cottages belonging to the Duchy of Cornwall. Further upstream, the road next passes through **Duntisbourne Rouse**. This also possesses a fine church, the tiny St Michael's, which has some fine features dating back to Saxon and Norman times. The 15th-century west tower has a rare saddleback roof and inside, there is a wonderful old Norman crypt and font.

The road fords Duntbrook in both **Middle Duntisbourne** and **Duntisbourne Leer**, two sleepy hamlets, the latter of which once belonged to the abbey of Lire in France. In **Duntisbourne Abbots** at the northern end of the valley, the old cobbled road actually follows the course of the stream as it flows through the village between two raised walls. This is a place where carters once cleaned their waggons and washed their horses hooves in the flowing water. Despite the risk of flooding, the present-day inhabitants continue to resist any plan to divert the course of the river. The mossy stone pool which was once the village water supply is also worth having a look at.

From Duntisbourne Abbots, we zigzagged northwest through the minor country roads until we reached the village of **Miserden**, home of the renowned **Miserden Park Gardens**. The centre of this characteristic Cotswold village is marked by a large sycamore tree; this stands near a 17th-century barn which still contains a working forge. The famous gardens are situated on the northeastern side of the village and contain a wide variety of planting including spring bulbs, roses beds, herbaceous borders and topiary. Open 10am to 4.30pm, Wednesdays and Thursdays between 1st April and 30th September. Admission charge payable (accompanied children free).

We continued northwest for two miles and found ourselves in the unique community of **Whiteway**. At first sight, this windswept village set high up on a Cotswold ridge seems a hotchpotch of rather inhospitable buildings, many of which look homemade. We soon found out that, indeed, many of them were constructed by their owners, a group of Tolstoyan anarchists, who set up the village in 1898 following their resettlement from Surrey.

The inhabitants of Whiteway set up an economy based on horticulture and cottage industry and at first, refused all outside interference such as police, post office and public transport in their pursuit of self-sufficiency.

This raised a few eyebrows amongst the surrounding inhabitants who spread rumours about their suspect moral code. (The villagers were said to walk around without clothes and to engage in partner-swapping.) However, unlike many similar utopian communities, the wooden shacks of Whiteway along with many of the principles they were founded upon, remain to this day (albeit in a much developed form) and the present-day village with its winding lanes, tall hedges and unconventional architecture is still the domain of creative, liberal-minded individuals.

From Whiteway, we joined the B4070 and drove northeast onto the A417 and then onto the A436. Our next stop was **Seven Springs** near Coberley, one of several sites which claims to be the source of the River Thames. Despite there being an inscribed stone marker to back up this claim, a spring eleven miles to the south at **Thameshead** seems a more likely contender. (This can be found by following a path across some fields behind the Thameshead Inn, a pub on the A433, three miles southwest of Cirencester.) Nevertheless, Seven Springs is the undisputed source of the River Churn.

Colesbourne Inn   Colesbourne   0242 870376

We now turned south onto the A435 Cheltenham to Cirencester road and after four miles, reached the pleasant village of **Colesbourne**. At the side of the main road, we discovered the impressive **Colesbourne Inn**. Run by Eric and Mary Bird, the welcome at this charming Cotswold inn is extended to all. The traditional bar offers excellent food and fine ales from the wood which you can enjoy whilst soaking up the atmosphere in front of a real log fire. The inn incorporates a first-class restaurant, **Brambles**, with a large patio which overlooks beautiful Cotswold countryside. Here, diners can choose from a selection of mouthwatering meals, with home-grown, freshly prepared produce being order of the day. Excellent accommodation is also offered in the recently converted stable block. This provides ten very comfortable en-suite bedrooms, all

198

equipped to the English Tourist Board four crown standard.

Fully restored, we headed south once more along the A435 until we came to **North Cerney**, site of one of the most attractive and unusually decorated churches in the Cotswolds. 'Graffiti' thought to be the work of Tudor masons is etched into the internal and external walls of this fine 12th-century structure, much of it depicting the mythological animals which appeared in the mediaeval *Bestiaries*, the 'books of beasts' which contained descriptions of real and mythical animals, many of which had a wider moral significance. For example, a congregation-eating manticore (half man, half lion) with three rows of teeth is scored onto the church's outer south wall, and similarly a long-tailed leopard appears on the west wall. Other faces look down from gargoyles, roof-bosses and corbels, and four peer out from the Norman tympanum above the south doorway.

Corinium Museum

Three miles further south, the A435 joins the A417 on the northern outskirts of Cirencester near the attractive village of **Stratton**.

The ancient market town of **Cirencester**, the capital of the Cotswolds, has a history dating back to the Roman occupation of Britain. In 47 AD, the Romans built the Fosse Way, one of the four royal roads of Britain, to link the prosperous wool-based centres of the South-West with Lincoln and the garrisons to the north. Along its length were constructed a number of defensive fortifications, one of which was sited at the junction with two other Roman highways, Ermin Street and Akeman Street. This fort quickly grew to become *Corinium Dobunnorum*, the second most important Roman settlement in England after Londinium. It was named after a conquered tribe of Britons, the Dobunni, who inhabited the southern Cotswolds.

Today, little evidence of Cirencester's Roman roots survives in situ. However, the award-winning **Corinium Museum** in Park Street houses one of the finest collections of ancient Roman antiquities in the country. Items on show include superb sculptures, domestic items and two remarkable floor mosaics, *The Four Seasons* and *The Hunting Dogs*. The museum also features life-size reconstructions of a Roman garden, dining room and kitchen, as well as a cut-away section of a surprisingly sophisticated central-heating system.

The Corinium Museum also covers the history of area from prehistoric to mediaeval times. Open Mondays to Saturdays, 10am to 5.30pm and Sundays 2pm to 5.30pm between 1st April and 31st October; Tuesdays to Saturdays 10am to 5pm and Sundays 2pm to 5.30pm between 1st November and 31st March. Small admission charge payable.

After a prolonged period of decline, Cirencester came under the domain of William FitzOsbern, the Earl of Hereford, following the Norman Invasion. In 1117, King Henry I founded the Augustinian Abbey of St Mary which was subsequently destroyed following Henry VIII's Dissolution of the Monasteries. Little of it now remains except for a single Norman arch which can be found in the northeastern corner of the **Abbey Grounds**. Today, the grounds form an attractive park containing a lake, trees and a population of wildfowl. An outline of the original abbey walls can be found here, along with the only remaining section of the old Roman fortifications.

Cirencester's **Church of St John the Baptist** was constructed in the 15th- and 16th centuries and is perhaps the finest example of a Cotswold 'wool' church. Like many other similar structures in the area, the building of the church was financed by a wealthy wool merchant who prospered during that period. (Such churches are often characterised by the fact that they were built to a grander scale than befits the size of the community they now serve.) The funds for its pinnacled tower, however, came from a different source, the Earls of Salisbury and Kent who rebelled against Henry IV and who were arrested by the burghers of Cirencester as they passed through the town in 1399. After executing the rebellious pair, King Henry allowed the townspeople to keep the contents of the earls' strongboxes, a sum which covered the builder's charge.

St Johns is built of golden Cotswold stone and stands in a magnificent position in the Market Place. Inside, the pulpit is shaped like an enormous wineglass, beside which is placed a 17th-century hourglass which was

200

used to keep a check on the duration of the preacher's sermons. A statue of a blue-coated boy stands beside the door to the south aisle. This was used in the 18th-century to collect funds for the church primary school which was founded in 1714 and still flourishes today.

The famous silver and gilt **Boleyn Cup** can also be found in the south aisle. This was made for Henry VIII's second wife in 1535, the year before she was executed for alleged adultery. Anne's personal insignia can be seen on the lid: a rose tree and a falcon holding a sceptre. Look out also for the cat chasing the mouse, a mediaeval craftsmen's joke which can be seen in the Lady Chapel.

Although no longer open at set hours, parties are welcome to climb the 120 foot **West Tower** by arrangement with the vicar. Visitors climb up past the peal of twelve church bells which were made by Rudhall of Gloucester and are thought to be the earliest of their type in the country. From the top, the birds-eye view of Cirencester's network of streets is breathtaking. These include **Spitalgate**, with its remains of the 12th-century Hospital of St John, and **Coxwell Street** with its row of original wool-merchants' houses and artisans' cottages. From the tower, there is also the chance to see over the 40 foot yew hedge which was planted in 1818 to conceal **Cirencester House**, the home of the Earl Bathurst.

Cirencester House stands on the western edge of town at the top of Cecily Hill and although not open to the public, its grounds are. Walkers and horse riders are permitted to roam freely over the 3000-acre **Cirencester Park** which has pathways stretching almost as far as Sapperton, five miles to the west. The park was laid out in the 18th-century by the First Earl Bathurst with the assistance of his friend, Alexander Pope. **Pope's Seat**, a summerhouse standing at a point where ten pathways meet, was one of the poet's favourite places of contemplation.

Also to the west of the town are the remains of the **Bull Ring**, a once-glorious Roman amphitheatre which is perhaps one of the largest and best-preserved examples of its kind in Britain. Best approached from Querns Hill and Cotswold Avenue, the remains consist of an oval arena with twin entrances and a series of sloping earth banks which would have supported rows of timber seating.

On leaving Cirencester, we made a short diversion northeastwards along the B4425 to visit the attractive Gloucestershire village of **Barnsley**, a conservation area which until a few years ago was owned by a single family. Almost all the buildings are constructed of the same locally-quarried golden limestone giving the community a unified yet unplanned character. At one time, all the houses in the village were lived in by local farmworkers; however, today, the estate is owned by a charitable trust which seems prepared to sell off vacant properties to outsiders.

In the centre of the village there is a pub, a village hall and a church with an Elizabethan tower. Also situated here is **Barnsley House**, a former rectory which is renowned for its beautiful gardens. These are usually open to the public on Wednesdays, and amongst other noteworthy features, contain two 18th-century summerhouses (one classical, one Gothic). **Barnsley Park** on the outskirts of the village is a baroque Georgian mansion which was probably designed by Hawksmoor. It is open to visitors by prior appointment only.

Glebe Farm Cottages   Cirencester   0285 659226

On leaving Barnsley, we noticed a sign to **Glebe Farm Holiday Cottages**, a collection of four outstanding barn conversions which are set in the heart of the peaceful Cotswold countryside just two miles outside Cirencester. These first-rate holiday cottages offer beautifully furnished and excellently equipped self-catering accommodation. Sleeping up to six (plus a cot), 'Calf Pens' is ideal for a large group or family, whilst accommodation in 'The Dairy' comprises one double and one twin bedroom. Both provide well furnished open plan kitchen, dining and sitting room areas, as well as a private patio. Additional shared facilities include a washing machine, tumble dryer and freezer. 'Granary One' and 'Granary Two' offer accommodation of the same high standard and, should you require it, there are babysitting and maid services available.

Heading south, the minor country roads led us to **The Ampneys**, three small villages which are connected by Ampney Brook. Furthest upstream is **Ampney Crucis**, a pleasant community with a large mansion (Ampney Park), an old mill, an attractive vicarage and a part-Saxon church with an unusual carved stone cross in its churchyard and mediaeval paintings on its interior walls.

The village of **Ampney St Mary** was moved to its present position following the Black Death in the 1300s. All that remains of the original mediaeval settlement is its 12th-century church which stands on its own

202

in the middle of a field half-a-mile away. **Ampney St Peter** is perhaps the most attractive of the three villages. It has a small green, a Saxon church with a gabled tower, and some noteworthy buildings including a large Cotswolds residence designed by architect Sidney Gambier-Parry in the 1900s.

Poulton Fields Farms   Poulton   0285 851830

Before continuing our journey south, we made a point of finding **Poulton Fields Farms**. Situated five miles east of Cirencester and one mile north of Poulton, Poulton Fields is an arable and sheep farm set in 811 acres of lovely Cotswold countryside. Owned by Major Andrew Wigram and his wife Gaby, this is also the home of the outstanding **Poulton Chasers Course**.

This impressive equestrian course was opened in May 1992 and is some eight miles long; it has a varied selection of 32 well-constructed jumps, including a water obstacle and bank. The jumps are all five to seven metres wide and range from one-and-a-half to three feet in height, which means both experienced and novice riders are able to attempt them all. Whether your penchant is hacking, jumping or carriage driving, the Poulton Chasers Course is ideal.. It is open all year round by prior appointment subject to the condition of the course, and up-to-date information and bookings can be obtained by telephoning (0285) 850851.

Riders register in a portacabin in the large parking area at the edge of the farm building complex. Here, they can use the facilities to wash, change, make telephone calls and purchase refreshments, whilst nearby there is a hitching rail, water and hose, mounting block, WC and short-term grazing facilities. Open to members of the UK Chasers, the course is also available to non-members on purchase of a day membership pass. In addition, lessons can be provided at the Poulton Chasers Riding School which can include the use of a mount and the Chasers Course if required.

Poulton Fields Cottages offer top class self-catering accommodation

203

for visitors to the Wigrams' farm. Situated at the centre of the farm with attractive lawned gardens to the front, a patio to the back and enclosed by a Cotswold stone wall, this charming pair of cottages were extended and updated in early 1991. Both sleep up to six, with a communicating door enabling them to be let as a single twelve-bed unit if required. The facilities are excellent and include a fully equipped kitchen, colour television and convector/night storage heaters throughout. The quality of accommodation provided has earned Poulton Fields Cottages an English Tourist Board four-key commended rating.

To the south of Cirencester, the gentle dip slope of the Cotswolds creates a flat open landscape with river valleys so wide that they seem like gentle undulations in a rolling plain. This pleasant area of the upper Thames valley is also rich in valuable sand and gravel deposits which have been exploited by the building industry since the 1920s. The removal of the material has left a large number of hollows which have gradually filled with water to form shallow freshwater lakes. In recent years, the potential of this area as a leisure resource has been realised and today, the area is known as the **Cotswold Water Park**.

The Cotswold Water Park covers a total area of some 22 square miles and contains over 100 manmade lakes. As well as being an important centre for water-based sport, fishing and general recreational pursuits, it is also an internationally recognised nature conservation area. A large number of waterfowl breed and over-winter here, and several of the lakes and water meadows are designated Sites of Special Scientific Interest.

Poulton Fields Farms   Poulton   0285 851830

The water park lies to the west of the A419 Cirencester to Swindon road and is centred around the two villages of South Cerney and Cerney Wick. Though not a particularly pretty village, **South Cerney** contains some pleasant old manor houses, a street called Bow Wow and a church with a carved Norman doorway which contains a noted work of art, the carved wooden head and foot of Christ taken from a crucifix in Compostela.

Lying two miles to the southwest, the village of **Cerney Wick** is also a pleasant community. Those looking for first-rate refreshment or accommodation near the Cotswold Water Park should look out here for the celebrated 16th-century hostelry, the **Crown Inn**. Native Gloucestershireman, Colin Jackson, and his wife, Liz, take pride in serving the very best in beers, wine and food (try Liz's award-winning homemade steak and kidney pie). The Crown also offers a number of comfortable, quiet and welcoming letting bedrooms. *0793 750369*

South Cerney Riding   Cerney Wick   0793 750151

Cerney Wick is also the location of the renowned **South Cerney Riding School**. This top-class riding centre is situated just to the west of the A419 Swindon to Cirencester road in the heart of the Cotswolds Water Park conservation area. Here, a high standard of tuition is offered to riders of all ages and levels of experience.

A few miles further west, the **Somerford Lakes Reserve** near **Somerford Keynes** offers guided launch trips around a hundred-acre lake taking in an eel and trout farm and a variety of pens containing such exotic fauna as wallabies and ornamental pheasants. Open all year round to pre-booked parties of four or more. Admission charge payable.

From the Water Park, we drove east across a narrow spur of Wiltshire before reentering Gloucestershire near the village of **Down Ampney**, the birthplace of composer Ralph Vaughan Williams (1872-1958) who wrote the music to the hymn *Come Down O Love Divine* and named it *Down Ampney*. All Saints' church, where Vaughan Williams' father was incumbent, dates from 1265 and can be seen for miles around across the flat surrounding farmland. Inside, a reclining effigy of the mediaeval soldier, Sir Nicholas de Valers (or Villiers), can be seen in the south transept.

During the Second World War, Down Ampney was the site of an important airfield and some years later, a modern stained-glass window was installed in the church in memory of the airmen based here. Each year in September, a service is held to commemorate those lost in the Battle of Arnhem. Not far from the church, a high yew hedge hides Down Ampney House, a handsome Tudor mansion which was remodelled in 1799.

Heading further eastwards along the minor country roads, we again crossed a spur of Wiltshire before reaching **Kempsford**, a Gloucestershire village with strong Lancastrian connections. The interior of the church is decorated with Lancastrian roses and the tower is said to have been commissioned by Blanche, the wife of John of Gaunt who was also an heir of the first Duke of Lancaster and mother of Henry IV. Look out for the horseshoe on the church door which is rumoured to have been shed by the Duke of Lancaster's horse with tragic consequences. Kempsford is also said to be populated by number of unusual ghosts including a silent monk, a youth in lace and breeches, a distraught mother and a repenting knight.

St. Mary the Blessed Virgin, Fairford

From Kempsford, the road took us northwards to the large and bustling village of **Fairford**, a stop on the old stagecoach route which stands on the gently-flowing River Colne. Of architectural merit in the village is the church of St Mary the Blessed Virgin which contains a truly outstanding set of 15th-century stained-glass windows. At the time these were installed, Fairford was at the centre of a prosperous wool-producing area and a major church restoration was carried out by the wealthy wool merchant, John Tame. He is said to have commissioned the set of 28 windows which are thought to have been made by Henry VII's master glass painter, Barnard Flower, whose work appears in Westminster Abbey. St Mary's also contains some fine oak carving including Tame's original ceiling supports which are fashioned in the shape of angels. John Tame's memorial gravestone, along with those of his wife and son, are set into the floor of the church.

We now joined the A417 for the four-mile journey to **Lechlade**, a charming little town which is situated at the southeasternmost point of the county. Lechlade stands at the junction of the A417 and A361 and is consequently a rather busy place with wide streets and a bustling Market Place. It also stands at the point where the Rivers Leach (from which the town gets its name) and Coln join the River Thames; indeed Halfpenny Bridge, which is named after the halfpenny toll which was once payable, is the highest navigable point on the river. At one time, river barges used to line the wharves around St John's Bridge when they were being loaded with building stone bound for Oxford, London and beyond. Today, the barges have been replaced by pleasure craft which provide an enjoyable way to spend a few hours.

There are some fine Georgian buildings in Lechlade, many of them designed by an accomplished local architect called Pace. One of the characteristic architectural features of the town are its once highly-fashionable gazebos which were built at the bottom of every reputable garden. One such structure can be found in the garden of Church House and is said to be the place where in 1815 Shelley wrote his *Stanzas in Lechlade Churchyard*. The church itself has a tall spire which can be seen from miles away across the low surrounding water-meadows. Inside, there is an unusual carved roof boss above the nave depicting two wrestlers.

To the north Lechlade, a network of country lanes connect a number of interesting little villages. **Southrop** is an attractive and beautifully-kept community with a small green and a fine manor house. The manor is set behind a pair of distinctive gateposts in grounds containing a restored riverside mill, ancient barns and a charming church with Norman features. John Keble lived in the Old Vicarage from 1823-25, the period he was laying the foundations of the Oxford Movement with William Wilberforce and others. Southrop is also noted for the distinctive stone ball-finials which adorn many of the older buildings in the village.

A little further north, the two hamlets of **Eastleach Martin** and **Eastleach Turville** face each other across the River Leach. (Together they form the village known simply as **Eastleach**.) For many centuries, the two hamlets were owned by rival lords of the manor and so each contains its own church. Both date from Norman times and incorporate a number of fine architectural features. John Keble was appointed non-resident curate of both churches in 1815 and the ancient clapper footbridge across the River Leach which connects the two hamlets is known as **Keble's Bridge**.

A couple of miles to the west, we passed through **Hatherop**, a model village of solid stone-built cottages which was built between the estates of Williamstrip Park and Hatherop Castle (now a girls' school) in the 1860s. The Victorian village church contains the chapel of Barbara, Lady de Maulay designed by William Burges. He was also jointly responsible for remodelling the castle in the 1850s.

On the banks of the River Coln a mile to the southwest, the village of **Quenington** has a church with two exceptional Norman tympana. (Such is their importance that in the 1880s, two porches were added by the architect of Gloucester Cathedral, F S Waller, to protect them from the elements.) In the 12th-century, the church became a preceptory of the Knights Hospitaller and their presence is reflected in several local place names including Knights' Mill and Knights' Gatehouse.

Arlington Mill

The wonderful village of **Bibury** lies three miles to the north at the point where the B4425 bridges the River Coln. In the 19th-century, it was described by William Morris as the most beautiful village in England. Thankfully, little has changed since then. At its centre, the delightful village square is overlooked by the ancient church of St Mary, a much-altered building with parts dating back to Norman, mediaeval and Saxon times. In the churchyard, the lichen-speckled tombs and gravestones date from more recent times, their brilliant yellow mottle standing out in the moist Cotswold air.

The River Coln flows slowly past handsome stone-tiled buildings and under Bibury's late-18th-century road bridge. The river and its water meadows attract a wide variety of wildfowl and the National Trust-owned **Rack Isle Water Meadow** has been designated a bird sanctuary. **Arlington Row**, a short terrace of mediaeval stone-built cottages stands nearby and is also under the protection of the National Trust. Originally built in the 14th-century to house sheep, the cottages were converted into cloth-weaving workshops in the early 17th-century.

Fabric from here was supplied to nearby **Arlington Mill**, a water-powered fulling mill which was built on the site of a corn-mill mentioned in the Domesday Book. (*Fulling* was a process of cleansing and thickening woollen material by immersing it in water and beating it with mechanically-operated hammers.) Today, Arlington Mill is a museum which houses a fascinating collection of industrial artefacts, arts, crafts and furniture including items made in the William Morris workshops. There are seventeen display rooms in all, including a blacksmith's forge, a wheelwright's workshop and a number of machine rooms containing working equipment. Open daily 10.30am to 7pm, mid-March to mid-November. (Weekends only during winter months.) Admission charge payable.

The **Bibury Trout Farm** can be found adjacent to Arlington Mill. Originally established as a trout hatchery as long ago as 1906, it has grown into a flourishing working farm which welcomes visitors all year round. There is also a farm shop offering fresh and smoked fish, plants and gifts. Open 9am to 6pm, Mondays to Saturdays and 11am to 6pm Sundays. Admission charge payable.

In the 17th-century, Bibury was famous as a horse racing centre and at one time was the home of a racing club which was founded during the reign of Charles II, the oldest such club in the country. Much of the racing activity centred around **Bibury Court**, a splendid country house which was built on the site of Roman, Saxon and Norman remains. Now a hotel, the building is still a focus for horse-riding activities. It was once owned by the influential Sackville family who were involved in a famous law suit involving a contested will. The case lasted several decades and is said to have provided the background for Charles Dickens' vicious inditement of the legal profession, *Bleak House*.

Upstream from Bibury, the villages lying along the course of the River Coln are both beautiful and unspoilt. The first of these gems is **Ablington**, a community which was immortalised by J Arthur Gibbs in his chronicle of Victorian rural life *A Cotswold Village*. A high stone wall surrounds the Elizabethan manor (and its extensive landscaped grounds) which was Gibbs' home. On the manor's main doorway there are five delicately carved heads, one of which is of Queen Elizabeth herself. Another interesting building in the village is the 17th-century gabled **Ablington House** which is also partly concealed behind a high dry-stone wall. Its iron gateway is guarded by two stone lions rampant brought from the Palace of Westminster.

Chedworth Roman Villa

From Ablington, we continued northwest through the delightful communities of **Winson**, **Coln Rogers** and **Coln St Dennis** before crossing the A429 Fosse Way at **Fossebridge**. Two miles further on, we came to **Chedworth**, a village which gives its name to one of the most impressive attractions in the area, the National Trust-owned **Chedworth Roman Villa**, the finest and most extensively excavated example of its kind in the UK. Before going in search of the famous archeological site, we decided to have a look at Chedworth village.

210

The village is made up of a number of simple stone-built houses and farms which are huddled together in the shallow valley between Pancake Hill and Chedworth Beacon. As well as a handsome Norman church with a castellated tower, it possesses a number of fine gabled buildings including the Old Farm, Cromwell House and two rows of attractive 18th-century cottages known as Church Row and Ballingers Row.

The site of the Roman villa is situated in the wooded valley of the River Coln one mile north of the village (it is more easily approached via Yanworth). It is thought to have been built between the mid-second century and the early-fourth century AD, and was accidentally rediscovered by a gamekeeper in 1864. This prompted a series of excavations organised by the owner of the land, Lord Elton, which revealed a complex layout of rooms and a remarkably sophisticated plumbing and heating system. This included separate steam and dry heat 'saunas', a pool for taking a cold plunge and a system for circulating warm air underfloor.

A number of beautiful and richly-patterned mosaic floors were also uncovered including a wonderfully patterned dining room floor. This consists of eight panels decorated with nymphs and satyrs set around a central octagon; another series of mosaics depicts the four seasons. A short distance away, there is a shrine above the villa's fresh water spring which is adorned with water nymphs.

In 1924, the site was acquired by the National Trust who have since erected a visitors' centre. An earlier museum building dating from the 1860s houses a display of some of the smaller objects unearthed on the site. A ten-minute video giving further background information on Chedworth Roman Villa can also be viewed here. Site open daily 10am to 5.30pm, March to end-October (closed Mondays except Bank Holidays), plus restricted winter opening hours. Admission charge payable (free to National Trust members).

Our next port of call was **Northleach**, a small country town situated near the junction of the A40 and the A429 Fosse Way, three miles to the northeast of the Roman villa. In common with many other Gloucestershire communities, this was once a major wool-trading centre which at one time rivalled in Cirencester in importance; as a consequence it possesses the disproportionately large 15th-century Church of St Peter and St Paul which is only outshone by those in Cirencester and Chipping Camden. The church is built in light Perpendicular style with pinnacled buttresses, high windows and a massive square castellated tower. The interior is noted for its ornately carved font and its unique collection of brasses, one of the finest in the country (permits for brass-rubbing can be obtained from Cotswold Pharmacy and the materials from the post office).

After a period of decline following the Dissolution of the Monasteries,

Northleach reverted to a small market town before becoming an important stopping point on the Gloucester to Oxford coaching route in the mid-18th-century. In the 1780s, a **House of Correction** was built at the old crossroads where the main east-west and north-south routes met. This was a small prison which dealt out an early form of the 'short sharp shock' to offenders who had been found guilty of minor crimes. The 37 inmates were kept in relatively good conditions (for example, they were allowed washing facilities), but were subjected to hard labour including work on a treadmill.

St. Peter and St. Paul, Northleach

Today, the building has been converted into a fascinating museum of rural life, the **Cotswold Countryside Collection**, which features a prison cell maintained in its original condition. The central theme of the museum, however, is its collection of historic agricultural implements which were originally gathered by Olive Lloyd Baker, a local enthusiast with a special interest in the evolution of modern agriculture. Exhibits include a steam tractor, waggons, an early laundry and an interesting collection of below-the-stairs domestic items. Open daily 10am (2pm Sundays) to 5.30pm between 1st April and 31st October. Small admission charge payable.

Another highly entertaining museum, **Harding's World Of Mechanical Music**, is situated in a 17th-century merchant's house in Northleach High Street. This remarkable museum-with-a-difference houses a collection of antique music boxes, chiming clocks and an assortment of mechanically-driven musical instruments which are played to visitors during guided tours and demonstrations. Proprietor Keith Harding also restores clocks and music boxes and runs the on-site gift shop. Open daily, 10am to 6pm. Admission charge payable. Those interested in original works of art should also look for Fothergill's Gallery in the High Street.

An excellent place to stay in **Northleach** is **Bank Villas Guest House**, an attractive residence with white-framed leaded windows which is situated on the main village road leading to Northleach from the historic Fosse Way. This first-rate establishment makes an ideal base for exploring the beautiful Cotswold countryside and discovering the many local places of interest. The house is very well presented and deceptively spacious; the dining area is situated in a large double-glazed conservatory, and there is also a comfortable television lounge. Each bedroom has a washbasin and tea/coffee making facilities, whilst the family room also has en suite facilities. *0451 860464*

Don't forget....

To tell people that you read about them in The Hidden Places

On leaving Northleach, we joined the A40 and headed east towards Oxford. After four miles, we turned north of the main road to reach **Sherborne**, a delightful village of characteristic stone-built houses which are strung out in twos and threes along the course of Sherborne Brook. In the centre of the village, a number of grander buildings surround Sherborne House, a classical country mansion rebuilt in 1830 which has recently been turned into private flats. The nearby Church of St Mary Magdalene is filled with monuments to the Duttons, the local landowning family. The village is surrounded by picturesque National Trust-owned parkland and woods which contain a number of lovely waymarked walks and scenic viewpoints.

Two miles further east, we made a point of visiting **The Barringtons**, two superb villages which at one time were an internationally-renowned source of Cotswold limestone. Several of the Oxford colleges and the interior of St Paul's Cathedral in London were constructed of stone quarried here. Indeed, Wren considered Thomas Strong, the owner of quarries at Little Barrington, to be the leading mason of his generation. (When Strong died, he left money to build the causeway across the River Windrush which can be seen today.)

For many years, river barges were loaded with stone at a wharf near the Fox Inn which were then floated down the Windrush and the Thames to London. Today, both Great and Little Barrington are quiet feudal villages built of indigenous Cotswold stone which together create an idyllic, though not altogether genuine, picture of English rural life.

From Great Barrington, we took the minor road which follows the course the River Windrush past Great Rissington to **Bourton-on-the-Water**.

Rooftrees Guest House   Bourton-on-the-Water   0451 21943

Our route into this small yet bustling Cotswold town took us past **Rooftrees Guest House** in Rissington road. Situated in a quiet part of Bourton-on-the-Water just ten minutes walking distance from the centre, Rooftrees is a large, welcoming house built of Cotswold stone, with mullioned windows and a frontage adorned with attractive hanging baskets. The proprietors, Sylvia and Sean Farley, have gone to great lengths to provide top quality accommodation. This becomes immediately apparent on entering the master bedroom where a handmade four-poster bed with beautiful drapes and frills has been installed, a real showpiece. The same degree of care and thought has gone into the other rooms, an additional feature of which is the display of cuddly animals, all dressed in fine costumes and made by the proprietor. As well as a full English breakfast, first-rate evening meals are provided if requested; these are

214

prepared from fresh local produce and are usually served with a complimentary drink.

The centre of Bourton-on-the-Water has a magical feel. The River Windrush flows through its centre under a unique series of low-arched pedestrian bridges, two of which date from the late 18th-century. Narrow lanes run back from the willowed greens which line the river between small houses and cottages that are all constructed of the same golden Cotswold limestone. (In Sherborne Street, look out for the unusual dovecotes built into the walls.) The town possesses some fine buildings including St Lawrence's church with its 14th-century chancel and Georgian tower, and the Old Manse dating from 1784 which has since been converted into a hotel.

Coombe House   Bourton-on-the-Water   0451 821966

Our journey around **Bourton-on-the-Water** took us past **Coombe House**, a charming family-run guesthouse which stands in its own attractive lawned garden and enjoys a peaceful location within easy walking distance of the centre of this truly delightful town. Proprietors Graham and Diana Ellis have seven guest bedrooms available, all of them excellently equipped with en suite bath or shower; two are on the ground floor making them suitable for partially disabled guests. The sitting room and breakfast room are bright, fresh and airy, providing a comfortable and relaxing atmosphere. This is enhanced by the central heating and residential license. The quality of the establishment is reflected in its English Tourist Board two crown, highly commended rating. Graham and Diana are happy to provide their guests with information on places to visit and eat out. Please note, however, that there is a total non-smoking policy in the house, with a first floor balcony providing an ashtray for the desperate!

Because of its attractiveness, Bourton-on-the-Water has become something of a lure for tourists, especially during the summer months, so don't expect to find a secluded gem. However, there are some unique attractions which are worth visiting, particularly if the weather is unreliable.

Birdland is a three-and-a-half acre private zoological garden which is situated in the grounds of a Tudor manor. The zoo was founded in 1956 by local builder, Leonard Hill, who set out to realise his dream of creating a living sanctuary for exotic birds of all descriptions. Today, the gardens are filled with aviaries, ponds and densely-treed groves which are home to over a thousand brightly-plumaged birds. Macaws and parrots fly freely in the open, sunbirds and hummingbirds flit about the tropical houses, toucans and flamingos inhabit the aviaries, and penguins swim in a glass-sided pool. Open daily all year round. Admission charge payable.

Birdland, Bourton-on-the-Water

The gardens behind the enigmatically-named Old New Inn in the High Street are the location of another of Bourton-on-the-Water's attractions, its famous **Model Village**. During the 1930s, the present landlord's father and a team of skilled craftspeople built a one-ninth scale replica of the town complete with inn, church, shops, flowing River Windrush and working water wheel. All the buildings are made of Cotswold stone and there is even a miniature of the Model Village itself. Open daily all year round. Small admission charge payable.

The **Cotswold Motor Museum** occupies an 18th-century corn-mill in Sherborne Street. In addition to the thirty or so cars and motorcycles on show, the museum contains a fascinating range of memorabilia including a collection of antique children's toys and the largest display of historic advertising signs in the country. Open daily 10am to 6pm between February and November. Small admission charge payable. Those

216

interested in model railways should also make a point of finding the **Model Railway Exhibition** in the High Street.

The Lawns   *Bourton-on-the-Water*   *0451 821195*

Before leaving Bourton-on-the-Water, we called in at **The Lawns** in Station Road, one of the access routes leading from the historic Fosse Way. Surrounded by lovely countryside, the Lawns is a recently completed, stone-built detached house which offers first-rate bed and breakfast accommodation. Beautifully constructed with a splendid solid wood staircase and balustrade, solid timber beams in the ground floor rooms, and first-class furnishings and decor throughout, the house oozes quality and charm. The accommodation comprises five letting bedrooms, some of which are en suite family rooms; cot facilities are also available. For guests wishing to relax in these comfortable surroundings at the end of the day, an evening meal can be provided by prior arrangement.

From Bourton-on-the-Water, we drove west for three miles along the A436 to find the widely-renowned wildfowl and garden centre at **Folly Farm**. This interesting conservation farm has grown to become one of the largest private collections of domestic waterfowl and wildfowl in Europe. The collection was started before World War II by Tom Bartlett, a recognised expert in his field who has written and broadcast on the subject throughout his life. The visitor area now covers over fifty acres and is home to over 160 breeds of birds and animals, many of them rare and exotic. Open daily 10am to 6pm (3.30pm in winter), all year round. Admission charge payable.

Situated only a couple of miles north of Bourton-on-the-Water yet entirely different in character, we visited the twin villages known collectively as **The Slaughters**. Despite the gruesome connotations, the villages actually take their name from the innocuous Anglo-Saxon word, *slohtre*, meaning 'muddy place'. Set a mile apart and joined by the River Eye, Upper and Lower Slaughter are both examples of the archetypal

217

Cotswold village. Each consists of a cluster of honey-coloured limestone buildings set around a church and manor. Apart the renovation of some cottages in Baghot's Square by Sir Edwin Lutyens in 1906, no new houses have been built in Upper Slaughter since 1904. Francis Edward Witts, whose *Diary Of A Cotswold Parson* was published in 1978, was the rector here from 1808 to 1854. The villages are both very photogenic and best explored on foot. We suggest starting at the church in Lower Slaughter and following the riverside path to the Square and on past the 19th-century corn-mill with its working water wheel.

Lower Slaughter

Those wishing to stay in this beautiful village setting should make a point of finding the **Washbourne Court Hotel** in **Lower Slaughter**. Lying just off the A429 Cirencester to Stow-on-the-Wold road a mile-and-a-half north of Bourton-on-the-Water, this must be one of the most picturesque locations in the Cotswolds. A truly outstanding place to stay, the **Washbourne Court Hotel** is a magnificent 17th-century country residence which stands within four acres of superb riverside grounds near the centre of the village. The hotel's interior retains much of its original character with stone-flagged floors, beamed ceilings and stone-mullioned windows. In winter, guests can relax in front of roaring log fires and in summer they can sit out on the charming riverside terrace, a natural habitat for birds and wildlife.

218

The hotel is privately-owned and run by the Pender family. During a period of renovation, they took great care to harmonise the traditional character of the building with the luxuries expected of a modern first-class hotel. A choice of accommodation is now offered in the 17th-century main building, in the delightful beamed Barn, and in the recently-constructed cottage suites. All rooms have en suite shower- or bathrooms, colour televisions and the finest modern facilities. The hotel restaurant offers a high standard of cuisine which is prepared using fresh local produce wherever possible. Shortly after opening in March 1992, the AA awarded the restaurant their coveted rosette for food (the hotel was given a three-star rating), making this a truly exceptional place to stay for exploring the Cotswolds and the many surrounding places of interest.

Washbourne Court   Lower Slaughter   0451 822143

From Upper Slaughter, we joined the Cheltenham to Stow-on-the-Wold road and made a short diversion west to visit **Naunton**. From the road running along the top of the ridge, Naunton looks like a village in miniature. It was founded in Saxon times and features a 14th-century church and string of characteristic stone cottages which congregate around the upper River Windrush. According to local legend, Naunton's first inhabitant was an imp who fell to the ground and broke a wing when flying over the Cotswolds with his satanic master. Finding himself unable to fly, he decided to build himself a cottage of local stone.

Our return route along the B4068 took us past another pair of villages, this time connected by the River Dykler and collectively known as **The Swells**. **Upper Swell** contains a fine 17th-century manor house and the tiny part-Norman Church of St Mary the Virgin; **Lower Swell** is slightly larger and contains a wonderful old pub, the Golden Ball, and a large country house and garden, Abbotswood, which was designed by Lutyens in 1902.

The area around **Condicote**, two miles to the west, contains some interesting ancient remains including the Roman Ryknild Street, the imposing Iron Age fortification known as Eubury Camp and the site of a prehistoric *henge*, an enclosure marked by stones dating from around 2500 BC.

At 800 feet above sea level, **Stow-on-the-Wold** is the highest town in the Cotswolds. Because of its exposed position, it has earned itself the rhyme, *Stow-on-the-Wold, where the winds blow cold.* Eight roads converge near the town, although fortunately only one actually passes through its centre. Instead, Stow survives as an exceptional collection of 17th- and 18th-century stone houses clustered around a market cross.

Motor Museum, Bourton-on-the-Water

Two of the Stow-on-the-Wold's main thoroughfares are called Sheep Street and Shepherds Way, reminders of the days when the town's main economic activity was wool trading. At one time, large twice-yearly sheep fairs (one of which was recorded by Daniel Defoe) were held on the open Market Square which was also the site of the stocks once used for punishing minor offenders. Narrow alleys known as 'tures' radiate from the Square and on market days, these were used for counting sheep in single file. The sheep fairs were eventually replaced by annual horse fairs which continued until 1985.

The church of St Edward was named after the unfortunate King Edward the Martyr who was murdered at Corfe Castle by his wicked stepmother, Elfrida. It has been restored on a number of occasions throughout the centuries and is considered one of the outstanding Cotswold churches. It also contains a famous 17th-century painting of the Crucifixion by Gaspard de Craeyer of Antwerp. The town contains some other noteworthy old buildings, including the 15th-century Crooked House (now an antique shop), the 16th-century Masonic Hall and the 18th-century Talbot which was once the local corn exchange.

During the English Civil War, forces of both sides regularly passed through Stow-on-the-Wold and the town was regarded to be of great strategic importance. On 21st March 1646, a hilltop to the northwest of the town was the site of the last open battle of the first Civil War. Following the battle, the defeated Royalist forces withdrew into the streets of Stow and some were fortunate enough to reach the relative safety of St Edward's Church. Others, however, were cut down in the Square and according to local reports, ducks were seen bathing in the blood which flowed through the streets. A Royalist officer, Captain Keyte, is buried beneath a slate slab in the chancel of the church.

Stow-on-the-Wold

From Stow-on-the-Wold, we drove east along the A436 for four miles until we arrived in the delightful village of **Adlestrop**. This is another Cotswold gem, filled with honey-gold cottages and boasting a Georgian mansion, a 13th-century church and a 17th-century rectory which Jane Austen regularly visited at the beginning of the last century. The

221

mansion, Adlestrop Park, was built in Gothic style with grounds laid out by Humphry Repton. Sadly, neither are open to the public. The Church of St Mary Magdalene contains a number of memorials to the Leigh family who have lived at Adlestrop Park since 1553. Jane Austen's grandfather, Thomas Leigh, was incumbent here for many years. The rectory where he lived stands surrounded by mature cedar trees near a 19th-century school house and cottage.

Adlestrop is perhaps best-known, however, for being the title of a poem by Edward Thomas, a great lover of the English countryside who was killed in action during the First World War. The work was written following a brief halt at the now-demolished Adlestrop station which was actually situated some distance away from the village. The station nameplate which fired Thomas' imagination can now been seen in the village bus shelter along with a plaque inscribed with his famous poem.

Don't forget....

To tell people that you read about them in The Hidden Places

From Adlestrop, we drove north along a minor country road towards Moreton-in-Marsh, a journey which took us through the quiet country village of **Evenlode**. Here, we discovered **Portland House**, a charming double fronted period residence which offers first-rate bed and breakfast accommodation. Surrounded by countryside, every window offers a view over the surrounding landscape, creating a wonderful sense of peace and tranquillity. Despite carrying out a thorough renovation, the proprietors, Mr and Mrs Dancer, have take care to ensure the property retains its original character and charm. This is enhanced by some fine period furniture, beautiful drapes and tasteful decor in each room, making Portland House a simply charming place to stay. *0608 51653*

A two-mile walk across the Oxfordshire border to the east of Evenlode leads to **Chastleton House**, a magnificent mansion which has remained virtually unchanged since it was constructed in 1603. The interior contains period furniture and a secret room where a Royalist family is said to have been concealed during the English Civil War. A nearby garden contains some amusing examples of box topiary.

Moreton-in-Marsh is a bustling market town which stands at a busy junction on the A44 and the A429 Fosse Way. In its time, the town has been an important stopping place for stagecoaches and, unlike many of its Cotswold equivalents which were solely bound up in the wool trade, it was also a leading linen-weaving centre. The present-day centre is full of 18th- and 19th-century buildings which give it a great deal of period character. Some of the structures date from an earlier era such us the old town gaol and the unusual Curfew Tower with its bell dated 1633 which in its time has been used to summon the local fire brigade.

The Marshmallow   Moreton-in-Marsh   0608 51536

A walk down the High Street in Moreton-in-Marsh revealed a couple of other noteworthy stopping places. The **Marshmallow Licensed Restaurant** is one of four tea shops nominated for the 'Teashop of the Year' award; it is also highly praised in *The Teapot Trail* guidebook which lists the best tearooms in the country. This is a comfortable traditional tearoom with tastefully coordinated decor, exposed stone walls and old pine furnishings. Outside, there is a flagstoned patio surrounded by beautiful hanging baskets. The menu offers a selection of food to suit every palate. Lunchtime fare includes vegetable crumble, baked potatoes and daily specials, with Sunday lunches also being available. In the evening, the candlelit dinner menu offers such exotic-sounding dishes as 'coriander lamb with orange rice' or 'mushroom and nut fettucine', along with steaks and chef's specials. Table reservations advised at weekends.

At the northern end of Moreton-in-Marsh High Street, visitors will find the delightful **Townend Cottage and Coach House**, a first-rate bed and breakfast establishment and licensed restaurant which is run by Elizabeth Alderson and Stephanie Jenvey. Guests will particularly love

223

the 'Tree House' which is like a lovers' hideaway; situated on the top floor of the coach house, this unique en suite bedroom is accessed by a wooden stairway leading to a stable door. The room has a beautiful view of the garden with its many attractive hanging baskets and plants. On the ground floor of the cottage there is a beamed, licensed restaurant where food is available every day except Mondays and Wednesdays. Restaurant fare ranges from economically priced dishes for the 'pop-in' visitor to wonderfully presented home-baked dishes, all prepared using the finest local produce. Visitors can also purchase homemade cakes and crafts as a memento of their visit.

Townend Cottage   Moreton-in-Marsh   0608 50846

Moreton-in-Marsh also contains two specialist museums: the **Bygones Museum** at Aston Magna contains an interesting display of historic farm implements and folk memorabilia (open Wednesdays and Sundays between Easter and end-October), and the **Wellington Aviation Art** museum in Broadway Road contains a unique collection of World War II aircraft paintings, prints and models, together with details of the aircraft's historical background (open Tuesday to Sunday, 10am to 12.30pm and 2.30pm to 5.30pm; admission charge payable, profits to RAF Benevolent Fund).

Like Stow-on-the-Wold, Moreton-in-Marsh was strategically important during the English Civil War and King Charles I himself is reported to have stayed at the White Hart Inn during one fleeting visit. Those wishing to stay a little longer should make a point of finding **Treetops** in London Road.

Treetops is a detached stone-built house with a private drive which is set in a delightful secluded position. Run by Liz and Brian Dean, this first-rate establishment offers spacious overnight accommodation. The beautifully presented en suite bedrooms with their wide doors and easy access extend an obvious welcome to disabled guests. Only a few minutes' walk from the main street of this delightful market town, Treetops makes an ideal touring base for exploring the beautiful Cotswold countryside. *0608 51036*

From Moreton-in-Marsh, we headed west along the A44 and after a couple of miles found ourselves climbing a steep hill. At the top, we found ourselves in **Bourton-on-the-Hill**, a pleasant village with a fine part-Norman church and a mansion, Bourton House, which is surrounded by beautiful landscaped grounds containing a 16th-century tithe barn.

Chastleton House, Moreton-in-Marsh

One mile south of Bourton-on-the-Hill, we made a point of visiting another impressive country house and garden, this time the highly eccentric **Sezincote**. In 1805, the house was rebuilt for a director of the East India Company, Sir Charles Cockerell, by his architect brother. He was assisted in his task by the noted Indian artist Thomas Daniell, hence its distinctive copper-covered onion-shaped dome; this was once burnished but is now coated in thick blue-green verdigris. Sezincote was visited in 1807 by the future Prince Regent and its design is said to have provided the inspiration for Brighton Pavilion which he built some years later. The grounds also contain a number of Indian-influenced features including a wonderful water-garden laid out by Repton and Daniell. House open 2.30pm to 5.30pm on Thursdays and Fridays during May, June, July and September; gardens open 2pm to 6pm on Thursdays and Fridays all year round except December, plus Bank Holidays and selected Sundays. Admission charge payable.

The Market Hall, Chipping Campden

From here, we retraced our steps to Bourton-on-the-Hill before joining the B4479 for the journey to **Blockley**, a mile-and-a-half further north. The idyllic and unspoilt appearance of the present-day village hides an unexpectedly diverse industrial past. The fast-flowing Blockley Brook is fed by a large number of local springs giving it a constant head of water; as a consequence, the village became a popular site for water-powered mills and as many as a dozen were recorded in the Domesday

Book back in the late 11th-century. In the centuries which followed, the main industrial activity in the village was silk spinning, most of the output of which went to ribbon weavers in Coventry. At one time, however, the village also boasted a piano, a soap and a collar factory, as well as an iron foundry. Today, the picturesque silk mills have been made into desirable private homes and the village has an air of secluded wellbeing.

For a short period in the early 19th-century, Blockley became famous as the home of Joanna Southcott, an eccentric who announced to the world that she would give birth to Shiloh, the second Messiah. Following a series of disturbances in the village, her house was eventually burnt to the ground. Today, the rebuilt Rock Cottage is marked with a commemorative plaque attached to two sturdy gateposts.

Lower Farm Cottages   Blockley   0386 700237

Visitors seeking a truly idyllic country holiday need look no further than **Lower Farm Cottages**. Situated beside a brook in a quiet corner of Blockley, these exceptional self-catering cottages have been tastefully converted from period farm buildings to provide six luxury holiday homes. All are named after places and characters from *Wind In The Willows*: Ratty's Retreat is a tranquil hideaway for two people with a galleried bedroom and Victorian half-tester bed, Toad's Hall is the largest cottage which makes an ideal home for a large family or group, and Willow End, Mole's Cottage, Badger's Den and Otter's Abode are charming cottages which each accommodate either four or five people. Each cottage has a superb fitted kitchen, and visitors are welcomed with a pint of milk in the fridge and other essentials. (Guests can even arrange to have an order of groceries awaiting their arrival.) Outside, there are various slides, play equipment and even an immobilised tractor for children to play on, as well as a delightful little boat.

From Blockley, we drove north along a minor road towards Chipping Campden, a route which took us through the charming hamlet of **Broad**

227

Campden. The hamlet is noted for its former Norman chapel which was converted into a house for Indian philosopher Dr Coomaraswamy.

Chipping Campden itself is an ancient community of attractive gabled buildings which has remained largely unaltered for centuries. *Chipping* is a name which occurs several times in the Cotswolds and is derived the Old English word meaning 'market' or 'trading centre'. More a large village than a town, Chipping Campden was a regional capital of the wool-trade between the 13th- and 16th-centuries and many of the fine buildings that can be seen here today date from this era of prosperity. The Perpendicular 15th-century **Church of St James** with its 120 foot pinnacled tower is one of the finest wool churches in the Cotswolds (second only to Cirencester). Inside, there are several monumental brasses including one of William Grevel, which at eight feet by four feet, is thought to be the largest in the country. Presumably erected in an attempt to secure his immortality, its inscription (translated from Latin) reads 'the flower of the wool merchants of all England'. Also on view in the church is a glass display case containing a rare collection of embroidery including one example dating back to the time of Richard II.

Almshouses, Chipping Campden

Another noted 17th-century wool merchant and financier, Sir Baptist Hicks, was responsible for several of the finer Cotswold-stone buildings in the village including the unique Jacobean **Market Hall** with its open arcade and steeply-pitched gable ends which was completed around

228

1627. Fifteen years earlier, he endowed a group of attractive **Almshouses** built in the shape of the letter 'I' in honour of Kings James I (or Iacobus in the Latin of the day). Hicks was also responsible for building what was the largest residence in the village, **Old Campden House**. During the English Civil War, it was allegedly burned to the ground by Royalists to prevent it falling into the hands of the Parliamentarians. All that remains of it today are two unusual gatehouses near the church and the old stable block which was converted to a dower house some years after the end of the Civil War. Towards the end of his career, Hicks is said to have been so rich that even the King and members of his court asked to borrow from him.

Woolstapler Hall, Chipping Campden

Another unique character from Chipping Campden's past is **William Harrison**, an elderly rent collector who vanished in 1660. A woman and two of her sons were subsequently found guilty of his murder and hanged. Two years later, Harrison, the 'Campden Wonder', suddenly turned up in the village with an unconfirmable story of kidnapping, robbery and Turkish pirates.

Other points of interest in present-day Chipping Campden are the town hall, Grevel House and the Ernest Wilson memorial garden with its Chinese and Japanese botanical specimens. Also in the High Street is the **Woolstaplers' Hall**, a 14th-century former merchant's house which is now an interesting museum. Its eleven rooms contain a diverse collection

229

of historic memorabilia including kitchen items, cameras, office equipment, clothing and an apothecary's shop. Open daily 11am to 6pm between 1st April to 31st October. Small admission charge payable.

Campden Needlecraft Centre

Those interested in the art of embroidery should make a point of finding the **Campden Needlecraft Centre** in Chipping Campden High Street. A true heaven for needlecraft enthusiasts, this attractive 17th-century building positively bulges with a vast array of materials of every conceivable type and colour. There are canvases from all over the world and every kind of thread, braid and fabric imaginable. Visitors can even purchase footstools ready to be worked on. A nationally renowned business, the Campden Needlecraft Centre was originally opened by the mother of the current proprietor and has been established for over twenty years. Today, Helen Kirkup and her staff regularly dispatch orders abroad; they offer friendly, knowledgeable advice and can provide a fast and efficient postal service if required.

Between 1612 and the mid-19th-century, a natural amphitheatre above Chipping Campden known as **Dover's Hill** was the venue for an annual series of organised games. These 'Olimpick Games' partly followed the traditions of Ancient Greece and partly involved more vernacular activities such as shin-kicking and bare-knuckle fighting. After having flourished for almost 250 years, the lawlessness and hooliganism which had grown up around the games led magistrates to close them down in 1852. However in 1951, they were revived in a modern form and each year on the Friday following the spring Bank Holiday, a series of competitions takes place which ends in a spectacular torchlight procession.

Two miles east of Chipping Campden on the B4035 Banbury road we came to **Ebrington**, a quintessential Cotswold village of honey-coloured walls and neat thatched roofs. The village falls away to the north in irregular steps into a valley filled with apple and cherry orchards. There was a manor at Ebrington as early as the 13th-century, although the present-day house dates from around 400 years later. The village church, St Eadburgha's, contains a number of ancient features including a Saxon stone coffin, a Norman nave and a mediaeval tower. It also contains an unusual 17th-century pulpit and a statue of Sir John Fortescue wearing the full regalia of a mid-15th-century Lord Chief Justice.

From Ebrington, we turned north into a network of country lanes and after two-and-a-half miles came to the National Trust-owned **Hidcote Manor Garden** at Hidcote Bartrim. This exceptional garden is said by many to be one of the most beautiful built this century. In 1907, an American army officer, Major Lawrence Johnston, began a process which was to transform an exposed Cotswold escarpment into a series of delightful enclosed gardens. His only raw materials were a copse of mature beech trees, a lone cedar of Lebanon, a number of empty fields and a stream which flowed through a small valley. After creating several wide terraces, Johnston laid out a series of protective hedges which were deliberately made up of contrasting plant types (for example, yellow-leaved yew was interspersed with dark-leaved yew and copper beech with standard beech).

This created a series of sheltered compartments, each of which was planted with a carefully selected range of shrubs and plants which often followed to a recognisable theme (for example, some have flowers and foliage in a single colour). The water garden is less formal and consists of a rambling path overhung with trees which winds along the course of the stream between species shrubs and flourishing water-loving plants. There is also a large kitchen garden near the house with walls covered in clematis and old-fashioned climbing roses. Open daily (except Tuesdays and Fridays), 11am to 7pm between April and the end October. Admission charge payable (free to National Trust Members). In July, Hidcote Manor Garden also hosts outdoor performances of popular Shakespearean plays.

Another attractive garden, **Kiftsgate Court**, can be found adjacent to Hidcote. This also features a wide range of less well-known flora including tree peonies and old-fashioned roses. Open Sundays, Wednesdays and Thursdays between 1st April and 30th September. Admission charge payable.

A charming place to stay in this attractive northern tip of Gloucestershire can be found one mile to the northwest of Hidcote in the village of **Mickleton**. 'Brymbo', the home of Gene and Barry Jeffrey, is a former farm building which has been tastefully converted into spacious, comfortable accommodation comprising one twin, one double and one family room. Two rooms have en suite facilities, and all have television

231

and tea/coffee making facilities. Gene and Barry go out of their way to ensure their guests are informed about the best attractions and eating places in the area. They even offer an evening tour in a four-wheel drive vehicle around places which might prove inaccessible in a normal car. Their helpfulness, keen prices and prodigious supply of maps and local information have made 'Brymbo' a highly popular place with overseas visitors. Advance booking is strongly advised.

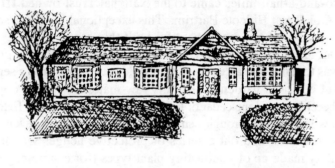

Brymbo   *Mickleton*   *0386 438876*

We left Mickleton on the B4632, and after passing through the pleasant Worcestershire town of Broadway, continued south into the area of Gloucestershire covered in our next chapter.

Gloucester and Cheltenham to the Hereford and Worcester Border

Tewkesbury Abbey

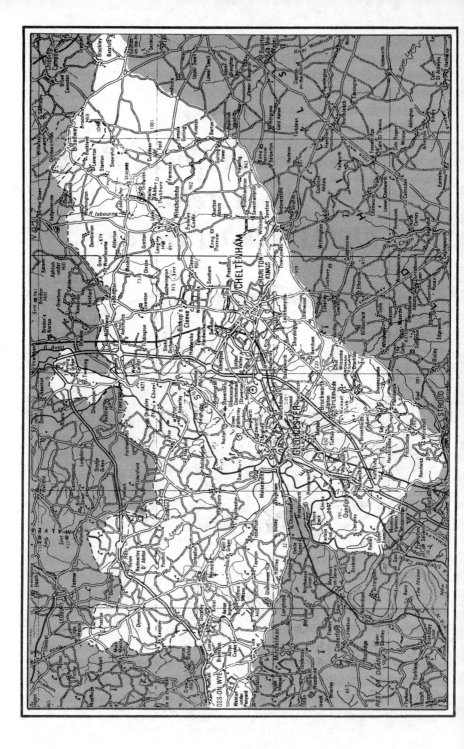

Index

The Abbey Mill Restaurant, Mill Street, Tewkesbury
Beechmount Guest House, Birdlip, Nr Gloucester
Brooklands Farm Caravan Park, Alderton, Nr Tewkesbury
City Museum and Art Gallery, Brunswick Road, Gloucester
Croft Farm Leisure Park, Bredon's Hardwick, Nr Tewkesbury
Damsels Farm B&B, Painswick, Gloucestershire
Dormy House Hotel, Willersey Hill, Broadway
Dryknapps House B&B, Painswick, Nr Stroud
The Fountain Inn, 53 Westgate Street, Gloucester
Gilbert's B&B, Gilbert's Lane, Brookthorpe
Gower House B&B, 16 North Street, Winchcombe
The Granary B&B, Kempley, Dymock
Hobnails Inn, Little Washbourne, Nr Tewkesbury
Home Farm B&B, Bredons, Norton, Tewkesbury
The Horseshoe Inn, Broom's Green, Dymock
Ireley Farm B&B, Winchcombe, Nr Cheltenham
Kings Arms Inn, Ross Road, Newent, Nr Gloucester
Kingshead House Restaurant and B&B, Birdlip, Nr Cheltenham
Linton Farm B&B, Highnam, Gloucestershire
Nature in Art Gallery, Wallsworth Hall, Twigworth
Newent Gold and Silversmiths, 15 Broad Street, Newent
The Olde Bakery Tea Shoppe, Winchcombe, Nr Cheltenham
Plaisterers Arms Inn and B&B, Winchcombe, Nr Cheltenham
Stanton Court Self Catering Cottages, Stanton, Nr Broadway
Stanway Grounds B&B, Toddington, Nr Cheltenham
Stanway House, Stanway, Cheltenham
Taynton Farm Shop, Hown Hall, Taynton, Gloucestershire
Tyms Holm Guest House, Apperley, Gloucestershire
The Vine B&B, Stanton, Nr Broadway
The White Hart Inn and B&B, Winchcombe, Nr Cheltenham
The White Hart Inn, Maisemore Village, Gloucester

Gloucester Cathedral

CHAPTER NINE

Gloucester And Cheltenham To The Hereford And Worcester Border

Our journey into northeast Gloucestershire took us through **Broadway**, an exceptionally attractive Worcestershire village which has earned a reputation for being the 'show village of England'. Many of the honey-gold Cotswold stone buildings which line the unusually long and wide main street date back to Tudor and Jacobean times. In recent years, some have been converted into interesting antique shops and other retail premises designed to cater for passing visitors. The village has a broad green overlooked by St Michael's parish church and the Broadway Hotel. A short distance away, the 16th-century Lygon Arms Hotel, formerly a private residence, stands beside the famous furniture workshops belonging to Gordon Russell Ltd.

We decided to stay just on the outskirts.Between Broadway and Chipping Campden, adjacent to Broadway Golf Club, you will find **Dormy House**. Dormy in golfing terms means 'unbeatable' and that is a very fair description of this fine hotel which offers the visitor the opportunity to relax in superb surrounings. Everything about Dormy House is tasteful. The bedrooms are all en-suite and furnished attractively with a mixture of antique and traditional pieces that lend charm to the rooms. Each bedroom has tea and coffee making facilities, colour TV and telephones. For people with young families there is a baby listening service which is always a boon to parents.

We dined by candlelight in one of the prettiest restaurants we have been to. It is broken up into a series of small intimate areas. The linen is in lovely pastels of beige and cream and every table has a single fresh rose. In such a relaxing atmosphere you feel absolutely right to enjoy the very best of English and French cuisine. We started our meal with an unusual terrine of Lobster and Asparagus with a basil sauce and followed it with Supreme of Guinea Fowl with wild rice and a creamed marsala sauce. These were just two from a range of nine starters and twelve main courses

237

on the a la carte menu. There is also a table d'hote menu which changes daily. The choice was hard to make and care is taken to ensure that you can have simply grilled or steamed fish for example if your diet demands it. With every main course there is a selection of fresh seasonal vegetables which come to the table cooked perfectly. Follow this with one of the delectable sweets, or cheese from the wide choice available from the cheeseboard and you will leave the table replete and happy. The fine wine list reflects the quality of the food and includes some superb vintages.

Dormy House is so well situated for anyone wanting to tour the Cotswolds. We thought it an excellent place for visitors from abroad to stay because it is just the sort of hotel that upholds all that is good about English hospitality.

Dormy House Hotel   Broadway   0386 852711

A mile-and-a-half to the southeast of Broadway, Fish Hill rises to over 1000 feet and is topped by a highly conspicuous folly, the 55 foot **Broadway Tower** which was built in 1800 by the Earl of Coventry solely so that it could be seen from his home at Worcester nearly twenty miles away to the northwest. The tower contains an elegantly-proportioned observation room and an exhibition on the history of Broadway and its famous folly. Open daily, April to early-October. A further exhibition, this time on local natural history, is housed in nearby Tower Barn; this stands at the centre of the network of footpaths and nature trails which crisscross the attractive area known as the **Broadway Tower Country Park**. Open daily, all year round.

A couple of miles further south, we made a point of calling in at the National Trust-owned country house, **Snowshill Manor**. This small yet elegant manor house dates from Tudor times and once belonged to Catherine Parr, the sixth wife of Henry VIII. The present-day building has an attractive 17th-century Cotswold stone façade and contains 21 rooms, most of which are open to the public.

238

These rooms now contain a fascinating collection of historic artefacts assembled over several decades by the last private owner, Charles Paget Wade. Articles on display include clocks, toys, bicycles, sedan chairs, oriental furniture and nautical items such as compasses, telescopes and model ships. There are also a number of exhibits relating to Wade's special interest in the occult. (Towards the end of his life, the collection became so large that Paget was forced to move in to one of the outbuildings.) Open Wednesdays to Sundays (and Bank Holiday Mondays) between May and September, and on Saturdays and Sundays only during April and October. Admission charge payable (free to National Trust members).

Broadway Tower

From Snowshill, we continued south on a small country lane, crossing the B4077 at Ford. A mile further south, we came to **Temple Guiting**, an exceptionally attractive north Cotswolds hamlet on the banks of the Upper Windrush which has a fine church and a handsome Georgian mansion. In the 12th-century, the Knights Templar founded a preceptory here. A couple of miles downstream, Temple Guiting's sister village, **Guiting Power**, consists of a delightful collection of Cotswold stone cottages clustered around a triangular green. In the 1970s, Richard Cochrane, a local property-owner who had acquired about half the cottages in the village, set up a trust to ensure that the housing here would continue to be offered to local people at affordable rents. This arrangement has done much to preserve the rural character of the village with its steep gables, mullioned windows and neat blue doors. Other noteworthy features here are the part-Norman St Michael's Church which was extensively remodelled in 1903, the memorial cross which was erected after the First World War, and the old bakery in Well Lane which has an unusual columned frontage dating back to the early 17th-century.

Midway between the Guitings, and approximately one mile to the east, stands the **Cotswold Farm Park**, a characteristic Cotswolds hill farm which contains one of the largest collections of rare farm animals in the country. Visitors are encouraged to meet the animals which include longhorn cattle, Gloucester Old Spot pigs and a local breed of thickly-fleeced sheep known as Cotswold Lions. Also on offer is a children's adventure park, pets corner, café and farm trail. Open daily, 10.30am to 6pm between Good Friday and 1st October. Admission charge payable.

Sudeley Castle

Our journey westward from the Guitings crossed the **Salt Way**, an ancient packhorse path which runs along the ridge between the Windrush valley and the vale of Sudeley. Because of the lack of winter foodstuffs, it was a common mediaeval practice to slaughter livestock in the autumn and then preserve the meat in barrels of salt. The mineral became a valuable commodity and a network of routes grew up between its source (in this case Droitwich in Worcestershire) and the rest of the country. The most accessible section of the Cotswolds Salt Way runs for seven miles south from Hailes Abbey to a point on the A436 three miles east of

Andoversford. Near its northern end, the route passes close to **Salter's Hill**, an impressive viewpoint lying two miles east of Winchcombe.

Our route westwards passed close to **Sudeley Castle**, the burial place of Catherine Parr which is located one mile to the southeast of Winchcombe. After outliving Henry VIII, Parr married her former lover, Sir Thomas Seymour of Sudeley, but sadly died in childbirth the following year. Not long after in 1549, her husband was executed for treason after unsuccessfully attempting to turn Edward VI against the Lord Protector, Seymour's own brother. The marble tomb of Catherine Parr can be seen in St Mary's Chapel. This, however, is not the original but a 19th-century substitute designed by Sir Gilbert Scott to replace the one destroyed during the English Civil War.

Winchcombe

Sudeley Castle was a Royalist headquarters during that war and was twice besieged, once in 1643 and again in 1644. The conflict left the castle badly damaged by cannon fire and a large gap can still be seen in the wall of the Octagon Tower. During the following two centuries, Sudeley was badly neglected and much of the stone was carted away by locals for use as building material. By the 1820s, it had degenerated into a common alehouse, the Castle Arms, and it wasn't until 1837 that the castle and sixty acres of land were rescued by the Dent family. Emma Dent was responsible for completing the period restoration of the exterior and for refurbishing the interior in sumptuous Victorian style. She was

241

also responsible for accumulating a a large number of priceless old masters, including work by Constable, Turner, Van Dyck and Rubens, as well as a unique collection of tapestries, period furniture, costumes and one of the largest private collections of toys in Europe.

As well as being able to tour of the interior, visitors can walk around Sudeley's extensive grounds which contain a lake, a formal garden and a fifteen-foot double yew hedge. A more recent addition has been a large adventure playground complete with replica castle. Castle open daily, 12 noon to 5pm between 1st April and 31st October. Admission charge payable.

The attractive small town of **Winchcombe** was once a regional capital of Saxon Mercia. One of the town's more enduring legends concerns, Kenelm, a popular child king who is said to have been martyred here by his jealous sister, Quendrida, in the 8th-century. As a way of calming a mob which had gathered to voice its disapproval at this murderous act, legend has it that she recited Psalm 109 backwards, an act which resulted in the divine loss of her sight. In mediaeval times, St Kenelm's shrine grew to rank second only to Thomas á Becket's as a destination for pilgrims, a factor which made the town one of the wealthiest tourist attractions in the country. Winchcombe grew to become a walled town with an abbot who presided over a Saxon parliament; however in 1539, the abbey was destroyed by Thomas Seymour of Sudeley following Henry VIII's Dissolution of the Monasteries. All that remains of it today is a section of a gallery which is on view at the **George Inn**.

Plaisterers Arms   Winchcombe   0242 602358

Our journey around Winchcombe led us past a fine country inn, the **Plaisterers Arms** in Abbey Terrace. This impressive establishment dates from the 18th-century and inside has oak-beamed ceilings and a wonderful traditional atmosphere. Landlord David Gould serves an excellent selection of hand-pulled ales and a range of bar meals including delicious homemade pies and a traditional roast lunch on Sundays. He also has three comfortable letting rooms available which are all pleasantly appointed and equipped with en suite facilities. The land to the rear of the inn slopes away sharply to form a delightful beer garden. An attractive patio area has been created here and in spring and summer, the whole area overflows with spectacular floral displays. The garden enjoys fine views over the surrounding landscape and also contains a charming pets' corner and large children's play area. Children are also very welcome in the pub's pleasant cellar bar.

Following the destruction of the abbey, the local merchants were forced to find an alternative source of income. This they found in a new crop which had just been introduced from the New World, tobacco. Despite the vagaries of the English climate, for several decades Winchcombe earned a healthy living growing this increasingly popular cash crop, a fact which is reflected in several present-day place names such as Tobacco Close and Tobacco Field. Unfortunately, this new-found prosperity was brought to an abrupt end in 1670 when an act of Parliament banned home-produced tobacco in favour of imports from the struggling colony of Virginia.

The Olde Bakery   Winchcombe   0242 602469

The long period of decline which followed this legislative interference has left the town with a great many unaltered buildings. These include the Tudor houses in Hailes Street and the splendid parish church with its forty leering gargoyles and alter cloth reputed to have been embroidered by Catherine of Aragon.

On the corner of Castle Street in the centre of Winchcombe, we found the delightful **Olde Bakery Tea Shoppe**. This handsome stone building is believed to be between 200 and 300 years old, and earlier this century, operated as a working bakery (the old bakehouse can still be seen at the bottom of the tea garden). Proprietors Sally and Colin Snell maintain the

243

tradition of home baking, with the vast majority of items being made on the premises (their special homemade carrot cake is renowned.) Customers can sit in either of the two tea rooms, in the vine-covered conservatory or, weather permitting, in the delightful walled tea garden. On Sundays, an excellent traditional roast lunch is served for which booking is advised. Sally and Colin also have two charming en suite letting bedrooms available.

The White Hart   Winchcombe   0242 602359

Also in the High Street, we called in at the excellent **White Hart Hotel**, a splendid inn which is believed to be one of the oldest in **Winchcombe**. This impressive half-timbered building has a private car park at the rear and for much of the year is covered in wonderful hanging baskets of flowers. Inside, it has lost none of its original character and charm with oak-beamed ceilings, open fires and an interesting collection of horse racing memorabilia, including several antique saddles. Proprietors Alistair and Mari MacPherson and John Steele-Scott offer a fine selection of traditional hand-drawn ales and an extensive bar meals menu, with dishes ranging from sandwiches and jacket potatoes to steaks and chicken Kiev. The White Hart also has several letting bedrooms available which are all comfortable, well-appointed and provide a good base for exploring the Cotswolds. Residents are also able to make use of the inn's snooker cellar and games room, though they should keep an eye open for the friendly ghost which is said to pay a visit from time to time.

Winchcombe also contains two interesting specialist museums. **Winchcombe Folk and Police Museum** is situated adjacent to the tourist information centre in the town hall. As well as information on the history of the town from neolithic times to the recent past, the museum also houses an intriguing collection of police equipment and uniforms, both from British and overseas forces. Open Mondays to Saturdays,

244

10am to 5pm between 1st April and 31st October. Small admission charge payable.

A half-acre garden behind an ordinary-looking Victorian house in Gloucester Street is the home of the **Winchcombe Railway Museum**, thought to be the oldest private railway museum in the country. All types of railway-related exhibits are on show with the exception of locomotives and rolling stock. There is even a working signal box, a booking office and a number of signals which visitors are encouraged to operate. Also on show is a collection of over 200 cast iron line-side signs and a large display of printed memorabilia, including tickets and posters. Open daily, 1pm to 6pm. Admission charge payable (accompanied children free).

Gower House   Winchcombe   0242 602616

Standing near the centre of Winchcombe at 16 North Street, we found the first-rate bed and breakfast establishment which has been run since 1984 by Mrs Sally Simmonds. **Gower House** is an attractive stone-built residence with an atmosphere which is exceptionally friendly and welcoming. The oak-beamed bedrooms are comfortable and well-appointed and have access to two guest bathrooms. Mrs Simmonds provides her guests with the warmest of welcomes and a traditional Cotswold breakfast which is guaranteed to set them up for the day. She also has an interesting collection of antique weighing scales. To the rear of the house, there is a delightful garden with its own well, raised beds and an unusual sundial on the wall.

Those preferring the relaxed atmosphere of farmhouse accommodation should make a point of finding **Ireley Farm**, a delightful bed and breakfast establishment which is run by Margaret and Ian Warmington. Situated just off the Broadway road on the edge of Winchcombe, Ireley Farm has a history going back to Roman and mediaeval times. It is centred around an elegant 18th-century residence built of golden Cotswold limestone which stands within 500 acres of beautiful rolling farmland. Inside, the house has a handsome panelled hallway, open fires and three spacious letting bedrooms, all oak-beamed and decorated in charming country style. Maggie and Ian provide the warmest of welcomes and a delicious farmhouse breakfast. Horse riding and rough shooting are also available nearby.

Ireley Farm   *Winchcombe*   *0242 602445*

On leaving Winchcombe, we joined the B4632 for the two-mile northeasterly journey to **Hailes Abbey**. The abbey was founded in 1246 by Richard, Earl of Cornwall, son of King John and youngest brother of Henry III, following his narrow escape from a shipwreck off the Scilly Isles. Unfortunately, it was built to such an ambitious scale that the Cistercian monks found it difficult to maintain financially; that is, until a wealthy patron donated of a phial which was said to contain the blood of Jesus Christ. Thanks to this holy relic, Hailes Abbey soon became one of Europe's most important pilgrimage destinations and was even referred to in Chaucer's *The Canterbury Tales*.

This state of affairs lasted until the Dissolution of the Monasteries in 1539 when the authenticity of the relic was questioned and the phial destroyed. The abbey then fell into disrepair and today, the only significant structures still standing are seventeen arches of the monastic cloister. Because of its illustrious past, however, a large number of artefacts have been found on the site including mediaeval floor tiles and fragments of elaborate stone sculptures. These are now on display to the public in an interesting museum which is open daily, 10am to 6pm between 1st April and end-September. Admission charge payable (free to National Trust and English Heritage members).

The nearby parish church of Hailes was constructed around 1130 and predates the abbey. Many of the floor tiles belonging to the abbey were transferred here following the Dissolution, and there are also some fine

14th-century wall paintings and a canopied pulpit dating from the 1600s.

Our next stop was **Stanway**, a charming village which lies tucked under the western ridge of the Cotswolds a couple of miles to the north. The view down to the village from the A4077 on the escarpment above is one of the loveliest in Gloucestershire. Stanway itself contains a number of interesting architectural features including a 14th-century mediaeval tithe barn, an unusual bronze of St George on the war memorial, and private cricket pavilion built on curious mushroom-shaped staddle-stones. An ornate Jacobean gatehouse guards the entrance to Stanway House, a fine Tudor mansion built of mellow honey-gold Cotswold limestone which is one of the most remarkable houses in the county.

Hailes Abbey

Stanway House is an outstanding example of an English Jacobean manor house, built between 1580 and 1640 by the Tracys of Stanway, a landed family who owned property in Gloucestershire since pre-Norman times. Other than by inheritance, the estate has only changed hands once in the last 1200 years. Today, Stanway is the home of Lord Neidpath; he has personally written an excellent guide to the house which is on sale to visitors to help them enjoy a tour around the property. (It is also a pleasure to read the guide after a visit when it helps to refresh the memory of the many delights of the house.)

247

We brought away some outstanding memories of Stanway, for example, of the gatehouse which is situated between the church and the main house. This was built around 1630, it was believed, by Inigo Jones, though more recently it has been ascribed to Timothy Strong of Barrington. Whoever the designer, it is one of the gems of Cotswold architecture.

There is an interesting piece of history connected with the scallop shells which adorn the gatehouse. Sir William de Traci of Barnstaple was one of the four knights who murdered St Thomas á Becket in Canterbury Cathedral at the instigation of King Henry II. After the King repented of this horrendous crime, Sir William was obliged to go on pilgrimage to Jerusalem, and so, it is supposed, the Tracys adopted the scallop shell crest of St James of Compostella, the patron saint of pilgrims.

Stanway House   Stanway   0386 73469

The shuffleboard table along the west wall of the hall was built about 1620. The game of shuffleboard, an early form of shove-halfpenny, was very popular in the 16th- and 17th-centuries. As there are only three known to be in full working order complete with their brass counters, this is a rare example indeed. It is particularly special because it has a single piece of oak as the playing surface. The table has a moulded frieze on the side which is visible from the hall, but none on the side nearest the west wall, suggesting that it has always stood in its present position.

In the bay window there is a Chippendale exercising chair; at one time, half-an-hour's vigorous bouncing each day on this was considered to be good for the health. We also saw two fine Broadwood pianos which, until recently, lay neglected in an unheated, unlit, unventilated and uninhabited room. Despite hardly ever having been played, they have remained in excellent condition. Each piano cost forty-six guineas in 1810; when you compare that with the price of a Broadwood Grand today, the rise in the cost of living really hits home. Stanway is filled with fine paintings, many

248

The Mediaeval Village Cross, Stanton

of them portraits of family ancestors, all of which add to the atmosphere and well-being of this lovely house.

Stanway House is also known for being the home of Thomas Dover, the sea captain who rescued Alexander Selkirk from a deserted island, an event which gave Daniel Defoe the inspiration to write *Robinson Crusoe*. We hope you will enjoy a visit to Stanway House as much as we did.

Stanton Court Cottages   Stanton   0386 73551

Stanway's sister village, **Stanton**, lies a mile further north. This exceptional Cotswold village consists almost entirely of steeply-gabled limestone cottages built during the 16th- and 17th-centuries. One of the reasons Stanton is so well-preserved is that it was owned by the architect Sir Philip Stott between 1906 and 1937. Stott's home, **Stanton Court**, is an elegant Jacobean residence which was built by the Chamberlain to Queen Elizabeth I when the original 16th-century manor, Warren Farm House, had become outmoded. The house is set within attractive landscaped grounds which are occasionally open to the public on summer Sundays.

Attached to Stanton Court, we found the superb **Stanton Court Cottages**, a collection of eight top-class self-catering holiday cottages which were constructed of local Cotswold limestone in the 16th- and 17th-centuries. Now luxuriously renovated, the cottages provide the ideal place to get away from the daily trials of life and completely unwind. The cottage buildings are set around a wonderful old courtyard and stand within five acres of impressive landscaped gardens containing orchards, sweeping lawns and beautifully-kept flower beds. The grounds also contain a heated outdoor swimming pool (open during the summer months), a tennis court (open weekdays) and a games room containing table tennis, table football and darts.

The eight holiday cottages sleep from two to seven people and are appointed to an extremely high standard. All have full gas central heating, direct-dial telephones, fully-equipped modern fitted kitchens, attractively decorated dining/sitting room areas with colour televisions, modern bathrooms with showers and plenty of hot water, and bedrooms with all linen and continental quilts provided. There are also excellent laundry facilities on site. The cottages are luxurious and stylish, yet comfortable and informal, and provide the ideal environment in which to relax and enjoy the beautiful surroundings and many nearby places of interest. Open all year round.

Stanton's village Church of St Michael's and All Angels has a number of noteworthy features including a fine Perpendicular south aisle and porch, an east window containing stained glass from the ruined abbey at Hailes, and a number of mediaeval pews whose ends have been deeply scarred by the leashes of dogs said to belong to local shepherds. A number of early-20th-century additions were made to the church by the architect Sir Ninian Comper; these include the organ loft, the rood screen and a number of stained-glass windows which can be identified by the designer's signature, a wild strawberry.

Those looking for first-rate farmhouse accommodation in the delightful village of Stanton should make a point of calling in at **The Vine**. Lying just to the east of the B4632 between Winchcombe and Broadway, this exceptional place to stay can also be reached on foot via the Cotswolds Way. The Vine is a friendly, family-run bed and breakfast establishment which is run by Jill Gabb. Her substantial 17th-century stone-built farmhouse stands within a beautiful low-walled garden and was once the home of the local bailiff. Inside, the atmosphere is warm and relaxing with open log fires, a superb dining room and three spacious letting bedrooms, each with a four-poster. Mrs Gabb is happy to offer accommodation to unaccompanied children who come to take advantage of the excellent riding facilities which are offered at the nearby stables.

The Vine   *Stanton*   *0386 73250*

Before turning west, we made a short detour to the northeast to visit the village which is believed to possess the oldest rectory in England. **Buckland** is a quiet and picturesque settlement which is situated under the crest of **Burhill**, just to the east of the B4632 Broadway road. The ancient rectory dates from the Middle Ages and includes a 14th-century great hall which has unusual hammerbeams carved with angels. One of the rectory windows dates from the 15th-century and has a design attributed to the Malvern Priory school of glass making. John Wesley is said to have preached at the rectory which is open to visitors 11am to 4pm on Mondays only during May, June, July and September. Admission free.

There is also a fine Perpendicular church in Buckland with a 15th-century east window which was restored in the 19th-century on the instructions of William Morris. The lovely little building is surrounding by an interesting churchyard containing an unusual table tomb and the graves of several local luminaries.

Stanway Grounds   Toddington   0242 620079

From Buckland, we retraced our steps southwest along the B4632 for three miles before turning west onto the B4077. Toddington Station, the northern terminus of the privately-owned **Gloucestershire-Warwickshire Railway**, is situated close to this road junction. From here, it is possible to take a steam train for an enjoyable six-mile return trip through some of the loveliest countryside in Gloucestershire. The restored Great Western Railway station is open to the public all year round and includes a signal box and a goods shed. Small admission charge payable. Train trips at an extra charge depart between 12 noon and 5pm on Saturdays and Sundays between March and October.

A mile or so further west, we turned north off the B4077 Tewkesbury to Stow-in-the-Wold road to visit the delightful village of **Toddington**. Here, we went in search the renowned bed and breakfast establishment which is run by Mrs Pratley at her spacious country home, **Stanway Grounds**. Set within beautiful open countryside, this handsome late-Victorian farmhouse can be found approximately one mile northeast of the village. (For accurate directions, telephone the owner on 0242 620079.) Mrs Pratley has three spacious and comfortable letting bedrooms available (either double or twin), all with tea/coffee making facilities and either en suite facilities or a private bathroom. For those keen on horse-riding, a stables is attached to the building which offers riding lessons and accompanied pony trekking rides. Children and pets welcome.

The Hobnails   Little Washbourne   0242 620237

Approximately three miles to the west of Toddington, we found ourselves in **Little Washbourne**, a charming village which lies in the broad valley which sweeps down from the Cotswolds to the River Severn.

Here, we stopped at the **Hobnails Inn**, a renowned country pub which dates from 1474 and has been run by the same family since 1743. The present landlords, Stephen and Vanessa Farbrother, have built up an excellent reputation for good pub food, and in particular, for their range of Scottish baps which they serve with a huge variety of delicious fillings. They also offer an imaginative range of vegetarian dishes, homemade entrees and a mind-blowing selection of desserts. A good selection of traditional ales is served in the bar which, like the dining room, lounge and games room, is full of traditional atmosphere. Queen Elizabeth I is believed to have stopped at the here on her way to visit Catherine Parr, and Harry the friendly poltergeist is rumoured to be a regular visitor to this day!

One mile to the northwest of Little Washbourne, the village of **Alderton** is home to the impressive **Brooklands Farm Touring Caravan Park**. This small and attractive family-run caravan park stands within twenty acres of rolling farmland just six miles to the east of junction 9 on the M5. Set around a small lake, the site enjoys fine views over the surrounding countryside to Gretton Hill and beyond. It has been run since 1988 by Caravan Club members Sue and Simon Greener, a very friendly couple who have done much to improve the facilities on offer. There is now an excellent toilet block with showers, hair dryers and laundry facilities, a large games room with indoor bowls and table tennis, electric hook-ups and a small site shop selling, amongst other things, bottled butane and propane. Coarse fishing is also available in the lake during the season.

Brooklands Caravan Park   Alderton   0242 620259

Driving westwards once more, we soon came to the junction with the A435 Tewkesbury to Evesham road. The upland area to the north of here, **Bredon Hill**, is a spur of the Cotswolds which extends from the main range across the Hereford and Worcester border. Undeterred, we turned northeast into the country lanes and found ourselves in the pleasant village of **Ashton under Hill**.

Home Farm   Bredons   0684 72322

Our onward journey took us through a series of attractive villages which eventually led us to the western side of Bredon Hill. Some of the

254

finest farmhouse accommodation in the area can be found at **Home Farm** in the historic village of **Bredon**. Owned by Anne and Mick Meadows, Home Farm is a lovely brick-built farmhouse which forms part of a 150-acre family-run working livestock farm. Guests are assured of a warm welcome at this cosy friendly establishment, the central part of which dates from the late 17th-century and was originally quite small, containing only a kitchen, sitting room and four bedrooms, two at attic level. Today, there are three comfortable letting rooms available, two with en suite facilities and all tastefully furnished and centrally heated. Anne provides superb home-cooked food, much of which is prepared from her own produce (make a point of sampling her delicious homemade jams). Evening meals are also available by prior arrangement. For those preferring self-catering accommodation, the Meadows also have a well-equipped three-bedroom cottage which sleeps up to six people.

Croft Farm   Bredons Hardwick   0684 72321

Heading towards Tewkesbury once more, our journey south took us through the village of **Bredon's Hardwick**, the location of the renowned **Croft Farm Leisure and Water Park**. Situated just to the north of the B4080, this impressive leisure facility is a mecca for enthusiastic windsurfers of all ages and levels of ability. Formerly a market garden, the site was taken over in 1976 by a sand and gravel company whose excavations led to the formation of the lake which can be seen today. Proprietors Alan and Agneta Newell offer fully qualified instruction at their RYA recognised windsurfing school. They also offer excellent value caravanning and camping facilities between 1st March and 31st October at two attractive lakeside sites. For further information or to book in advance, telephone (0684) 72321.

From Croft Farm, it was only a short journey across the Gloucestershire border to **Tewkesbury**, a historic and strategically important town which stands at the confluence of the rivers Severn and Avon. Because its geographical position restricted outward development, Tewkesbury grew as a series of narrow streets packed with unusually tall buildings, many of which were constructed during the 15th- and 16th-centuries. Thanks to the period of relative decline which followed this late-mediaeval period of prosperity, a great many black and white half-timbered structures remain; these are best seen on foot.

Tewkesbury Abbey

Tewkesbury's three main thoroughfares, the High Street, Church Street and Barton Street, form a 'Y' shape around the abbey. The area in between is filled with narrow alleyways and hidden courtyards which contain some wonderful old pubs and mediaeval cottages. At the centre of the 'Y' stands the spectacular **Tewkesbury Abbey**, a parish church of cathedral-like proportions which was originally founded in the 8th-century and re-consecrated at the end of the 11th-century. It was once the church of the mighty Benedictine Abbey of Tewkesbury and was one of the last monasteries to be dissolved by Henry VIII; in 1540, it was saved from destruction by the astute town burghers who bought it from the Crown for just £453.

Inside, one of its most striking features is the double row of massive Norman pillars; these support some fine early-14th-century roof vaulting which in recent years has been restored to its original colour. In the central quire, there are seven superb stained-glass windows containing panes dating from the 14th-century. Two other outstanding features are

256

the abbey's Milton organ, which has pipes dating from around 1620 that are thought to be some of the oldest in the country still to be in regular use, and the high alter which consists of a single massive slab of Purbeck marble over 13 feet in length.

At 132 feet high and 46 feet square, Tewkesbury Abbey's colossal main tower is believed to be the largest Norman church tower still in existence. Those making the climb to the top will be rewarded with a breathtaking view of the town and the surrounding landscape. Indeed, the tower was used as a lookout position during one of the bloodiest and most decisive confrontations of the Wars of the Roses, the **Battle of Tewkesbury**.

Tewkesbury

The battle took place on Saturday 4th May 1471 in a field to the south of the town which ever since has been known as **Bloody Meadow**. Following the Lancastrian defeat, those who had not been slaughtered on the battlefield fled to the abbey where they were pursued by the victorious Yorkist troops. A further massacre took place before it was halted by timely intervention of Abbot Strensham; however, two days later the refugees, who included the Duke of Somerset, were handed over to the king and executed at the town's Market Cross. The seventeen year-old son of Henry VI, Edward Prince of Wales, was also killed during the conflict and a plaque marking his resting place can be seen in the abbey.

Almost two centuries later, Tewkesbury was again the scene of military action, this time during the English Civil War. It changed hands several times during the conflict and on one occasion, Charles I began his siege of Gloucester by requisitioning every pick, mattock, spade and shovel in the town.

Those keen on finding out more about the town's turbulent military history should follow Tewkesbury's **Battle Trail**, an informative guide for which is available at the Tourist Information Office. Alternatively, there is an interesting model of the battlefield in the **Tewkesbury Town Museum**. This fascinating museum is housed in a mediaeval timber-framed building in Barton Street and contains a number of displays on the social history and archeology of Tewkesbury and its surrounding district. Open daily, 10am to 1pm and 2pm to 5pm between Easter and the end of October. Admission charge payable.

Two other specialist museums can be found almost adjacent to each other in Church Street. The **Little Museum** is situated in a timber-framed merchant's house which dates from around 1450. The building was fully restored in 1971 and is laid out as a recreation of a typical Tewkesbury merchant's home and workplace during the late-Middle Ages. Open Tuesdays to Saturdays (and Bank Holiday Mondays), 10am to 5pm between Easter and October. Admission free.

The nearby **John Moore Countryside Museum** contains a huge variety of artefacts relating to the Gloucestershire countryside, past and present. It was opened in 1980 in commemoration of the work of John Moore, a well-known local writer, broadcaster and natural history enthusiast who was born in Tewkesbury in 1907. Items on show include agricultural implements, domestic equipment and a wide range of unusual rural memorabilia; most of the exhibits are set out to be particularly appealing to children. The museum also concerns itself with nature conservation and the effects of human intervention on the natural environment. Open Tuesdays to Saturdays (and Bank Holiday Mondays), 10am to 1pm and 2pm to 5pm between Easter and October. Small admission charge payable.

Another place in Tewkesbury well worth visiting is the **Abbey Mill** in Mill Street. Standing in a lovely position by the river, this charming restaurant can cater for up to 140 people. A mill began operating on the site in the 8th-century which was run by a monk, most probably from the abbey. In the 17th-century the building was rebuilt in Tewkesbury brick and, more recently, it was converted to a comfortable, modern restaurant. A large working waterwheel stands next to the attractive patio which is open throughout the summer. Customers can drop in at the Abbey Mill for morning coffee, lunch or afternoon tea, or book in advance to join one of their famous fun evenings; these include mediaeval banquets, Cockney nights and Bavarian evenings.

Tewkesbury is also known for its literary associations. Charles Dickens set part of *The Pickwick Papers* in the town's Royal Hop Pole Hotel, and the Victorian romantic writer, Mrs Craik, based her novel *John Halifax, Gentleman* on the people and places of the borough.

Abbey Mill   Tewkesbury   0684 292287

A three-mile detour across the River Severn to the west of Tewkesbury led us to **Forthampton**, an unspoilt Severn Vale village with a genuine historic character. The village consists of an assortment of 16th- and 17th-century timber-framed farmhouses and cottages which are loosely grouped around a knoll containing the part-13th-century church of St Mary's. A series of narrow lanes cuts through the village offering a number of beautiful walks past some of the most delightful old buildings in Gloucestershire. These include the **Sanctuary**, with its 15th-century great hall, the imposing 18th-century **Forthampton House**, and the similarly-aged **Southfield House** with its handsome brick-built dovecote. The grounds of Southfield House are occasionally open to the public and contain the former country retreat of the abbots of Tewkesbury, **Forthampton Court**.

After retracing our steps, we passed through Tewkesbury and drove in a southerly direction along the A38 towards Gloucester. After about two miles, turned west onto the B4213 to reach the attractive Severn-side hamlet of **Deerhurst**. The tiny present-day village disguises the fact that in Saxon times, it was of much greater importance. Indeed, this was the site of the most powerful monastery of *Hwicce*, the Anglo-Saxon principality of the lower Severn. The village church is one of the oldest in Britain and has parts dating back as far as the 7th-century, the period when the monastery would have been at the height of its influence. The building has a distinctive Celtic flavour; the elaborate double east

259

window is unique to Deerhurst and is considered to bear more resemblance to a window in Ethiopia's Debra Damo monastery than it does to any equivalent construction in Britain. The interior of the church contains some unusual Saxon carvings, including an angel in the apse which probably dates from the 9th-century and an exceptionally fine carved font which was found buried in a local farmyard. This also dates from the 9th-century and is carved with a Celtic trumpet spiral, a vine scroll and an unusual Northumbrian motif. The present-day base has different origins and originally belonged to a carved Saxon cross.

St Alphege, who went on to become Archbishop of Canterbury and was subsequently martyred by the Danes, was a monk here during the 10th-century, and some decades later, a nearby island in the Severn was the place where the Saxon king, Edmund Ironside, signed a treaty of cooperation with Canute, King of the Danes. The church also contains a number of memorial brasses dating from the late-14th-century commemorating the Cassey family, the owners of the estate one mile to the south which now encompasses the handsome 16th-century residence, Wightfield Manor.

The floor of nearby Abbots Court once concealed the remains **Odda's Chapel**, another Saxon treasure which was founded in 1056 by the Earl Odda, a trusted friend of Edward the Confessor. A stone inscribed with the date of consecration was discovered in 1675 and is now on view in the Ashmolean Museum in Oxford. A copy of this **Odda Stone** can be seen inside the chapel which is now administered by English Heritage.

Tyms Holm Guest House   *Apperley*   *0452 780386*

One mile southwest of Deerhurst, we came to the attractive village of **Upper Apperley** where we discovered the impressive **Tyms Holm Country Guest House**. This fine establishment is owned and personally run by Ann Sabin and her husband, two extremely thoughtful people whose care and attention to detail make this delightful guesthouse really

260

stand out. On booking their accommodation, guests are sent comprehensive details on how to find the place, along with a wonderful little guide, beautifully hand-drawn, showing all the places of interest which lie within easy reach. Produced and detailed by Richard Harrow, these little maps show, for example, Apperley to Bibury via the Coln Valley, or Apperley to Snowshill or Worcester.

Situated in the ancient parish of Deerhurst, Tyms Holm lies midway between Tewkesbury, Cheltenham and Gloucester making it ideal for exploring the Malverns, Cotswolds and the Forest of Dean. The guesthouse is set within an acre of beautiful lawned and shrub-filled gardens which give it almost total seclusion, and is reached along a lovely tree-lined drive. The building is a very old cottage which has been restored and enlarged. In fact, the present dining room was originally called Hawkers Cottage; a charming place, it features lovely old Jacobean-style furniture, including an original monk's bench. Guests certainly eat well here on the fine home cooking. Delicious morning coffees, lunches and afternoon teas are served in the licensed restaurant, as well as first-rate breakfasts and evening meals. (Because the food is so tempting, diners can put on pounds if they are not careful!)

The accommodation comprises one single, two twin and two double rooms, with one double and one twin offering en suite facilities. The Sabins take the business of running a successful guesthouse all in their stride and manage to create a wonderful relaxed atmosphere. Children are very welcome and the proprietors are happy to cater for any practical request during your stay. Tyms Holm has been awarded two crowns by the English Tourist Board and is open all year round except during Christmas week. In winter, roaring log fires supplement the central heating, making this a truly splendid place to stay. Mind you, we have always found the Cotswolds and Severn Vale to be outstandingly beautiful whatever the time of the year.

We set off from Upper Apperley in an easterly direction and made our way to **Cheltenham** via the B4213, A38 and A4019. Unlike most of the other settlements we had so far visited in Gloucestershire, Cheltenham's history is relatively short, really only beginning in the 18th-century. Indeed, the only surviving mediaeval building here is the parish church of St Mary's in Clarence Street which has parts dating back to the 12th-century. This building is worth a visit, partly to make a comparison with the rest of the town and partly to view some of its exceptional features. The most noteworthy of these is the circular east window which is renowned for its delicate 14th-century tracery; there are also some fine Victorian stained-glass windows and an unusual 13th-century Sanctus bell in the chancel.

Until the beginning of the 18th-century, Cheltenham was a small market town consisting of one main street. However in 1715, a local farmer accidentally uncovered a saline spring in one of his fields, an occurrence which would eventually change the character of Cheltenham out of all recognition. Twenty years later, his son-in-law, the retired privateer Captain Henry Skillicorne, saw the potential of the discovery and built an enclosure around the spring along with a meeting room, a ballroom and a network of walks and rides to provide access. (These grew to form the modern tree-lined Promenade.) Later, he added a stylish Long Room to the complex of buildings.

As the reputation of Cheltenham Spa grew, a number of other springs were discovered locally, including one in the High Street around which the first Assembly Rooms were constructed. In 1788, the prosperity of the town was assured following a visit from George III who, along with his queen, daughters and assorted members of the court, spent five weeks in Cheltenham taking the waters. This royal endorsement made the town into highly fashionable resort and a period of spectacular development followed. The local luminaries of the day commissioned a team of eminent architects to plan an entirely new town which would incorporate the best features of neoclassical Regency architecture. The scheme turned out to be so successful that it attracted many prominent figures of the day, including the Duke of Wellington who spent several weeks in Cheltenham in 1816 treating a liver complaint he had contracted in the tropics.

Today, Cheltenham continues to attract visitors to its splendid Regency streets which are best explored on foot. These include **Suffolk Place**, **Lansdown Place** and **Montpellier Walk**. Montpellier Walk is modelled on the Athenian Temple of Erechtheion, though the **Rotunda** at its southwestern end has more in common with the Pantheon in Rome. One of the common features of Cheltenham's Regency architecture is the delicate ironwork which is built into many of the upstairs balconies and verandas.

This golden era of architecture reached its high point with the completion of two unique structures in the late-1820s. The **Promenade** is noted for its superb fountain of Neptune, and the **Pittville Pump Room** is an extravagant masterpiece which stands within spacious parkland to the north of the town centre. The latter was designed by John Forbes and features a great hall fronted by a colonnade of Ionic columns and topped by a domed gallery. It was built for Joseph Pitt MP as a place to entertain his circle of friends, though by the time of his death in 1842, its construction had left him heavily in debt. Cheltenham's famous spa water can still be sampled here today (it is also available at the Town

Hall). Said to be the only naturally occurring alkaline spring water in the country, it is believed to be instilled with beneficial medicinal properties. It is certainly an acquired taste.

Today, the building also houses the **Pittville Pump Room Museum**, an imaginative museum which brings to life Cheltenham's past from its Regency renaissance to the 1960s using the medium of original period costumes. There is also an interesting display of historic jewellery and tiaras which charts the changes in fashion that occurred between the Regency and Art Nouveau periods. Open

Tuesday to Sundays (also summer Sundays and Bank Holiday Mondays), 10am to 4.20pm between February and November. Admission charge payable.

The Promenade, Cheltenham

Two other worthwhile museums are situated nearer the centre of Cheltenham. The **Gustav Holst Birthplace Museum** in Clarence Road is housed in the terraced Regency house where the famous composer (of among other things, the *Planets Suite*) was born in 1874. Among the items on show in the music room are Holst's original concert piano and an interesting display giving the background to the composer and his music. The house has been refurbished in keeping with the 'upstairs-downstairs' way of life which would have prevailed in the late-Victorian era and includes a gracious Regency drawing room, a children's nursery filled with period memorabilia, and a working kitchen with a housekeeper's room, pantry, scullery and laundry. Open Tuesdays to Saturdays, 10am to 4.20pm, all year round. Admission free.

The **Cheltenham Art Gallery and Museum** in Clarence Street is also worth a visit, especially by those interested in furniture and silver. The museum possesses a fine collection of Cotswold-made pieces inspired by William Morris, the founder of the much-respected Arts and Crafts Movement in the 19th-century. Other work on show includes an impressive display of oriental porcelain, English ceramics, pewter, glassware and a permanent collection of paintings by Dutch and British masters. Information on the social and archeological history of Cheltenham is also available here, along with a fascinating collection of personal items belonging to Edward Wilson, one of the members of Captain Scott's ill-fated team of Antarctic explorers. Open Mondays to Saturdays, 10am to 5.20pm, all year round and on Sunday afternoons between June and August (closed Bank Holidays). Admission free.

Each year, Cheltenham hosts a number of top class arts' festivals. In May, a two-week **Festival of Music, Speech, Drama and Dance** is held; this is followed in July by the **International Festival of Music**, again lasting two weeks and featuring a wide variety of classical concerts, opera and recitals; then in October, the **Festival of Literature** features readings, exhibitions and a range of literary events. The **Everyman Theatre**, Cheltenham's former opera house, provides an excellent venue for performed work of all kinds.

A **Cricket Festival** has been held in Cheltenham each August since 1877, and the town is also the home of one of the nation's premier horse racing events, the Cheltenham Gold Cup, which takes place each year in March. **Cheltenham Racecourse**, Britain's top-rated steeplechasing venue, is situated at Prestbury Park, two miles north of the town centre and just to the west of the A435. The nearby village of **Prestbury** contains an abundance of thatched, timber-framed buildings, a couple of welcoming pubs and the lost remains of a mediaeval bishop's palace. Its largest claim to fame, however, relates to the unusually large number of ghosts which are said to inhabit the village. These include Old Moses the groom, a young woman playing a spinet, a lone strangler, a black abbot and a man on a bicycle.

A spectacular view of Cheltenham and the surrounding landscape can be obtained from **Cleeve Cloud**, which at 1083 feet above sea level is the highest point in the Cotswolds. The summit is situated four miles northeast of Cheltenham and can be reached by walking southeast along the Cotswold Way for one-and-a-quarter miles from the village of **Cleeve Hill**. The view from the Cotswold ridge is spectacular; Tewkesbury Abbey, Herefordshire Beacon and the distant Brecon Beacons can all be seen on a clear day.

One of the finest examples of a neolithic long barrow can be found two miles east of Cleeve Cloud (it can either be approached from Cleeve Hill or in the opposite direction from the village of Charlton Abbots). Known as **Belas Knap**, the grass-covered 180 foot by 60 foot barrow was constructed by New Stone Age people around 5000 years ago. Excavations discovered four burial chambers which together contained the remains of thirty people. One of the most remarkable features of Belas Knap is its false entrance at the broader northern end which was probably installed to discourage grave robbers and unwanted spirits. The burial chamber hidden nearby was found to contain the remains of a man and five children who had possibly been buried as part of some ancient sacrificial rite.

Another dramatic hilltop site can be found two-and-a-half miles south of Cheltenham and just to the east of the B4070 Birdlip road. **Leckhampton Hill** is an imposing limestone crag with a bare cliff face and a grassy crest on which an Iron Age fortification once stood (evidence of more recent Roman and Saxon occupation has also been found here). Just below the summit stands the fragile rock column known as the **Devil's Chimney** which is rumoured to have been 'sent straight from hell'. The hill is best approached from the north along a path which rises sharply from the B4070. After some distance this divides, offering the choice of a direct route to the top or a circular route around the summit to the west which allows a spectacular view of the Devil's Chimney.

Much of the fine limestone which was used to face Cheltenham's splendid Regency buildings was quarried at or around Leckhampton Hill and the old quarry workings add to the rugged character of the landscape. **Leckhampton** village has a 14th-century manor house and a church of a similar age which contains some unusual brass monuments.

The exposed ridge of the Cotswolds escarpment winds southwest from Leckhampton Hill, taking with it the course of the **Cotswolds Way**. This impressive long-distance footpath offers spectacular views across the Severn Vale to the Severn Bridge and Brecon Beacons to the southwest, and across the Vale of Gloucester to Bredon Hill and the Malverns to the north. This superb three-mile stretch also takes in a number of dramatic promontories. The first of these is **Cooper's Hill**, a nature reserve covering 137 acres of common land which is now owned by Gloucestershire County Council. This was once the site of some of the most extensive Iron Age fortifications in the area, though since the early Middle Ages, it has been set aside as common agricultural land. Owners of local farms are still entitled to special commoners' rights including estover, the right to collect wood for fuel, and pannage, the right to allow pigs to feed freely.

Each year at Whitsun, Cooper's Hill is the site of the famous and highly risky **cheese rolling ceremony** where participants chase a whole cheese down the steep slope from a maypole on the ridge above. The event is thought to have formerly taken place on Midsummer's Day as part of a prehistoric sun-worshipping ceremony. Sheltering in a coombe half-a-mile from Cooper's Hill are the remains of **Great Witcombe Villa**, a once-grand Roman villa with a bath wing and some fine mosaic floors.

A little further to the southwest, evidence of occupation by neolithic people has been found at **Crickley Hill**. (This was also the location of an Iron Age fort some centuries later.) Today, this magnificent National Trust-owned site is run as a country park in conjunction with a neighbouring tract of land owned by Gloucestershire County Council. The area is filled with unusual geological and archeological feature, and a number of interesting walks are described in the leaflets which are available at the information point.

Those interested in geology should look out for the nearby memorial to the young geologist, Peter Hopkins. This is constructed of five different rock types, all of which can be found within the Cotswold and Malvern Hills. The third viewpoint on this stretch of the Cotswold ridge, **Birdlip Hill**, is approached from the A417 through attractive private mixed woodland. The famous bronze **Birdlip Mirror**, now in Gloucester City Museum, was found in an Iron Age burial mound known as Barrow Wake which lies just to the north of the Birdlip village.

Kingshead House   *Birdlip*   *0452 862299*

The pleasant community of **Birdlip** stands near the junction of the B4070 and the A417 Ermin Way, close to the point where the old Roman road descends into the Vale of Gloucester. One of the highest villages in Gloucestershire, this is where we discovered the renowned **Kingshead House**, a restaurant with a national reputation for owner Judy Knock's

266

distinctive and imaginative cooking. Customers entering this 16th-century former coaching inn are welcomed into a relaxing oak-beamed bar which is presided over by Warren Knock. On the day we visited, the dinner menu included chicken liver and spinach paté, guinea-fowl accompanied by Judy's superb lemon and garlic sauce, and 'chocolate Alcazar', a rich truffle topped with dark chocolate. A varied lunchtime menu is available on weekdays, with a more traditional three-course lunch being served on Sundays. For those who can't tear themselves away, Kingshead House also offers a large and attractive letting bedroom equipped with en suite bathroom.

Beechmount   Birdlip   0452 862262

Those preferring first-rate guesthouse accommodation in Birdlip should look for the family-run **Beechmount Guest House**. An extremely friendly place to stay, Beechmount has been owned and run since 1978 by Pauline and Mike Carter. Originally built as a temperance hotel, this imposing stone-built residence stands within easy reach of the Cotswolds Way. Inside, there is a large lounge, an impressive dining room and seven spacious guest bedrooms, two of which have en suite facilities. The rooms to the rear look out over attractive gardens to open fields beyond. Pauline and Mike offer an excellent choice of breakfast dishes and also provide first-rate evening meals by prior arrangement. With most of the Cotswolds lying within 45 minutes drive, this English Tourist Board two-crown commended guesthouse provides an ideal base for exploring the area.

On leaving Birdlip, we joined the B4070 Stroud road for a couple of miles before turning north to reach the village of **Cranham**, home of the famous **Prinknash Abbey** and the neighbouring **Prinknash Bird Park**.

The Abbey at Prinknash (pronounced *Prinnage*) consists of two separate buildings set on opposite sides of a beautiful wooded estate. The old abbey was built between the 14th- and 16th-centuries for the

Benedictine monks of Gloucester Abbey. For a short period following the Dissolution of the Monasteries it became the country retreat of the Bishops of Gloucester before passing into private hands for over 400 years. The most recent private owner, Thomas Dyer-Edwardes, became a devout Roman Catholic in his declining years and gifted the property to a community of Benedictine monks who were struggling to eke out a living on Caldey Island off the south Wales' coast.

When the white-robed monks returned to Prinknash in 1928, they found a cluster of attractive honey-gold buildings, including a fine mediaeval chapel with some elaborate carved woodwork and stained glass. They soon realised, however, that the old buildings were unsuitable for the needs of their expanding brotherhood, and in 1939 the foundation stone for a modern abbey was laid. The new Cotswold stone structure was designed with practical simplicity in mind and was eventually completed in 1972.

Painswick

Today, the monks of Prinknash are involved in a number of home-based economic activities including the production of world-renowned **Prinknash Pottery**. Members of the public are welcome to visit the pottery workshops which were established on the site following the discovery of clay deposits during construction work. Viewing gallery open daily, 10.30am to 4.30pm (2pm to 5pm Sundays), all year round. Although the brightly-coloured earthenware is not to everyone's taste, a

268

range of other hand-crafted items are available in the abbey's gift shop including carved woodwork, stained glass, incense, wrought-ironwork and fresh produce from the home farm.

A nine-acre section of the abbey grounds is run as a separately-managed establishment, the **Prinknash Bird Park**. As well as being the home to a wide variety of free-roaming peacocks (including white, black-shouldered and Indian blue) and waterfowl (including mute swans, black swans and snow geese), the bird park contains a number of interesting animals including African pygmy goats and fallow deer. A lovely woodland path leads though the Golden Wood to a haunted 16th-century Monk's fish pond which was built before the Reformation and is still stocked with large trout. Open daily, 10am to 5pm between Easter and October. Admission charge payable.

From Prinknash, we stayed on the small country lanes and headed south for approximately two miles towards **Sheepscombe**, a pleasant unspoilt community of gabled Cotswold stone farmhouses and small cottages. One of the first Sunday schools in the country was opened here by a local weaver in 1780 and is thought to have provided Gloucester's Robert Raikes with the inspiration for founding the national Sunday School Movement shortly after. Not far from Sheepscombe, the National Trust-owned **Ebworth Estate** offers some fine walks through three attractive woodland areas: Workman's Wood, Lord's and Lady's Woods and Blackstable Wood. Access is via public rights of way, however, parking is limited.

Two miles to the west of Sheepscombe, a minor country road brought us to the beautiful small town of **Painswick**. This attractive community had been dubbed 'The Queen of the Cotswolds' and is full of characteristic pale grey limestone cottages built of stone quarried at Painswick Hill, a mile to the north. Between the 15th- and 18th-centuries, Painswick was a prosperous wool trading and cloth manufacturing centre, and a number of substantial merchants' houses dating from this period can be found in and around Bisley Street. The churchyard, too, is filled with elaborate table-top graves, many of which are inscribed 'clothier'.

Painswick churchyard also contains a large quantity of carefully-manicured yew trees. Local legend has it that only 99 yew trees will ever grow here, the Devil having pledged to do away with any more. Some of the trees were planted as long ago as 1714 and together they form a series of skillfully-clipped arches, cones and hedges, creating the atmosphere of a living sculpture garden.

Each year on the Sunday following September 8th, **St Mary's Churchyard** is the venue for the annual Clipping (or Clypping) ceremony. Here, garlanded children join hands to encircle the church before dancing around it singing hymns. Afterwards, each child receives a silver coin, a traditional Painswick bun and a slice of 'puppy dog pie', a traditional pie whose ingredients include a china dog. The church itself dates from around 1378 and contains some unusual corbels thought to represent Richard II and his queen. Its colossal 172 foot spire contains a peal of twelve bells and can seen for many miles around. (One of the finest views of Painswick is from the top of **Bulls Cross** to the southeast, a mystical place referred to by Laurie Lee in *Cider With Rosie*.)

St Mary's Church was the site of a skirmish during the English Civil war when a party of Parliamentarian soldiers came under fire whilst sheltering here, resulting in considerable damage to the building. Earlier in the conflict, Charles I is said to have stood at the top of nearby Painswick Beacon and enquired as to the name of woodland below. On hearing it had none, he replied, 'let it be called *Paradise*', a name which has stuck to this day. A month after confidently supervising the campaign to take Gloucester, he passed this way again, defeated.

Rococo Gardens, Painswick

The streets of Painswick village contain a number of interesting features including a set of unusual 19th-century 'spectacle' stocks in St Mary's street, the Tudor **Byfield House** with its elegant 18th-century façade, Dennis French's renowned **Painswick Woodcrafts** in New Street, and the fine half-timbered **Post Office** dating from 1428 which is said to be the oldest functioning post office in the country. There are also

270

two impressive manor houses in Painswick, **Court House**, which was built in 1604 for a local cloth merchant, and **Castle Godwyn**, a small 18th-century manor owned by the Milne family which is open to visitors all year round by written appointment only.

Dryknapps House   Painswick   0452 813652

Tucked away off Edge Road on the southern side of Painswick, we found the charming bed and breakfast establishment, **Dryknapps House**, which is run by Hamish McLean and his family. This Grade II listed residence was built around 250 years ago and at one time was believed to have been used as the local police station. Inside, it has oak-beamed ceilings and a wonderful warm and friendly atmosphere. The guest rooms are comfortable and spacious and enjoy wonderful views across the valley to Edge village and beyond.

Painswick House is located on the northern edge of the village, and although the interior of this splendid Palladian mansion is not open to the public, its six-acres of grounds are. **Painswick Rococo Garden** is hidden in a broad coombe and contains a number of old gardeners' outbuildings and some delightful woodland walks. Open Wednesdays to Sundays (and Bank Holiday Mondays), 11am to 5pm between February 1st and mid-December. Admission charge payable.

Those looking for top quality farmhouse accommodation in this idyllic part of the Cotswold should make a point of finding **Damsels Farm** on the edge of Painswick. This is charming Grade II listed farmhouse dates back to the 14th-century and was originally the Dower House for Painswick Manor; later, it was used by Henry VIII as a hunting lodge. Proprietors Michelle and Peter Burdett have 100 acres on which they rear sheep and cattle. They also offer cosy accommodation in the farmhouse in three twin/family rooms, and have a first-rate self-catering cottage available which sleeps up to four. Children are welcome at Damsels Farm and can delight in feeding the ducks, geese, calves and orphaned lambs. Michelle is chairman of *Stay On A Farm* in Gloucester and can put visitors in touch with other members of the organisation within the area; she can be contacted on (0452) 812148.

Damsels Farm   Painswick   0452 812148

The upland area to the west of Painswick offers some magnificent views of the Severn Vale and the Forest of Dean. The National Trust-owned **Haresfield Beacon** overlooks the River Severn as it bends around the Arlingham peninsula and is the site of a once strategically-important Roman hill-fort. A short distance away, the outline of an early-British encampment known as Broadbarrow Green can also be detected. At 700 feet above sea level, it is possible to see for over fifty miles from here on a clear day.

The village of **Haresfield** lies tucked below the headland and is the home of the widely-renowned **Countryside Centre**. These attractive wildlife gardens contain a large walk-through aviary, a collection of owls and other birds of prey, a pets' and small animals' corner, and a number of interesting nature trails. A wildlife rescue unit and sanctuary is also based here. Open daily, 10am to 4.30pm, all year round. Admission charge payable.

The country lanes to the northeast of Haresfield led us to **Brookthorpe**, a pleasant village containing a 13th-century church with an unusual saddleback tower. This is where discovered **Gilbert's**, a truly charming country house built around 400 years ago using stone from the Cotswold Hills and timber from the Forest of Dean. Originally Whaddon Manor and later a farmhouse, it was subsequently divided into cottages. Restored in 1939, it is now a Grade II listed building which is run as a charming bed and breakfast guesthouse by Jenny Beer. The house has been upgraded through the addition of central heating and double glazing, whilst still retaining the charm and character of its 16th-century origins. There is still a 1930's AGA (fondly referred to by Jenny as 'Agatha') which helps to

272

provide the English part of the delicious wholefood breakfast. The AGA is the focal point of the attractive kitchen where guests breakfast around the large table. At Gilbert's, the emphasis is on wholesome, home-cooked food, and the owners even have a smallholding which ensures a plentiful supply of delicious organic produce, vegetables and fruit.

At Gilbert's, there are four en-suite letting bedrooms available (one single, one double, one twin and one honeymoon room), all with excellent facilities, including colour televisions. Downstairs, there is a lovely, cosy sitting room where guests can relax in front of the wood-burning stove or browse through the plentiful supply of books listing local places of interest. With an English Tourist Board two crown, highly-commended rating the standard of comfort can be relied upon to be high, so if you are looking for first-rate bed and breakfast accommodation with a difference, Gilbert's is the place to stay.

Gilberts   Brookethorpe   0452 812364

As we continued northwards along the A4173 into the centre of Gloucester, we passed through **Whaddon**, a small community consisting of few cottages set around a 13th-century church with an unusual mediaeval font.

The city of **Gloucester** has a surprising amount to offer the visitor, partly because of its long and distinguished history, and partly because of the revitalisation that has taken place in recent years around the old docks area. Although there was a settlement here in the days of the Iron Age, it was the Roman legions who made an indelible impression on this strategically important site following their invasion of southern England in the first century AD. Their first undertaking was to build a fort to guard what was then the lowest crossing point on the Severn; this was followed about twenty years later by the construction of a much larger fortress on higher ground. The central point of these later fortifications can still be seen in the modern street plan of the city at the place now known as

Gloucester Cross where the four streets of Westgate, Northgate, Eastgate and Southgate converge. Within a few years, the new Roman settlement of *Glevum* had become an important military base which was to play a vital strategic role in confining the rebellious Celts and Britons to the bleak uplands of Wales.

Gloucester Cathedral

Following the founding of a Saxon monastery in the 7th-century, a number of other ecclesiastical buildings were constructed in Gloucester during the following four centuries. The next important influence on the town, however, came with the Norman invasion. William the Conqueror followed the Saxon tradition of holding a Christmas Court at Gloucester and it was here in 1085 that he took the decision to commission the Domesday Book. Four years later, he instructed the Norman monk, Serlo, to restore the Saxon abbey, a task which took 33 years to complete and which resulted in the construction of the great church which went on to become **Gloucester Cathedral**. The following centuries led to a series of renovations resulting in a structure which skillfully combines the Norman, early English, Decorated and Perpendicular styles of architecture.

Two rows of colossal Norman pillars dominate the cathedral's 174 foot long nave, the original timber roof of which was replaced in 1242 by stone vaulting in early English style. The Norman presbytery and choir were replaced in the 14th-century, and the west end of the nave was rebuilt in Perpendicular style during the 15th-century. At 72 feet by 38

274

feet, the great east window is largest surviving mediaeval stained-glass window in the country. It was built to celebrate the victory at the Battle of Crécy in 1346 and depicts the coronation of the Virgin surrounded by a colourful entourage of saints, popes and monarchs.

The exquisite cathedral cloisters were constructed around an attractive garden in the 14th-century and contain some of the finest fan tracery still in existence. From here, an excellent view of the 225 foot cathedral tower can be enjoyed; this was rebuilt in the 15th-century is estimated to weigh over 600 tons. Several interesting monuments can be seen in the cathedral, most notably the wooden effigy of Robert Duke of Normandy dating from 1134 and the elaborate carved tomb of Edward II, murdered at Berkeley Castle in 1327 by his queen and her lover. The cathedral also houses a recently-opened exhibition of Anglican church plate from the **Cathedral Treasury**. Open Mondays to Saturdays, 10.30am to 4pm between Easter and November. Admission free.

Fountain Inn   Gloucester   0452 522562

On leaving the cathedral we decided to call in at the **Fountain Inn**, a first-rate pub and eating place which is hidden down Westgate Street in the heart of Gloucester. The Fountain has a history dating back as far as 1216, although the handsome present-day building dates from Tudor times in the 16th-century. The inn is associated with William of Orange who, in order to show his contempt for his predecessor, James II, is said to ridden his horse up a shallow flight of external stairs leading to an upper room where some known sympathisers of the Jacobite cause were holding a meeting. There is a relief portrait of William on his horse commemorating the event which is set above a doorway in the inn's picturesque courtyard. Today, the courtyard is laid out with tables and chairs, and customers can sit here to enjoy a drink or tasty bar meal. Visitors will find a large and varied menu, and at the weekend, the drudgery can be taken out of preparing the Sunday roast by treating the family to a meal from the Sunday carvery which is served at the inn's hot counter.

The old part of the city centred around Gloucester Cross contains a number of interesting old buildings. Among them is the fine late-19th-century **Guildhall** in Eastgate Street, the ancient church of **St Mary de Crypt** in Southgate Street, **St Johns Church** in Northgate Street, and the home of **Robert Raikes**, founder of the Sunday School Movement, in Ladybellegate Street. A good way to explore the city is to join one of the guided walks which leave the tourist information centre at St Michael's Tower at 2.30pm on Wednesdays and Sundays (daily during August). A map of the **Via Sacra**, a self-guided tour around old Gloucester, is also available here.

City Museum   Gloucester   0452 24131

Three great inns were established in Gloucester during the 14th- and 15th-centuries to cater for pilgrims who came here to visit the tomb of Edward II. Two these remain today: the magnificent galleried **New Inn** was founded by a monk from the abbey in 1450 and can be found close to Gloucester Cross in Northgate Street, and the **Fleece Hotel**, which has a stone-vaulted undercroft dating from the 12th-century, can be found in Westgate Street.

Another building well worth finding is **Maverdine House**, a luxurious four-storey residence which was occupied by the commander of the Parliamentarian forces during the infamous Civil War siege of 1643. Despite most of Wessex being in Royalist hands, the strategically-important city of Gloucester held out for Cromwell and survived a month-long attack which was personally commanded by Charles I. Colonel Massey's headquarters can be reached via a passageway adjacent to No. 26 Westgate Street.

Gloucester's **City Museum and Art Gallery** is situated opposite the Gloucestershire College of Art in Brunswick Road, near the city's main

276

shopping centre. The honey-coloured stone façade hides a treasure of rare and beautiful artefacts originating from both the city and county of Gloucester. A three-ton column in the entrance hall is a relic of the Roman city; this provides a foretaste of the exhibits which gleam in the darkened interior of the archaeology gallery. The Birdlip Mirror, made in bronze for a Celtic chief just before the Roman conquest, is a superbly engraved abstract ornament. Two tombstones depict Romans involved in the conquest: one a horseman spearing a British foe, the other a merchant muffled in a thick cloak. Several altars and votive tablets are carved with simple images of the Roman gods. The gallery floor is cut away to reveal the Roman city wall which passes under the building.

There is also a Norman backgammon (or *tables*) set here, dating from about AD 1100 which is unique in Europe; the bone counters are carved with zodiac signs and the board is engraved with a hunting scene and covered in a bone veneer. Also, be sure not to miss the closing ring from St. Nicholas' Church which was made about AD 1300 and has an escutcheon in the form of two grotesque human heads. Upstairs under the elegant plaster ceiling, is a magnificent set of walnut furniture from the Queen Anne period. On the hour, the gallery echoes with the chimes of grandfather clocks made by Gloucester and London makers of the 18th-century, including a fine Gloucester-made clock which only needs to be wound once a year. The early walnut barometers on display are amongst the finest in the country, and include three examples by the doyen of barometer makers, Daniel Quare (1649-1724).

Visitors should also look out for the collection of Cromwellian silver spoons, which were found under the floorboards of a shop in Cirencester's Market Place, and the apostle spoons made by a silversmith who was Sheriff of Gloucester in 1675. Several English landscape paintings of the 18th- and 19th-centuries are on display, including works by Gainsborough, Richard Wilson and Turner. (The gallery stages a varied programme of special exhibitions throughout the year.) A small aquarium and a beehive, ever popular with children, stand at the entrance to a gallery dedicated to the natural history and geology of Gloucestershire. A sixty foot dinosaur and plesiosaur 'sea-dragon' were recently found in the north Cotswolds and their massive bones are on display here. Open Mondays to Saturdays, 10am to 5pm, all year round. Admission free.

The 16th-century timber-framed house known as **Bishop Hooper's Lodging** can be found in Westgate Street. This is said to be the place where the martyred Protestant Bishop spent his last night before being burnt at the stake in 1555. Today, the building and its immediate neighbours house one of the most highly regarded folk museums in the country, the **Gloucester Folk Museum**. Here, the social history of

Gloucester and its county are brought to life in a series of beautifully laid-out displays. These include a reconstruction of an 18th-century pin making factory, a cobbler's workshop, a dairy, and a 19th-century schoolroom. Artefacts on show include historic farm implements, tools, kitchen equipment, toys, dolls and a number of relics from the Civil War siege. A series of special exhibitions are held at regular intervals, and outside there is a lovely secluded courtyard with its own herb garden. Open Mondays to Saturdays, 10am to 5pm, all year round. Admission free.

Within 200 hundred yards of the Folk Museum, a small collection of historic vehicles has been assembled at the **Gloucester Transport Museum** in Bearland. Exhibits on show include a horse-drawn tram from around 1880, a fire engine from around 1895, and an early-19th-century baby carriage.

Children of all ages will be interested in the **World of Beatrix Potter** at 9 College Court. The shop was used as the model for her much-loved story, *The Tailor Of Gloucester*, which was based on a local folk tale. Today, this commercially-run gift shop displays a number of interesting features relating to the life and work of Beatrix Potter, including a working model of the mice stitching the Mayor of Gloucester's waistcoat. Admission free.

For centuries, Gloucester has been an important river port on the busy route between the Midlands and the Bristol Channel, a state of affairs which was recognised by Queen Elizabeth I when she granted the city formal port status in 1580. However, the introduction of larger vessels during the 18th-century necessitated the building of a canal which would directly link Gloucester with the deep water of the Severn estuary. After once being abandoned due to lack of finance, the canal project was finally completed in 1827, resulting in a greatly increased level of commercial activity which continued for several decades.

From the 1860s onwards, however, the area around **Gloucester Docks** began to suffer a steady decline due to competition from more efficient rail and road transport. By the end of the 1970s, the docks were virtually derelict and a radical solution was needed to secure the area's future. After much consideration, an ambitious project of renovation was initiated which was to transform the 23-acre site into a vibrant cultural centre which today should be included on every visitor's itinerary. The handsome old warehouse buildings have been brought back into use as flats and commercial units, and a stylish new shopping area, **Merchants' Quay**, has been constructed on the waterfront. A converted barge, the *Semington*, now operates as an **arts centre** and café, and there is also a bustling **antique centre** containing a large number of retail units where

278

anything from a small item of bric-a-brac to an expensive piece of antique furniture can be found.

Three floors of the recently converted Llanthony Warehouse are taken up by the **National Waterways Museum**, a fascinating establishment devoted to the 200-year period when Britain's inland waterways carried the goods of the nation. The warehouse building forms part of the museum and is named after Llanthony Priory, a ruined monastery on the eastern edge of the Welsh Black Mountains which in its heyday was one of the wealthiest and most influential in the country. The museum features working engines and models, live craft demonstrations, archive film presentations and hands-on computer simulations of canal navigation. A number of barges and narrowboats are moored outside on the quayside, one of which, the *Queen Boadicea II*, takes visitors on short cruises around the docklands area. The site also contains a working forge, a massive 'No. 4' steam dredger, a stable with a shire horse, an activity room for younger children and a number of canal-related workshops. Open daily, 10am to 6pm (5pm in winter), all year round. Admission charge payable.

National Waterways Museum, Gloucester

Gloucester's **Victoria Dock** is now a thriving marina. This is where we found the Albert Warehouse, a converted storehouse which houses another specialist museum, **Robert Opie's Museum of Advertising and Packaging**. Robert Opie is an enthusiastic collector of commercial ephemera who, in the last twenty years, has assembled around 30,000 packaging and advertising items. The result is a fascinating exhibition which offers a real insight into the presentation of consumer products since the mid-1800s. As well as consumer packaging, the museum contains a interesting collection of posters, enamel signs and point-of-sale promotions which together map the changing trends in popular taste. A continuous screening of vintage television commercials is also featured. Open daily, 10am to 6pm between May and September (and Bank Holidays); Tuesdays to Sundays, 10am to 5pm between October and April. Admission charge payable.

Gloucester's old custom house in the Docks is the home of the recently-modernised **Regiments of Gloucestershire Museum**. Winner of the prestigious 1991 Museum of the Year Award for the best small museum, this absorbing exhibition gives an animated account of the county's two army regiments, the 'Glorious Glosters' and the Royal Gloucestershire Hussars, over their distinguished 300-year history. Open Tuesdays to Sundays, 10am to 5pm, all year round. Small admission charge payable.

Nature in Art   Twigworth   0452 731422

Our visit to Gloucester almost over, we made a two-mile detour northwards along the A38 Tewkesbury road to visit **Twigworth**, home of the internationally-renowned museum of wildlife art, **Nature in Art**.

Nature In Art is housed in a fine Georgian mansion, Wallsworth Hall, which dates from the 1740s and set in its own grounds on the northern outskirts of Gloucester. The building is owned and managed by the Society for Wildlife Art of the Nations, an organisation which sets out to fill an important gap in the collections of art which are available to the public. The Society strives to give honour where honour is due by encouraging the pursuit and appreciation of wildlife art and the

280

conservation of wildlife through the stimulation of fresh insights which only truly fine art can generate.

Nature in Art is a museum with a growing and ever-changing collection. At the time of writing there were 600 items by 350 artists from 40 countries spanning 1400 years. In its scope, appeal and stature, the collection is unrivalled. Although paintings in every medium make up the bulk of the items on display, visitors are also able to see sculptures (both inside and outside), tapestries, ceramics, glass engravings, prints and many other items such as Japanese netsuke and Chinese painted bottles. Each provides an exciting way of depicting nature and, in its own way, is a fine example of its artistic type. Between February and November, there is a full programme of artists in residence which gives visitors the opportunity to see international artists working in a wide variety of media. The museum is fully accessible to wheelchair users and is open Tuesdays to Sundays (and Bank Holiday Mondays), 10am to 5pm, all year round. Admission charge payable.

Without returning to the centre of Gloucester, we drove across the eastern channel of the River Severn to the northwest of the city before turning north onto the A417. Shortly after crossing the river's western channel, we came to the lovely village of **Maisemore** where we discovered a very pleasant inn, the White Hart.

The White Hart   Maisemore Village   *0452 526349*

The White Hart is a delightful 400 year-old inn which is full of character and warmth. The front of the inn is adorned with a beautiful array of hanging baskets and window boxes, and inside, there are original beams in the lounge and an open fire during the winter months. Run by Christine and Ralph Creed, the inn is renowned for its excellent home-cooked food. The extensive menu includes a variety of ploughman's platters, 'designer toasties' in a variety of fillings, and the particularly popular 'sizzle platters', succulent pieces of steak or gammon served on

281

a hot plate. Visitors to the White Hart can also admire Christine's unique collection of chamber pots which adorn the ceiling of the bar.

Those looking for first-rate farmhouse bed and breakfast accommodation within easy reach of Gloucester and the Forest of Dean, should make a point of finding **Linton Farm** bed and breakfast at **Highnam**, two miles southwest of Maisemore. Linton Farm is a large traditional farmhouse run by keen vegetable and arable farmers, Caroline and Richard Keene. They offer three simply-furnished letting rooms (two large, one small) and welcome guests into their comfortable lounge and dining room. Just three-quarters-of-a-mile further down the road, their son Robert runs **Over Farm Market**, a marvellous fruit and vegetable shop offering a vast selection of homegrown produce, local cheeses and homemade pickles, chutneys and jams, all of which make ideal holiday gifts. (For those staying at Linton Farm there is a 10% discount here provided you remember the magic password, 'Hidden Places'!) Outside, visitors will find an assortment of livestock, including donkeys, goats and even ostriches.

Linton Farm   *Highnam*   *0452 306456*

We rejoined the A417 and continued our journey northwards towards Staunton. Just north of Hartpury, we turned east off the main road to reach the delightful Severnside settlement of **Ashleworth**. The focal point of the village is the 12th-century Church of St Andrew and Bartholomew which has some unusual herringbone masonry and a 14th-century spire. The church stands surrounded by attractive mediaeval buildings, including an enormous 15th-century **Tithe Barn** which features two projecting stone porches and an elaborate system of interlocking roof timbers with queenposts. The barn is owned by the National Trust and open daily, 9am to 6pm between April and the end of October. Small admission charge payable (free to National Trust members).

The surrounding estate, which once belonged to the Abbey of St Augustine in Bristol, contains two splendid 15th-century manor houses: the handsome stone-built **Ashleworth Court** and the timber-framed **Ashleworth Manor**. The latter was originally built as the abbot's summer residence and has since been enlarged. Both are open to the public by written arrangement only (for information, telephone 045270 241 and 350 respectively). The village pub, the **Boat Inn**, has been in the hands of the Jelf family for over a hundred years. During the English Civil War, one of their ancestors is said to have rowed Charles I across the Severn and as a reward was granted a monopoly to ferry passengers at this point. **Foscombe**, an elaborate 19th-century Gothic mansion standing on a low hill overlooking the river, was once owned by the Rolling Stones' drummer, Charlie Watts.

A little further up the A417, we came to the charmingly-named village of **Snig's End**. The nucleus of the settlement is a crescent of attractive sturdily-built stone cottages which date from the days when the village was at the centre of a Chartist land colony. Founded in 1847 by Feargus O'Connor, the movement placed great importance on education and constructed a sizable school building to serve the few dozen resident families who formed the community of self-supporting smallholdings. However, thanks to a combination of inadequate financing, confused aims, poor soil, inaccessible markets and a population of townspeople ill-suited to rural life, the project failed within six years. Today, all that remains of the Chartist utopia is a collection of well-built cottages and the old schoolhouse which now functions as the Prince of Wales Inn.

A couple of miles northwest of Staunton, the A417 passes to the east of **Pauntley Court**. Although today you will find a private country residence dating from more recent times, in the 14th-century, this was the birthplace of **Dick Whittington**, three times mayor of London between 1397 and 1419. Whittington was no poor boy who made his fortune with the assistance of a quick-witted cat; rather, he was the offspring of a wealthy landed family who went on to grow even richer as a mercer in the City of London. (The only other fact that is consistent with the original folk tale was that he married Alice Fitzwarren, the daughter of a wealthy Dorset knight.)

Why the famous pantomime legend grew up around Sir Richard Whittington of Pauntley is unknown, although similar rags-to-riches stories are said to exist in countries all over the world. One event which helped to create the myth was the discovery of a carving in the foundations of a mediaeval house in Gloucester in 1862. This carved figure of a youth holding some kind of animal became widely known as 'Dick and his Cat' and was responsible for establishing the legend in the British Isles.

Today, the carving can be seen in Gloucester's Folk Museum.

From Pauntley Court, the minor country lanes took us in a northwesterly direction across the M50 near Bromsberrow Heath. Continuing westwards, we arrived in the small hilltop village of **Dymock**, a delightful collection of cottages loosely arranged around the early-Norman Church of St Mary. The church contains some unusual artefacts, including Dymock's last railway ticket dated September 1959, and stands beside the pleasantly shaded Wintour's Green. The old buildings in northeast Gloucestershire differ from those in the east of country in that they are often built of red brick instead of Cotswold stone. Dymock contains some fine examples of early redbrick building including the White House and the Old Rectory near the church, and the Old Grange which is situated three-quarters-of-a-mile to the northwest and incorporates the remains of the Cistercian abbey of Flaxley.

In the years immediately prior to World War I, a group known as the Dymock Poets based itself in the area, causing the village to become something of literary centre. The group, which included Rupert Brooke, sent their quarterly poetry magazine *New Numbers* to addresses throughout the world from Dymock post office.

The Horseshoe Inn   Broom's Green   0531 890385

Run by Ken Thomson and Jackie Julier, the **Horseshoe Inn** at **Broom's Green**, Dymock is a small friendly pub well favoured by local people who go out of their way to make visitors feel welcome. Outside, there is a large garden with a children's play area, whilst inside, the traditional beamed bars are cosy and welcoming, with horseshoes, brasses and harnesses on the walls adding to the character of the establishment. A free house, the Horseshoe offers a selection of fine real ales, and there is also a charming restaurant where diners can enjoy such excellent local fare as 'pork in Hereford cider sauce', prepared using

284

fresh, local produce. Ken and Jackie are always keen to know if visitors have discovered the Horseshoe through the pages of *Hidden Places*.

A couple of miles to the west of Dymock, we made a point of visiting the famous **Church of St Mary** in **Kempley**. This unlikely gem was built between 1090 and 1100 and stands a short distance to the south of the present-day village. Inside, the chancel contains a virtually complete set of 12th-century frescoes, some of the most widely regarded in the region. It is believed that these fine works of art were created to assist the local priest in conveying the rudiments of the scriptures to his uneducated congregation. A series of 14th-century tempera paintings can also be found in the nave. In the mid-16th-century, both sets of paintings were concealed behind a whitewash coating and weren't rediscovered until 1872. Then during the 1950s, a major renovation successfully restored these exquisite frescoes to their former glory.

The Granary   *Kempley*   *0531 890301*

The village of Kempley contains another interesting church, the red sandstone **Church of St Edward the Confessor** which was built in 1903 in line with the finest traditions of the Arts and Crafts Movement. Most of the fabric was made by local craftspeople using readily-available materials; look out for the imposing scissor beams which were fashioned from green oak taken from the nearby Beauchamp estate.

The Granary is a charming farmhouse situated at **Lower House Farm** in Kempley. Situated close to the Forest of Dean and Dymock Woods, it offers delightful nature walks including the 'Daffodil Way', an eight mile stretch of countryside where wild daffodils grow in profusion. As well as excellent farmhouse bed and breakfast accommodation, owners Jill and Glyn Bennett offer self-catering accommodation in an adjoining wing. They also have their own horses and ponies on the farm and provide first-rate riding holidays. Being central to the Cotswolds, the Wye Valley and the Malvern Hills, the beautiful location of the Granary makes it a walkers' paradise. Visitors can contact the Bennetts on (0531) 890301.

From Kempley, we made our way southeast towards the old market town of **Newent**, the capital of the area of northwest Gloucestershire known as the Ryelands. Our route into the town from the north passed the **Three Choirs Vineyard**, a working vineyard producing good quality English wines which members of the public are welcome to sample and buy. Open daily, 9am to 5pm, all year round.

The Shambles, Newent

Newent stands at the centre of the broad triangle of land known as 'Daffodil Crescent' where in spring, the delicate small flower known as the Lent lily grows freely in the wild. The rich, brightly-coloured soil of the Leadon Valley was traditionally used for the growing of rye and the raising of Ryeland sheep, an ancient breed which produced wool of such quality that it sold for twice the price of its Cotswold equivalent. As a result, the town grew to become one of Gloucestershire's principal wool-trading centres, a factor which accounts for the large number of 18th-century merchants' houses that can still be seen today.

The nave of Newent's mediaeval church had to be completely rebuilt after Royalist troops removed the lead from the roof to make bullets, causing it to collapse during a heavy snowfall in 1674. (Reconstruction only went ahead after Charles II agreed to donate sixty tons of timber from the Forest of Dean.) Newent's most distinctive building, however, can

286

be found on the old Market Square – the splendid timber-framed **Market House**. Originally constructed as butter market in 1668, its upper floors are supported on sixteen oak pillars which form a unique open colonnade.

Those interested in finding out more about the history of Newent should make a point of visiting **The Shambles Museum of Victorian Life** in Church Street. This impressive museum is laid out as a Victorian town complete with cobbled streets, gas-fired street lamps, shops and workrooms. The core of the museum a four-storey house which has been furnished throughout as a Victorian draper's home. (The house in fact belonged to a butcher, the name 'shambles' coming from the Old English word for slaughterhouse.) To the rear, the narrow streets and alleyways contain over thirty shops and workshops, including a chemist's, a dairy, a pawnbroker's, an ironmongers' and a blacksmith's, each of which is stocked with its own unique collection of historic artefacts. The museum also contains a modern gift shop and tearoom. Open Tuesdays to Sundays (and Bank Holiday Mondays), 10am to 6pm between mid-March and December. Admission charge payable.

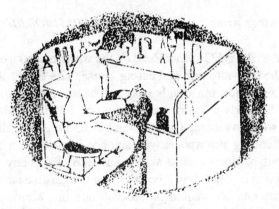

Newent Silver and Gold   *Newent*   *0531 822055*

A fine collection of original handcrafted silver and gold pieces can be found at **Newent Silver and Gold** in Broad Street. This unique establishment was founded upon the design skills, talent and craftsmanship of gold- and silversmith, Ken Vowles. Ken has a particular feeling for the materials and techniques of his craft, and it is quite amazing to watch him take a dull piece of metal and transform it into an article of beauty. Ken designs all his own work and many of his hand-crafted creations are on sale at the studio. A very welcoming place, Ken does not seem to be disturbed at all by visitors browsing around. He accepts commissions and is especially delighted when someone asks him to design an item as a special gift.

A tradition of glass making was established in Newent by French Huguenot refugees in the 17th-century. In recent years, this highly-skilled practice has been revived at the **Glassbarn** in Culver Street. Here, visitors can view the delicate process of glass-blowing and examine the items of finished glassware in the gallery. Open Mondays to Fridays, 10am to 5pm, all year round. Small charge payable for tours of the workshop.

The Kings Arms   *Newent*   *0531 820307*

Adjacent to the B4221 Ross Road on the western outskirts of Newent, we found the first-rate pub and eating house, **The Kings Arms**. This attractive family-run inn stands next to a handsome redbrick building which was formerly a Victorian workhouse. Landlord Martin Young provides a warm welcome for both visitors and regulars alike. Inside, there is a charming atmosphere with an open log fire and a collection of traditional pub pastimes such as skittles and shove halfpenny. This is also a good selection of hand-drawn beers and an imaginative bar meals menu which on the day we visited included 'duck in Chinese five spice'. (Booking is advised for evening meals.) Martin also has four comfortable letting bedrooms available which are all spacious and well-appointed.

Another of Newent's attractions is the **Butterfly Centre** in Birches Lane, just to the north of the town centre. As well as being able to see exotic butterflies flying freely in the tropical house, members of the public can visit the menagerie, aquarium, natural history exhibition and garden centre. Open daily, 10am to 5pm between Easter and October. Admission charge payable.

Newent's famous **National Bird of Prey Centre** can be found on the western side of the B4216, one mile south of the town. The centre boasts the largest private collection of birds of prey in Europe, including eagles, hawks, owls, falcons, condors and vultures. There are also a number of aviaries which have been set aside for breeding purposes. The site incorporates the widely-renowned **Falconry Centre** where visitors are offered the exhilarating experience of observing trained birds in free-flight. Up to four flying demonstrations take place each day, weather permitting. Open daily, 10.30am to 5.30pm between February and November. Admission charge payable.

A couple of miles further south, we came to **Taynton**, an attractive hamlet which in spring is filled with golden daffodils. The village church is unusual in that it was constructed during Oliver Cromwell's Commonwealth government; it was the view of the Puritans that the presence of God had no geographical limitations, and so it was built along a north-south axis rather than along the conventional east-west. Nearby, Taynton House has three impressive barns, one of which dates from 1695.

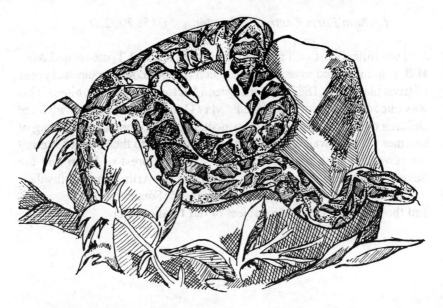

The Butterfly Centre, Newent

Hown Hall in Taynton is the home of the widely-renowned **Taynton Farm Centre**, a wonderful open farm run by Priscilla and John House. The farm has been in their family for four generations, and the 16th-century renovated farmhouse now has an attractive tearoom and farm shop where visitors can purchase delicious homemade produce. All cakes are baked by Priscilla, and cream teas are a speciality, with clotted cream supplied by the farm's Jersey cows. As well as specialising in duck breeding, the Houses keep a variety of other livestock, including rare breed cattle; pony rides are also available on most weekends. The farm centre is open daily, 9am to 7pm between 1st March and 31st October;

between 1st November and the end of February, the shop and tearoom are open from 10am to 6pm.

Taynton Farm Centre   Taynton   0452 790220

Two miles west of Taynton stands the National Trust-owned **May Hill**, a dramatic and mystical place which is crowned by an unusual copse of trees planted in 1887 to mark Queen Victoria's golden jubilee. This was once the scene of the annual 'May Games', an event in which the children of the area would meet in mock battle to celebrate the coming of summer. Today, walkers taking the pleasant stroll to the 969 foot summit are rewarded with magnificent views of the Forest of Dean and the Severn's distinctive horseshoe bend around the Arlingham peninsula.

From the foot of May Hill, we set off towards Southwest Gloucestershire and the Forest of Dean, the subject of our final chapter.

CHAPTER TEN

South West Gloucestershire

Westbury Court

291

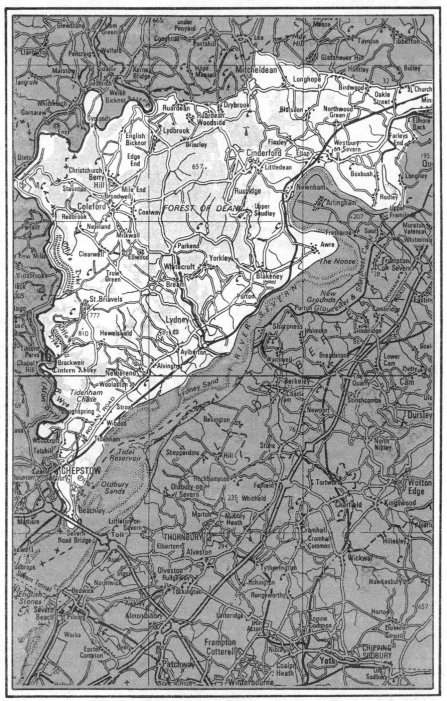

CHAPTER TEN

Index

Cinderhill House B&B, St Briavels, Gloucestershire
Dean Heritage Centre, Camp Hill, Soudley
Lydbrook House B&B, Lydbrook, Gloucestershire
Parkend House Hotel, Parkend, Nr Lydney
Poolway House Hotel, Gloucester Road, Coleford
Tan House Farm B&B, Newland, Coleford, Gloucestershire
Tudor Farmhouse Hotel, Clearwell, Nr Coleford
Wong's Cuisine, 11 Hill Street, Lydney
The Yallup Art Gallery, Llandogo, Monmouth, Gwent

Littledean Hall

CHAPTER 10

South West Gloucestershire

Our journey into Southwest Gloucestershire began along the A4136 Gloucester-Monmouth road. We turned north off this road in the hamlet of Nailbridge to reach our first stopping place, the lovely old village of **Ruardean**. The village church is known for its stone plaque on which two highly-unusual fish are carved. These are thought to have been sculpted by craftsmen from the Herefordshire School of Norman Architecture during the Romanesque period around 1150. The carving is thought to have once belonged to a frieze which was set in one of the church's exterior walls. However around 100 years later, it was removed, most probably by local people looking for readily available building materials, and was considered lost until 700 years later, an inspection of a bread oven in a nearby cottage revealed the two fish set into the lining. Today, these have been returned to the church and can be seen on one of the inside walls near the font.

From Ruardean, we followed the narrow country lanes in a southwesterly direction towards the two sister villages of **Upper** and **Lower Lydbrook**. For many centuries, the Forest of Dean was an important iron ore and coal mining area, and the position of these two communities on its northwest fringe made them ideally suited for the processing of ore into metal. Indeed, the first commercially-viable blast furnace in the area was sited here at the beginning of the 17th-century and, despite it being hard to imagine today, at one time Lydbrook rivalled Sheffield as a producer of pig iron.

Lower Lydbrook also stands at the point where the River Wye comes closest to the mineral extracting areas of the Forest of Dean and for several centuries, flat-bottomed barges were loaded with coal here before being hauled upstream to Hereford. (Before the completion of a tow-path suitable for horses in 1811, this was done by manpower alone.) This river trade continued until the 1840s when it was superseded, first by the Gloucester-Hereford Canal, and then the Severn and Wye Railway.

Today, the two villages are relatively quiet and secluded, and reveal little of their energetic industrial past. The house where tragedian actress Sarah Siddons lived as a child can be seen here, and there are also a number of excellent places to stay.

Lydbrook House   *Lydbrook*   *0594 861267*

Among these is **Lydbrook House**, a charming 18th-century Georgian building set in large, neatly laid out gardens, with outstanding views over the River Wye. Guests receive a warm welcome at this informal, friendly household. The proprietor, Anne Hayes, provides three letting bedrooms, one of which is en suite, all tastefully furnished in character with the house. In addition to bed and breakfast, Anne is happy to supply an evening meal by prior arrangement. The house is surrounded by many local beauty spots, and guests can enjoy lovely walks, canoeing and even fishing if they so wish. Guests should not be surprised to see rabbits hopping around the gardens of Lydbrook House, since Anne's daughter Holly owns several which roam around quite freely.

Deciding to explore the Forest of Dean at a later opportunity, we drove further westwards along the A4136 before turning north onto B4432 **Symonds Yat** road. Symonds Yat is an imposing outcrop of rock which forms part of Huntsham Hill, the promontory which juts out into the Wye Valley forcing the river to make a spectacular horseshoe deviation to the north. Though strictly in Hereford and Worcester, we made a point of visiting this popular place, partly to enjoy the magnificent views of the Wye Valley and partly in the hope of catching a glimpse of the wild peregrine falcons which inhabit the barren slopes of **Yat Rock**. This dramatic 500 foot rock is reached along a quarter mile forest trail which can be joined at the Symonds Yat car park. Parking fee payable; refreshments and toilet facilities available here during summer months.

On the riverbank below Yat Rock there is an usual man-powered rope ferry which takes passengers across to **Symonds Yat West**. Here, there are some first-rate visitor attractions including the widely-known **Jubilee**

Park Museum of Mazes which is run by the Heyes brothers, two keen maze-building enthusiasts. As well as containing a great deal of interesting background information on the art of maze design, the museum has an internationally-renowned centrepiece, the Jubilee Puzzle hedge maze, which visitors are encouraged to tackle. Open daily throughout the year except during January. Admission charge payable.

There is a useful visitor centre at Symonds Yat West, as well as a heritage centre on the nearby Doward hillside. This stretch of the River Wye is also renowned for its leisure and watersports activities. As well as a wonderful series of walks and trails, there are excellent facilities here for canoeing, rock climbing, abseiling, and even hot-air ballooning.

We crossed back to Symonds Yat East and retraced our steps onto the A4136 before turning west to reach the village of **Staunton**. This pleasant community has a Norman church and a row of charming almshouses which were built in the 1600s with funds donated by Benedict Hall. The church has been twice altered, first during the early English period and again in the 15th-century, episodes which have left the east window oddly offset from the nave. Look out also for the two stone fonts, one of which is claimed to be a converted Roman altar, and the unusual corkscrew staircase which leads up past the pulpit to the belfry door.

Ruardean Church Carvings

Two enormous mystical stones, the **Buck Stone** and the **Suck Stone**, lie a short walk from the centre of Staunton. The famous twelve-foot high sandstone monolith known as the Buck Stone can be reached along a path leading up onto Staunton Meend Common from the White Horse Inn. From here, the views in all directions are breathtaking. The Suck Stone can be reached by following a track from the village across Highmeadow Woods. Look out also for the Bronze Age standing stone which can be seen beside the A4136 at Marion's Cross, just to the east of the village.

Two-and-a-half miles southeast of Staunton, we came to **Coleford**, a lively and aptly-named former mining centre on the western edge of the Forest of Dean. In the 17th-century, the town received a royal charter from Charles I in recognition of its loyalty to the crown. By then, it had already grown to be an important iron processing centre, partly because of the availability of local ore deposits and partly because of the easily obtainable forest timber which was used to fuel the smelting process. (In order to generate the high temperatures this process required, the timber had first to be converted into charcoal.)

As the industry began to grow towards its peak in the 13th-century, an ever-increasing amount of wood was required to sustain it (it is said 5000 cubic feet of timber were needed for every iron bar produced). At this time, as many as 72 furnaces were operating in and around the Forest of Dean, resulting in deforestation on a massive scale. This began to worry the nation's naval commanders who also required large numbers of mature oaks for shipbuilding.

In the end, the navy was given priority and severe restrictions were placed on the felling of trees for conversion into charcoal. This sent the local iron industry into decline, a trend which continued until the beginning of last century when coke was introduced to replace charcoal in the smelting process. Within a few decades, however, the iron industry in the Forest of Dean had been driven to the brink of extinction by a series of technological advances and competition from other UK iron producing areas.

Nevertheless, Coleford has a special place in metallurgical history for it was here that the Mushets, a father and son team of local free miners, made many discoveries which were to revolutionise the iron and steel industry. Indeed, it was here that the son, Robert Forester Mushet, discovered the importance of *Spiegeleisen* (an alloy of iron, manganese, silicon and carbon) in the reprocessing of 'burnt iron'. This led him to develop a system for turning molten pig iron directly into steel, a system which predated the now-familiar process developed by Sir Henry Bessemer. Tragically however, Robert Mushet failed to pay stamp duty on his patents and allowed them to lapse, an oversight which must have resulted in untold financial consequences for him.

Today, Coleford continues to be regarded as the capital of the Royal Forest of Dean and is a busy commercial centre with an interesting church and a number of unusual industrial relics. It is also the home of the **Great Western Railway Museum**, an old GWR goods station dating from 1883 which contains a number of large-scale model steam locomotives and an interesting display of railway photographs and memorabilia. Open Tuesdays to Sundays (and Bank Holiday Mondays), 2.30pm to 5.30pm between Easter and end-October; also Saturdays only during the winter months. Admission charge payable.

Poolway House   *Coleford*   *0594 833937*

The beautiful 16th-century manor known as **Poolway House** stands on the B4228 in Coleford. Now a charming hotel, it is reputed that Colonel E Worgen sheltered King Charles I here following the battle of Edge Hill in 1642. Poolway House is run by Nick and Audrey Anstice and their son Michael, who is the resident chef. Guests will delight at the quaint rooms, all of which have their own character and identity. The bedrooms are all en suite and have excellent facilities, whilst downstairs, the oak-beamed and panelled restaurant is cosy and intimate. Also open to non-residents, Michael offers diners an extensive and imaginative range of dishes which are prepared using only the finest fresh produce. The food really is superb, and the menus are varied according to the season and availability of fresh vegetables, fruit and game. The combination of excellent food and top class accommodation make Poolway House a truly wonderful place to stay.

From the centre of Coleford, we drove south for a mile along the B4228 to reach Lower Perrygrove Farm, the site of the ancient woodland mine workings which were imaginatively landscaped during the last century to form **Puzzle Wood**. This historic place first became a centre for open-cast iron ore mining during the early Iron Age over 2700 years ago. One of its most active periods was during the Roman era when the site formed part of the famous Lambsquay mine workings; indeed in 1848, workmen discovered a small cave containing three spherical earthenware jars which turned out to be filled with over 3000 Roman coins from the third century AD.

For much of the site's history, the mining of iron ore was carried out using hand tools only and initially, most of it was recovered from the high quality deposits which lay near the surface. However, as these were gradually exhausted, the miners were forced to look for fresh deposits which often lay trapped between layers of solid rock. Before the invention of explosives, the tightly-compressed ore had to be loosened using the 'fire-setting' method of mining; this involved lighting fires against the exposed rock face, and then dowsing the hot stone with water, causing it to crack.

By the late-19th-century, the fourteen acre site was virtually exhausted. It was then that it was bought as a private woodland estate by the Turner family who decided to build a network of trails between the steep moss-covered outcrops and mine workings. However, instead of laying out the paths according to a logical plan, they constructed a series of confusing maze-like circles, a deed which accounts for the wood's unusual present-day name. This unique and historic place has now been open to the public for over fifty years. In 1981, both Puzzle Wood and Perrygrove Farm were acquired by their present owner, Ray Prosser, who installed an attractive tea garden and souvenir shop. Open Tuesdays to Sundays (and Bank Holiday Mondays), 11am to 6pm between Easter and end-October. Admission charge payable.

Before continuing south to Clearwell, we made a short diversion west to visit the charming village of **Newland**, home of the so-called 'Cathedral of the Forest'. This is the nickname given to the vast local Church of All Saints which has an aisle almost as wide as its nave and a huge pinnacled tower which needs the support of flying buttresses. Like many other churches in Gloucestershire, it was built during the 13th- and 14th-centuries and later remodelled by the Victorians. Inside, it has a number of noteworthy features, including a 17th-century effigy of a reclining archer and an unusual monumental brass featuring a mediaeval miner holding a pick and a hod and with a candle in his mouth. This is thought to depict Sir John Greyndour, a former Sheriff of Gloucester who, along with a company of miners from the Forest of Dean, accompanied Henry V's forces to France where they went on to capture and hold the town of Harfleur.

The sturdily-bred artisans of the Forest have a long history of assisting in military campaigns and were often called on by the monarch of the day

Puzzle Wood

to operate as an early form of special task force. Indeed, the 'Free Miners of Dean' were given their title by King Edward I after he had successfully put their demolition skills to use undermining the Scottish fortifications around Berwick-on-Tweed.

Newland contains an unusual number of large and well-maintained buildings reflecting a stable and prosperous past which seems to have endured into the present. Among the most distinctive of these are the almshouses near the church which were built for eight men and eight women in 1615 and then thoughtfully updated during the 1950s. There is also a charming 16th-century pub, the Ostrich, and an excellent farmhouse bed and breakfast establishment, Tan House Farm.

Tan House Farm   Newland   0594 832222

Tan House Farm is an immaculate Queen Anne period house which stands within fourteen acres of lush green fields. (According to architectural historian Nikolaus Pevsner, it resembles an '18th-century dolls' house'.) Throughout the year, it is used as a mediaeval field study centre offering courses covering such topics as Gothic architecture and stained glass. When courses are not being run, the proprietors Peter and Christie Chamberlain provide members of the public with first-rate bed and breakfast accommodation. They have several tastefully furnished twin-bedded rooms available, all with washbasins, and four with additional en suite shower and toilet. An informal relaxed air pervades the house giving it a comfortable and homely feel. If you are looking for peace and quiet, then Tan House Farm at Newland is an ideal place to stay.

A two-mile journey through the lanes to the southeast of Newland led us to the famous **Clearwell Caves**, the site of ancient iron mines which were worked for over 2500 years from the dawn of the Iron Age until 1945. The mines were originally a natural cave system which over a long period became filled with rich deposits of iron ore. These deposits were gradually removed to form a labyrinth of interconnecting passages and

302

chambers which in recent years have been renovated and opened as a fascinating museum.

Eight large caverns (or 'churns') are now open to the public, most of which contain special displays showing the primitive techniques that were employed (and atrocious working conditions that had to be endured) by mine workers throughout the ages. (For example, it was common practice for the ore to be manhandled to the surface by youths who were expected to carry over half a hundredweight at a time.) The deepest point normally open to the public is 100 feet below the surface, although the ancient mine workings extend into the hillside for another 500 feet; tours into these deeper levels can be made by special arrangement.

The last stop on the tour, the Engine Room, contains a marvellous collection of vintage mining equipment and mine engines which on the day we visited included a compressor built by Ingersol Rand in 1915, a 30-horsepower horizontal engine built by Fielding in 1924, and a 20-horsepower horizontal engine built by Crossley in 1925. The site also contains a tearoom and an interesting shop stocked with souvenirs, mineral samples, geological maps and books relating to the world of mining and geology. Open daily 10am to 5pm between 1st March and 31st October (also during December for special Christmas attraction). Admission charge payable.

Clearwell Caves

Nearby **Clearwell** village contains a number of interesting features, including a 14th-century sandstone standing cross, the Wyndham Arms inn, which is believed to date from the same century, and the extravagantly decorated 19th-century Church of St Peter. The church was built by Caroline Wyndham, Countess of Dunraven, to replace an earlier building which once stood at the other end of the village. She was the last member of her family to live at **Clearwell Castle**, the ornate neo-Gothic mansion which was built in the 1720s by her ancestor, Thomas Wyndham. The house was constructed around an Elizabethan great hall and was used as a base by the notorious Judge Jeffries when he travelled around Wessex trying and sentencing (usually to death or transportation) the supporters of the Duke of Monmouth's ill-fated rebellion of 1685.

The building was practically destroyed by fire in 1929, and despite being rebuilt, by the 1950s it was again in desperate need of major structural repairs. An unlikely rescuer came in the form of the son of a castle gardener, Frank Yeates, who had been brought up in Clearwell and gone on to earn his fortune as a baker in the North. Yeates bought the neglected estate and proceeded to spend the last years of his life in a labour of love, restoring it to its former glory. The castle and grounds now operate as a hotel, although they are open to the public on Sundays only between Easter and October.

Tudor Farmhouse Hotel   *Clearwell   0594 833046*

The **Tudor Farmhouse Hotel** is an outstandingly beautiful 13th-century listed building set within fourteen acres on a hillside on the edge of Clearwell. A hotel with a difference, it retains several important historical features, including its original wall panelling. (Oliver Cromwell is said to have stayed here whilst on hunting expeditions.) The cosy lounge boasts a large inglenook fireplace, and the dining room, with its open stonework and oak beams, provides the ideal setting in which to sample the establishment's varied and imaginative cuisine. The six guest bedrooms are reached via a 15th-century oak spiral staircase. All are traditionally and tastefully furnished and have excellent en suite facilities; two also have four-poster beds. In the courtyard to the rear of the hotel, there are two cottages and one stable suite providing the same high quality accommodation.

On the edge of the Clearwell, we passed a sign to the curiously-named Stank Farm, a term, we were assured, referring to the fact that this was once was the site of the local manor's carp pond, rather than to the farm's propensity for creating unusually high levels of wind-borne pollution.

Two miles south of Clearwell, and just to the west of the B4228, lies the impressive village of **St Briavels**. The community was named after a 5th-century Welsh bishop whose name appears in various forms throughout Celtic Wales, Cornwall and Brittany, but at no other place in England. In the Middle Ages, this was an important administrative centre for the Forest of Dean; it was also a major armaments manufacturing centre supplying weapons and ammunition to the Crown. (In 1223, Henry III is believed to have ordered 6000 crossbow bolts (or quarrels) from workshops in St Briavels.)

The somewhat oversized village church was built in Norman times to replace a Celtic chapel on the same site. It was significantly enlarged in the 12th- and 13th-centuries, and further remodelled by the Victorians who, perhaps rashly, demolished and rebuilt the original chancel. Each year on Whit Sunday, the Pound Wall outside the church is the site of a unique custom, the **St Briavels Bread and Cheese Ceremony**. Following the evensong service, a local forester stands on the wall and throws small pieces of bread and cheese to the assembled villagers below. This action is accompanied by the chant, *'St Briavels water and Whyrl's wheat, are the best bread and water King John can ever eat.'*

The ceremony is thought to have originated over 700 years ago when the inhabitants of St Briavels successfully defended their rights of estover (the right to collect wood from common land) in nearby Hudnalls Wood. As a gesture of gratitude, each villager agreed to pay one penny to the church warden towards feeding the poor, an act which in turn led to the founding of the bread and cheese ceremony. At one time, this annual charitable event took place inside the church; however, by the middle of last century, the festivities had become so rowdy that the whole procedure was banished to the wall outside. Local legend has it that the small pieces of bread and cheese bring good luck; they were traditionally cherished by Forest of Dean miners who believed, being like the bread of holy communion which was said never to perish, they would keep them from harm.

St Briavels also possesses an impressive castle which, perhaps due to its unassailable position on a 900 foot promontory above the River Wye, never saw any military action. It was founded in the early-1100s by Henry I and was considerably enlarged during King John's reign in the 13th-century when it was used as a hunting lodge. Much of the original structure, including the keep, collapsed during the 18th-century; however, the two fortress-like gatehouse towers survived along with a number of 13th-century castle buildings, most of which now function as a youth hostel. Some other parts of the castle are open to the public, including the court and jury rooms and the castle dungeon with its poignant graffiti. The structure is bordered by a grassy flower-filled moat, creating an atmosphere more characteristic of a fortified country house than an important military stronghold.

Cinderhill House   *St Briavels*   *0594 530393*

Standing in peaceful seclusion on the hillside below St Briavels Castle, **Cinderhill House** is a delightful country residence offering first-class accommodation which enjoys outstanding views towards Sugar Loaf Mountain and the Brecon Beacons. This splendid 14th-century house is full of character, with open fires in the inglenook fireplaces and traditional exposed beams. Proprietor Gillie Peacock offers five beautifully furnished en suite bedrooms, two with four-posters and all with first-rate facilities. In the dining room, an imaginative and professionally-cooked menu is offered, with all dishes being prepared from fresh local produce, including such delicacies as poussin or Wye salmon. Cinderhill House also has three excellently equipped converted cottages within its grounds, including one specifically designed for partially disabled guests. Guests here can also book for dinner at the main house.

From St Briavels, we drove northwest along the narrow lane which eventually leads down to Bigsweir Bridge across the River Wye. This 160 foot single-span structure carries the main A466 Chepstow to

Monmouth road and is thought to have been designed either by Thomas Telford or Charles Hollis, the engineer of Windsor Bridge. An unusual toll house stands at its eastern end, while near the other end, Bigsweir House can be seen at the foot of Hudnalls Wood.

We decided to cross the river and continue south on the A466 towards Tintern. The Wye forms the border between England and Wales along most of the fifteen-mile stretch between Monmouth and the sea, and so we were, in fact, driving through Gwent at this point. Within a mile-and-a-half of crossing the river, we saw a signpost pointing west to the village of **Llandogo**. This idyllic little village is situated on the banks of the River Wye in a landscape latticed with former horse and donkey tracks which once were the only means of access to the pretty cottages dotted across the hillside.

Llandogo makes a perfect location for the **Yallup Gallery**, a fascinating establishment which is run by South African-born Pat Yallup, herself an accomplished artist. Formerly the village school, the gallery now holds regular monthly exhibitions of work by reputable artists, as well as permanent displays of sculpture, pottery and jewellery. It is open every day (including all day Sunday), and visitors are encouraged to call in and browse. Pat also runs painting courses and workshops for budding artists, whether beginners or more experienced. Set in an idyllic location, the Yallup Gallery is a true artists' haven.

Yallup Gallery   *Llandogo*   *0594 530940*

We continued southwards along the western bank of the River Wye and after approximately three miles came to the open water meadow which is the site of the superb remains of **Tintern Abbey**. Though now sadly roofless and beyond repair, this is one of the finest legacies of the late-mediaeval monastic period. Originally founded in 1131 by Cistercian monks from Citeau in France, the buildings which remain date mostly from the 13th- to 15th-centuries. The walls are still largely intact and

307

feature some fine Gothic architecture, including a delicate traceried rose window at the eastern end of the great church which measures over sixty feet in diameter. As well as some impressive arches, windows and doorways, the abbey site also contains the remains of several ancillary buildings, including the chapter house, refectory and kitchens. Open daily, 9.30am (2pm Sundays) to 6.30pm (4pm in winter), all year round.

The Cistercians were known for their austere and diligent lifestyle. They intensively farmed the surrounding monastic estate, using lay brothers to carry out some of the more arduous tasks. Some light relief, however, may have been provided by a predecessor of the present-day Anchor Inn which can be found on the nearby riverbank. The route from the inn to the water's edge passes under a 13th-century archway which was probably the abbey's water gate. On the other side of the river, a natural rock platform can be made out which is known locally as the **Devil's Pulpit**. Legend has it that Satan would stand here and scream insults at the Cistercian monks. Having survived this verbal barrage for several centuries, Tintern instead fell prey to Henry VIII's Dissolution of the Monasteries in 1539, and despite being concealed amongst the steep tree-covered slopes of the Wye Valley, it was abandoned soon after.

The **Old Station** at Tintern now functions as a delightful visitor centre. Built during the Victorian era as a halt on the picturesque Wye Valley line, it is surrounded by an attractive picnic area and also houses a small exhibition on the history of the local railways. The recently-published *Wye Valley Walk* map pack is also available here at a special discounted price. Open between April and end-October. Small car parking charge payable.

Retracing our steps along the A466 for half-a-mile, we crossed back into Gloucestershire near the village of **Brockweir**. Before the present bridge was built in 1904, this pleasant settlement of white-painted buildings was reached from the west bank by ferry. Some of the houses in the village date back to Tudor times, and there is also an unusual Moravian chapel which incorporates an assortment of architectural styles from Gothic to art nouveau.

Brockweir was once an important river port and boat-building centre. For centuries, small vessels of up to 100 tons were constructed along the quay, then in 1824 an improved facility was built which could handle craft of up to 500 tons. This was also a place where river barges bound for Monmouth, Hereford and even Hay, were filled with coal and iron ore from the Forest of Dean. These were then hauled upstream by gangs of men harnessed together in teams of eight. Working in relays, it took four such teams to cover the gruelling eight-mile stretch of river between Brockweir and Monmouth. It must have been thirsty work for during its heyday, as many as sixteen pubs were open in the village to serve the combined workforce from the wharves and boatyards. Both boat-building and the river-barge trade were brought to an abrupt end by the arrival of the railways in the second half of the 19th-century.

The River Wye continues to be a well-stocked salmon river thanks almost entirely to the efforts of a lone Brockweir campaigner, Frank Buckland. Until the 1920s, salmon netting was allowed along the river's entire length, causing an alarming decline in numbers. However, due to Buckland's successful campaign, the netting of salmon was strictly controlled below the village and was banned altogether above it.

Tintern Abbey

The course of the famous **Offa's Dyke** passes through Brockweir. This great earthwork ditch and rampart was built by Offa, King of Mercia, between 757 and 795 AD to define the western boundary of his kingdom. The original construction ran for nearly 170 miles from the River Severn in the south to the River Dee in the north, with gaps occurring only in areas of dense forest. The dyke was also used to defend Mercia from parties of marauding Welsh raiders, a role which continued throughout the mediaeval era. During this period, a line of motte and bailey castles was built to strengthen the border defences; many of these can be seen today, and although some are now in ruins, those in a suitable state of preservation are generally open to visitors.

Offa's Dyke long-distance footpath follows the course of King Offa's 8th-century ramparts. The eight-mile stretch between St Briavels and the sea contains a number of spectacular vantage points which look out across the Wye Valley to the Welsh mountains in the west and the Severn estuary in the south. In particular, there are two outstanding viewpoints, both of which lie within easy reach of the B4228 St Briavels to Chepstow road. The first is from the northern edge of the Ban-y-gor rocks where the road runs along a ridge above the River Wye. There are two dramatic vistas from here: straight down the almost vertical rock face to the river, or westwards across the Severn towards the Vale of Berkeley and the Cotswolds.

The second vantage point can be found three-quarters-of-a-mile further south at **Wintour's Leap**, the massive rocky outcrop which towers 200 feet above the Wye. At this point, the river is forced to make a hairpin turn after completing its circuit around the Lancaut peninsula and the abrasive action of the water has created a pronounced hook in the solid rock riverbank. The crag gets its name from Sir John Wintour (or Winter), a royalist officer who, whilst being chased by Parliamentarian forces during the English Civil War, is alleged to have ridden his horse over the edge of the precipice and swum across the river to safety.

The triangle of land lying between the B4228 and the A48 to the east of here is known as **Tidenham Chase**. This 1000-acre area once belonged to the lords of Chepstow who set it aside for the hunting of deer. In places, the underlying limestone breaks through the surface to form a series of rocky outcrops which make excellent standpoints for surveying the surrounding landscape.

The River Wye reaches the mouth of the Severn near the ancient Gwent market town of **Chepstow**. This strategically-important place was the location of the Normans' first stone-built fortress in Wales. **Chepstow Castle** was extended several times over the centuries and it now occupies a large site on a limestone ridge above the River Wye which in turn forms a natural moat along its eastern side. Visitors to this colossal structure will find four courtyards, a lofty keep and a series of massive castle walls interspersed with defensive towers. During the 13th-century, the tower which later became known as Martens Tower was added; this was where Henry Marten, a co-signatory of Charles I's death warrant, was confined until his death in 1680. Chepstow Castle is open daily, 9.30am (2pm Sundays) to 6.30pm (4pm in winter), all year round.

A short distance away, **Chepstow Museum** houses a permanent exhibition on the history of this important port and military stronghold. Here, the working life of the town, which once included wine shipping, shipbuilding and salmon fishing, is brought to life in a series of imaginatively devised settings. Also on display is an interesting collection of 18th- and 19th-century prints featuring Chepstow, its castle and the countryside of the Wye Valley.

From Chepstow, we joined the main A48 and drove northeastwards along the southern edge of Tidenham Chase. After about seven miles, we came to the pleasant village of **Alvington**, the centre of which is located to the north of the main road. The village churchyard contains the Victorian graves of the Wintours, one of the area's most illustrious families who in the 16th-century, played an important role in the defeat of the Spanish Armada. Just over half-a-century later, Sir John Wintour was involved in his remarkable escape from Cromwell's forces following the Battle of Lancaut (see Wintour's Leap).

Continuing northeastwards along the A48, our approach to Lydney took us past the entrance to the famous **Lydney Park Gardens**. Nowadays, this beautiful valley garden is filled with rhododendrons, azaleas, magnolias and other flowering shrubs which are at their best during May and early-June. During the Second World War, however, this eight-acre site was used for growing potatoes, and it wasn't until the second Lord Bledisloe and his head gardener, 'Mac' Stracey, set to work that the present-day woodland paradise was created. These breathtaking lakeside gardens are only open to the public for a short season each year, namely on Sundays, Wednesdays and Bank Holidays between Easter and early-June, also every day during the week of the Whitsun Bank Holiday. (To confirm opening times, telephone 0594 842844.)

The grounds of Lydney Park also contain herd of fallow deer and a number of unusual features which together form a fascinating record of human occupation in this part of the country. As well as the site of an Iron Age hill fort, the park contains the remains of a late-Roman temple dating from the 4th-century AD which was excavated by Sir Mortimer Wheeler in the 1920s. It is likely that the builders of this unusual temple complex were wealthy Romanised Celts, similar to those occupying Chedworth or Great Witcombe. The temple had a mosaic floor (now destroyed) depicting fish and sea monsters and was dedicated to the god Nodens, a Roman-Celtic god of healing, whose emblem, in common with other early symbols of curing, was a reclining dog.

A unique collection of Roman artefacts from the site, including the famous 'Lydney Dog', are now housed in the nearby **Lydney Park Museum**. The museum also contains a number of interesting items which were brought back from New Zealand in the 1930s by the first Viscount Bledisloe following his term there as the Governor General. Museum opening times similar to gardens. Admission charge payable. Lydney Park also contains evidence of Roman iron-mine workings and a line of earth fortifications of a similar age which were later reinforced by the Saxons.

The sprawling town of **Lydney** occupies a site midway between the River Severn and the Forest of Dean. The largest settlement between Chepstow and Gloucester, it has the locality's only remaining railway station. We decided to stop here for something to eat and called in at **Wong's Cuisine** in Hill Street.

Lovers of Chinese food will appreciate Jimmy Wong's excellent restaurant in the centre of Lydney. With its attractive decor and cosy, relaxing atmosphere, Wong's Cuisine makes the ideal venue, whether for that intimate dinner or a party booking. With eighty covers, Wong's can also cater for banquets and receptions. Open seven days a week, Jimmy provides an extensive, quality menu, and is happy to cater for any special tastes by prior arrangement. In the summer, the restaurant is air conditioned for the comfort of customers. The popularity of Wong's Cuisine is self-evident judging by the number of visitors who return time and again to sample Jimmy's outstanding cooking.

Wong's Cuisine   *Lydney*   *0594 844555*

Those interested in the evocative world of steam railways should make a point of visiting the **Norchard Steam Centre** on the northern outskirts of Lydney. This is the headquarters of the **Dean Forest Railway** which was originally built in 1809 to haul coal and iron ore from Parkend in the Forest of Dean to the docks on the Severn. The line operated as a horse-drawn tramway until 1868 when it was updated to a broad gauge railway. Despite regular passenger services ceasing in 1929, British Rail continued to utilise the line for transporting coal and ballast until 1976.

In the early 1980s, members of the Dean Forest Railway Society acquired the decaying line and began the first major stage of restoration. This was completed in 1991 when a short stretch of track was reopened between Norchard and a new station at Lydney Lakeside, four miles to the south. Further work is currently in progress to reinstate the entire line between Lydney and Parkend, a project which will take several years to complete.

Today, visitors to the Norchard Centre can see a unique collection of steam locomotives and rolling stock, many of which are still undergoing restoration; they can also visit the Society's railway museum with its huge display of signs, nameplates, posters, photographs, number plates and other railwayana including many from the local Severn and Wye line. There is also an on-site picnic area and a sizable shop offering a wide variety of gifts and souvenirs.

Norchard Steam Centre

On certain designated 'steam days', a number of locomotives are made ready and excursions are offered along the restored stretch of line. The eight-mile return trip takes 35 minutes and includes a fifteen-minute stop at Lydney Lakeside. Steam days: all Sundays and Bank Holidays between April and September, plus Wednesdays in June and July, and Tuesdays, Wednesdays and Thursdays in August. Admission charge payable (lower on non-stream days), plus additional charge for train rides.

We rejoined the A48 and drove northeast for four miles to reach the attractive small village of **Blakeney**. At this point we decided to join the Forestry Commission's designated **Scenic Drive** through the central area

313

of the Forest of Dean. (The suggested entry point for this 25-mile circular route is at its most northwesternmost point at Cannop, near Coleford; however, because of our overall journey plan and because the first stop on our chosen itinerary would be the Dean Heritage Information and Interpretation Centre, we found it much more satisfactory to set out from Blakeney.)

The first stage of our journey took us up the twisting route of the **Soudley Valley**. Here, the road follows the course of the steep-sided river valley, resulting in a series of challenging gradients and bends. At Blackpool Bridge, the scenic drive crosses a recognisable section of the old Roman road which once ran between Lydney and Ariconium, near Ross-on-Wye. The bridge itself dates from the same period and was constructed to replace a ford which crossed Blackpool Brook at this point.

By now were getting close to the heart of the **Royal Forest of Dean**, a place with a long and fascinating past. Throughout its history, this ancient forest has been a wildwood, a royal hunting ground, an important mining and industrial area and a naval timber reserve, and because its geographical location effectively isolated it from the rest of England and Wales, it has developed its own unique character which endures to this day.

As the trees gradually returned to western Britain at the end of the last Ice Age, 53 species established themselves as our native trees. During this period, the Forest of Dean became established and grew to cover an area of some 120,000 acres between the Rivers Wye, Severn and Leadon. Around 4000 BC, the farmers of the New Stone Age began a process of field clearance and crop cultivation and gradually, large numbers of trees were cleared using highly-prized flint axes. The cut timber was used for many purposes including building materials and fuel, and it was also around this time that the process of *coppicing* was devised where the new shoots growing from the bases of felled trees were cultivated for periodical cutting.

Many species of animals and birds continued to inhabit the forest, and indeed the presence of deer led to it being designated a royal hunting forest by King Edmund Ironside early in the 11th-century. Later that century, King Canute established the **Court of Verderers**, an ancient council which had overall responsibility for everything that grew or lived in the forest. The court still meets ten times a year at the **Speech House** near Cannop Ponds, a unique building, now part of a hotel, which was built as a courtroom to settle disputes between the foresters and the new wave of 17th-century iron-founders.

Iron ore deposits were first discovered in the forest over 2500 years ago along an irregular arc which runs between Staunton and Lydney in

314

the west and south, and Ruspidge and Wigpool in the east and north. Although these were widely exploited by the Romans, it wasn't until the Crown allowed areas of the forest to be leased to commercially-motivated entrepreneurs in the 1600s that mineral extraction began to take place on a grand scale. Far more devastating, however, was the demand for timber to fuel the iron-smelting process; such was the scale of the requirement that by the 1660s, the once-magnificent forest had been reduced to a few hundred trees.

Seriously concerned about the shortage of mature oaks for naval shipbuilding, the government finally acted in 1668 by passing the Dean Forest (Reforestation) Act, one of the earliest examples of conservation legislation, and by cancelling all the mineral leases. This led to an extensive replanting programme which eventually restored the forest to something approaching its original state. The Napoleonic Wars prompted further restocking and by 1840, nearly 20,000 acres had been replanted, mostly with young oaks. However, by the time these trees had reached maturity, steel had replaced timber as the principal shipbuilding material and they were never required. (Some examples of the early-19th-century replanting can still be seen in the Cannop Valley Nature Reserve.)

During the Victorian era, coal began to be extracted in large quantities from the Forest of Dean and at one time, up to a million tons were removed each year, mostly from open cast workings. Large-scale coal extraction came to an end during the 1930s, although a few seams are still being worked today by groups of 'free miners', the individuals who exercise their traditional right to extract minerals from the forest. Although centuries of outcrop mining has left large areas scarred and unfit for agriculture, the forest has gradually reclaimed these 'scowles', or surface workings, often concealing them in a dense covering of moss, trees and lime-loving plants.

Today, the wooded area of the Royal Forest of Dean covers some 27,000 acres and although still under the ownership of the Crown, it has has been vested in the Forestry Commission since 1924. The forest is known to be one of the organisation's most successfully managed areas; it has opened up a large number of waymarked woodland walks, most of which are fully described in an excellent series of leaflets and guides, and has also been responsible for laying out a number of tastefully-landscaped picnic areas and car parks. Its principal task, however, has been to manage the commercial woodlands, half of which are planted with broad-leaved deciduous trees, predominantly oak with beech, ash and sweet chestnut, and the balance being non-native conifers such as larch, fir and spruce.

Further information on the background and history of the forest and its inhabitants can be obtained at the **Dean Heritage Centre**, the first stopping place on our circular drive. Standing in a cleft in the wooded hills, this fascinating place lies on the B4227 at Camp Mill on the edge of **Lower Soudley**.

Dean Heritage Centre   Camp House   0594 822170

Situated deep in the very heart of the forest, the Dean Heritage Centre is a real gem. It is a tranquil spot where time slows to a leisurely place and where a new face of the Forest unfolds to entrance the visitor with every changing season: the fresh greens of spring, the dark leafy greens of high summer, the russets of autumn and the brown greys of winter. In this unique haven, you can catch a glimpse of the unique heritage of the Forest of Dean and understand its very essence. Visitors are welcomed here every day of the year, with the exception of Christmas Day and Boxing Day.

The Dean Heritage Centre is housed at Camp Mill, an old corn mill standing on a site with a varied industrial history stretching back over the four hundred years. During the 17th -century there was a foundry here; then some years later, the buildings were modified to form a leatherboard mill where heel stiffeners and shoe insoles were manufactured. More recently, Camp Mill has been a saw mill and a piggery, then in 1981, it was presented to the Dean Heritage Museum Trust as as a prospective home for a Forest of Dean Museum. (At that time, its most eye-catching feature was the rusty remains of a car dump and scrap-yard.) However, within just two years, the first specialised displays of the new Dean Heritage Centre were opened to the public.

Since then, the displays have been extended and improved following the Trust's aim 'to preserve the heritage, information, objects, culture and sites of the Forest of Dean in perpetuity for the community, by the provision of museum services'. There is now a reconstructed miner's cottage within the mill complex with a living room, bedroom and wash

316

house which was built around 1900. (The contrast between modern homes with their many labour saving devices and the basic living conditions which existed at the turn of the century is all too apparent.) An example of the miner's workplace can be found near the cottage where one can imagine the rigours of life underground. The absence of explosive gases within the Forest of Dean coalfield enabled the miners to work with naked flames, candles at first, then later, carbide lamps. However, the mines here were subject to flooding and many of the deeper pits periodically filled with water, sometimes with disastrous consequences.

The social history of the Forest people is shown through domestic artefacts and documents which have been given to the museum by the local inhabitants. The importance of the close community spirit is felt; the Forest folk are fiercely independent, a result of their geographical isolation from both Wales and England. (Before the advent of the car and the Severn Bridge, this plateau area of closely wooded hills and deep valleys was relatively impenetrable.) The Forest folk developed their own customs, rights and even law courts, as well as a deep suspicion of outsiders.

The Centre houses a beam engine which was built by Samuel Hewlett around the turn of the 18th-century on this very site when it operated as a foundry. Recently, a twelve foot overshot water wheel was constructed within the original wheel pit of the mill to emphasise the importance of water power in the industrial development of the area. Outside, there is a typical Forest smallholding, complete with an orchard and some Gloucester Old Spot pigs, and nearby there are some old agricultural carts and a reconstructed cider press. Charcoal burning was a traditional Forest occupation, and a charcoal burner's hut and demonstration charcoal stacks have been constructed at the Centre. Each year, several batches of charcoal are made by this traditional method which requires them to be tended day and night over several days until the burning process has been completed. Excellent for barbecues, the end product is on sale to the public.

Several nature trails radiate from the Centre. Visitors can stroll through ancient oak and beech woods, past old stone quarries, and on through fir plantations along waymarked paths. There is also a level, all-weather footpath leading for about half-a-mile around the beautiful Soudley Pond, a Site of Special Scientific Interest for its aquatic insect life, in particular, dragonflies.

Local craftspeople carry out a variety of crafts at the Dean Heritage Centre. These include pottery, wood painting, stone sculpture, iron-working, and glass and wood engraving. Unusual hand-crafted gifts, ideal as extra-special presents, can be found in the shop and gallery. We also enjoyed the home-baking in the Heritage Kitchen where the menu offers a wide choice from snacks to three-course meals; they also serve an excellent pot of tea. (Parties are welcome if booked in advance).

The facilities on site include ample coach and car parks, toilets (including a mother and babies room), and good access and facilities for disabled visitors. A large and much praised adventure play area is situated near the car park. Picnic tables can be found both under the trees on the slope of Bradley Hill and beside the car park on the mossy banks of Soudley Brook. There are also several barbecue hearths which can be booked in advance. Throughout the year, special events, displays and art exhibitions are regularly staged. Guided tours of the Dean Heritage Centre and the surrounding woodlands are also available, making this the ideal place to take your family and friends for a day of interest, fun and education, whatever the weather.

On leaving the Heritage Centre, we returned to the scenic drive and soon passed the attractive small lakes known as Soudley Ponds. Then, just past the White Horse pub, we turned north onto the Littledean road to make the short diversion to visit the **Blaize Bailey** viewpoint; this can be reached by turning east after a mile or so onto a forest track. Once there, visitors are rewarded with breathtaking views over the village of Newnham and the Vale of Gloucester to the Cotswold Hills beyond. Another wonderful view, this time of Soudley village, can be obtained from a lay-by which is passed on the return to the scenic drive.

Heading anti-clockwise along the circular route once again, we passed through the old mining community of Ruspidge before turning west onto the B4226 on the outskirts of **Cinderford**. This sizable town is sometimes referred to as the capital of the east forest; however, we found it relatively unattractive with little to offer the visitor. Our next stop was the famous **Dean Sculpture Trail**, a unique collection of eleven outdoor sculptures which are spaced along a delightful woodland walk. The artists have all used the forest setting as their theme, for example, the final piece on the trail is an impressive stained-glass window known as *The Cathedral* which depicts the forest trees and wildlife. The Sculpture Trail is accessible either from the picnic area adjacent to the stained-glass window, or from the award-winning Beechenhurst picnic site a mile or so further west; both are sited on the northern side of the B4226.

Situated on the southern side at this point is the **Speech House Arboretum**, a fascinating place for those interested in finding out more about the world of trees. Visitors are welcome to inspect the large collection of native and imported specimen trees which are laid out along a pleasant woodland trail. A little further west, we passed the historic

318

Speech House Hotel, the official meeting place of the ancient Verderers' Court, before we descended abruptly towards Cannop. At Cannop Crossroads, we turned south onto the B4234 and very soon after, a sign directed us east to the **Cannop Ponds** picnic area. These picturesque pools were originally hollowed out in the 1820s to provide a regular water supply for the local iron smelting works.

Continuing southwards, our next stop was the wildlife reserve at **Nagshead** near Parkend. The Forest of Dean has long been a haven for a huge variety of animals and birds, including deer, badgers, woodpeckers and the famous forest sheep which have been permitted to range freely in the forest for centuries. The Nagshead reserve is particularly noted for its resident population of pied flycatchers and its visiting peregrine falcons. The attractive former mineral extracting community of **Parkend** stands at the northern terminus of the still-to-be-reopened Dean Forest Railway. Those looking to break their journey should look out here for the first-rate Parkend House Hotel.

Parkend House   Parkend   0594 563666

Situated within three acres of parkland containing a private croquet lawn, the **Parkend House Hotel** offers guests total seclusion. Run by Mrs Bobby Poole and Andrew Lee, it is a small country house hotel, over 200 years old, which provides excellent facilities whilst still retaining its original character and charm. The bedrooms are all en suite with colour televisions, hot drinks facilities and direct-dial telephones. Three of the rooms are on the ground floor, offering easy access to disabled guests. Children are also welcome and several family rooms are available. The restaurant offers a varied menu and Bobby is happy to cater for vegetarian and special diets. All meals are prepared using fresh produce, including unusual and exotic vegetables; Andrew and Bobby also make their own chutney and marmalade, the latter of which is served at breakfast.

On the northern edge of Parkend, the scenic drive turns southeast off the B4234 onto the former B4331. After one mile, we made a short diversion north to visit the charmingly-named **New Fancy View**, a delightfully landscaped picnic area which was once the site the New Fancy Colliery. It's worth making the effort to climb to the top of the nearby hill for the breathtaking views over the surrounding landscape.

Half-a-mile after returning to the main circuit, we made another detour to the north, this time to visit the beautiful **Mallards Pike Lake**. This is another good place for a short walk; however, for those wishing to press on, the track follows a circular route back onto the main scenic drive. The final place worth mentioning on our tour around the forest is the **Wenchford** picnic site. This is situated a mile further east and can be reached by turning north onto the Soudley road, and then immediately east onto an old railway track which leads the parking area (toilets available here).

Two miles further on and we found ourselves back on the A48 near Blakeney. We rejoined this road and drove northeast for three miles to reach the pleasant Severnside village of **Newnham**. This is said to be one of the best places for viewing the famous **Severn Bore**, the natural wave formation which is created when the incoming tide from the Bristol Channel meets the water flowing seawards from the Severn. Although small-scale bores occur throughout the year, during certain tidal conditions, a wave of some nine feet in height can be generated, usually on the spring tides of early spring or late autumn. The phenomenon is popular with surfers and canoeists who like to 'catch the wave'. Information on times and the best viewing points can be obtained from local retailers.

At Newnham, we turned away from the river and drove westwards up a steep lane towards **Littledean Hall**. This remarkable country house is surrounded by sweeping informal grounds and occupies a dramatic position overlooking the great horseshoe bend on the Severn. (It lies only a short distance from Blaize Bailey viewpoint we visited on our scenic drive around the Forest of Dean). Littledean Hall has a rich history and claims to be one of the oldest continuously occupied country residences in England. In 1984, the remains of one of the largest rural Roman shrines, Springhead Temple, were discovered in the foundations, and there is also evidence here of a great hall dating from Saxon times. The Norman core of the present-day house dates from the 11th-century when it was built for the Dene family. This was later replaced in 1612 by a new Jacobean building, carved wood panelling from which is still much in evidence throughout the interior. However, the new hall did not escape further alterations and was itself remodelled on a number of occasions between 1664 and 1896.

Perhaps Littledean Hall's main claim to fame, however, are its many ghosts, most of which seem to have their origins in the period since the 17th-century. One of the earliest apparitions dates from the English Civil War when the royalist garrison based here was surprised by a Parliamentarian attack. Following the royalists' surrender, one of their troops unfortunately killed one of the Roundhead soldiers, an act which resulted in the entire garrison being massacred. Royalist colonels Congreve and Wigmore were standing next to the main fireplace when they were put to the sword and today, phantom bloodstains are said to appear at this spot which no amount of cleaning can remove.

Another event which is said to account for some of the present-day poltergeist activity took place a century later. According to legend, the owner of the house, Charles Pyrke, was murdered by his black manservant in 1744, despite them having been friends since childhood; Pyrke was alleged to have been responsible for making his servant's sister pregnant and for subsequently murdering the baby. Today, the ghostly butler is said to haunt the landing outside his garret bedroom high in the east wing.

Some years later, the Pyrke family were involved in another incident when two brothers in love with the same woman ended up killing each other during an argument at the dining table. Their spirits are still said to inhabit the dining room. One unfortunate result of all this poltergeist activity is that one of the best guest rooms, the Blue Room, is alleged to be so disturbed by the sound of footsteps and the clashing of swords that no one has dared to spent the night there for over forty years. Littledean Hall is open daily, 10.30am to 6pm between April and October. Admission charge payable.

Leaving the secret passageways and haunted garrets behind, we turned east onto the A4151 and drove on through **Littledean** village towards our final stopping place in Gloucestershire, **Westbury-upon-Severn**. This is the home of the unique National Trust-owned **Westbury Court Garden** which, having been built between 1696 and 1705, is the earliest surviving example of a formal Dutch water garden in the country. When the Trust acquired the property in the 1960s, it was in a state of extreme dilapidation. The house had been demolished, the lawns were like hayfields, the canals were silted up, and garden walls and yew hedges were in a serious state of disrepair. However, with the help of an engraving of the original garden plan, the records of the initial plantings and a series of special grants, the Trust were able to begin a programme of restoration which was finally completed in 1971.

Today, these most attractive and unusual gardens stand as a unique example of the style of formal landscaping which existed before the onset of emparking later in the 18th-century. The only surviving building, the pavilion, is an elegant two-storey redbrick structure with a tower and weather vane which stands overlooking the garden's delightful waterlily-filled canals. Another particularly appealing feature of Westbury Court Garden is that it was exclusively replanted with species known to have been available in this part of England before 1700. Open Wednesdays to Sundays (and Bank Holiday Mondays), 11am to 6pm between April and end-October. Admission charge payable (free to National Trust members). These beautiful gardens at Westbury-upon-Severn provided us with a delightful and fitting conclusion to our most enjoyable tour of Gloucestershire and Wiltshire.

Westbury Court

We do hope you have enjoyed this book and that it prompts you to spend some time in this beautiful part of England. We would like to thank all those people who showed us such warm hospitality on our travels and we would be grateful if you mention that it was "The Hidden Places" which prompted you to visit.

Safe Journey.

Tourist Information Centres

AMESBURY, Flower Lane, Tel: (0980) 623255

AVEBURY, The Great Barn, Tel: (06723) 425

BRADFORD-ON-AVON, Bridge Street, Tel: (0225) 865797

CHELTENHAM, 77, Promenade, Tel: (0242) 522878

CHIPPENHAM, High Street, Tel: (0249) 657733

CHIPPING CAMPDEN, High Street, Tel: (0386) 840101

CIRENCESTER, Market Place, Tel: (0285) 654180

COLEFORD, Market Place, Tel: (0594) 836307

DEVIZES, St John's Street, Tel: (0380) 729408

GLOUCESTER, The Cross, Tel: (0452) 421188

MALMESBURY, Town Hall, Tel: (0666) 823748

MARLBOROUGH, George Lane, Tel: (0672) 513989

MELKSHAM, Church Street, Tel: (0225) 707424

MERE, The Square, Tel: (0747) 861211

NEWENT, High Street, Tel: (0531) 822145

NORTHLEACH, Cotswold Countryside Collection,
        Tel: (0451) 860715

PAINSWICK, Stroud Road, Tel: (0452) 813552

SALISBURY, Fish Row, Tel: (0722) 334956

STOW-ON-THE-WOLD, The Square, Tel: (0451) 831082

STROUD, George Street, Tel: (0453) 765768

SWINDON, Brunel Centre, Tel: (0793) 530328

TETBURY, 63, Long Street, Tel: (0666) 503552

TEWKESBURY, 64, Barton Street, Tel: (0684) 295027

TROWBRIDGE, St Stephen's Place, Tel: (0225) 777054

WARMINSTER, Central Car Park, Tel: (0985) 218548

WESTBURY, Edward Street, Tel: (0373) 827158

WINCHCOMBE, High Street, Tel: (0242) 602925

Town Index

A

Ablington	210
Adlestrop	221
Aldbourne	113
Alderbury	7
Alderley	169
Alderton	253
Alton Barnes	100
Alvington	311
Amberley	185
Amesbury	95
Ampney Crucis	202
Ampney St Mary	202
Ampney St Peter	203
Ansty	33
Arlingham	179
Ashbury	115
Ashleworth	282
Ashmore	32
Ashton Keynes	133
Ashton Under Hill	254
Atworth	60
Avebury	83
Avening	187
Avenis Green	193

B

Barnsley	201
Bathford	66
Beckington	53
Berkeley	173
Berwick St John	26
Beverstone	166
Bibury	209
Birdlip	266
Bisley	194
Blakeney	313
Blockley	226
Blunsdon St Andrew	124
Bournes Green	193
Bourton-on-the-Hill	225
Bourton-on-the-Water	214
Box	67
Bradford-on-Avon	62
Bredon Hill	254
Bredon's Hardwick	255
Bremhill	136
Britford	10
Broad Blunsdon	124
Broad Campden	227
Broad Chalke	25
Broad Hinton	118
Broadway	237
Brockweir	308
Buckland	252
Burcombe	24

C

Cadley	103
Calne	77
Cam	172
Castle Combe	140
Castle Eaton	124
Cerney Wick	205
Chalford	193
Chedworth	210
Cheltenham	261

Chelynch	45	Duntisbourne Leer	197
Chepstow	310	Duntisbourne Rouse	197
Cherhill	77	Dursley	171
Cherhill Down	78	Dymock	284
Chicklade	35		
Chilmark	34	**E**	
Chilton Foliat	112		
Chippenham	138	Eastcott	92
Chipping Campden	228	East Gomeldon	17
Christian Malford	137	East Kennet	100
Cinderford	318	Eastleach	208
Cirencester	199	Eastleach Martin	207
Clearwell	304	Eastleach Turville	207
Cleeve Hill	264	Easton Grey	150
Codford	36	Ebble Valley	25
Codford Circle	36	Ebrington	230
Codford St Mary	36	Edington	46
Codford St Peter	36	Epney	179
Colesbourne	198	Erlestoke	92
Coln Rogers	210	Evenlode	222
Coln St Dennis	210		
Condicote	220	**F**	
Coombe Bissett	9		
Corsham	67	Fairford	206
Corston	151	Farleigh Hungerford	54
Cranham	267	Farleigh Wick	65
Cricklade	126	Ford	144
Crickley Hill	266	Forthampton	259
Crofton	105	Frampton Mansell	196
Crudwell	157	Frampton-on-Severn	177
		France Lynch	193
		Froxfield	106
D		Fyfield Down	101
Daglingworth	196		
Deerhurst	259	**G**	
Devizes	88		
Didmarton	168	Garsdon	157
Dinton	25	Gloucester	273
Doulting	45	Great Badminton	147
Down Ampney	205	Great Barrington	214
Downton	6	Great Bedwyn	105
Duntisbourne Abbots	197	Great Durnford	18

Great Wishford	22	Lover	5
Guiting Power	239	Lower Goatacre	135
		Lower Lydbrook	295
H		Lower Slaughter	218
		Lower Soudley	316
Hanging Langford	22	Lower Swell	219
Haresfield	272	Lydiard Millicent	120
Hatherop	208	Lydiard Tregoze	121
Heytesbury	37	Lydney	312
Highnam	282		
Highworth	124	**M**	
Holt	61		
Honeystreet	100	Maisemore	281
Hook	119	Malmesbury	152
Horningsham	41	Manton	102
		Marden	98
I, K		Market Lavington	92
		Marlborough	102
Imber	38	Marshfield	145
Iford	56	Marston	91
Kellaways	136	Marston Meysey	125
Kempley	285	Melksham	59
Kempsford	206	Melsham Forest	59
Kingswood	169	Mere	39
Kington Langley	137	Mickleton	231
		Middle Duntisbourne	197
L		Middle Woodford	18
		Milton Lilbourne	99
Lacock	71	Minchinhampton	185
Lake	18	Miserden	197
Latton	125	Monkton Farleigh	65
Lechlade	207	Moreton-in-Marsh	223
Leckhampton	265	Moreton Valance	180
Leigh	133		
Leighterton	168	**N**	
Little Badminton	147		
Little Barrington	214	Nailsworth	186
Little Clarendon	25	Naunton	219
Little Langford	22	Nettleton	146
Little Washbourne	253	Nettleton Shrub	146
Llandogo	307	Netton	18
Lockeridge	100	Newent	286

New Fancy View 320
Newland 300
Newnham 320
North Cerney 199
Northleach 211
North Newton 98
North Nibley 173
Norton St Philip 53
Nunney 43
Nunton 8
Nympsfield 171

O

Oaksey 157
Odstock 8
Ogbourne St George 113
Old Sarum 15
Orcheston 20
Ozleworth 170

P, Q

Painswick 269
Parkend 319
Pewsey 99
Porton 17
Porton Down 17
Potterne 91
Prestbury 264
Prinknash 267
Purton 120
Quenington 208

R

Ramsbury 112
Redlynch 5
Rodden 43
Roundway Down 87
Ruardean 295

S

St Briavels 305
Salisbury 10
Sandy Lane 76
Sapperton 196
Savernake Forest 104
Seven Springs 198
Shaftesbury 32
Sheepscombe 269
Sherbourne 213
Sherston 149
Slimbridge 177
Snig's End 283
Somerford Keynes 205
Sopworth 148
South Cerney 204
Southend 113
Southrop 207
Stanton St Quentin 150
Stanway 247
Stapleford 22
Staunton 297
Steeple Ashton 51
Steeple Langford 22
Stinchcombe 173
Stockbottom 17
Stokescroft 186
Stonehenge 19
Stourton 40
Stow-on-the-Wold 220
Stratford-sub-Castle 16
Stratton 199
Stroud 183
Swindon 122
Symonds Yat 296

T

Taynton 289
Teffont Magna 34
Teffont Evias 34

Temple Guiting	239
Tetbury	163
Tewkesbury	255
Thameshead	198
Tidenham Chase	310
Tisbury	34
Toddington	252
Tollard Royal	31
Trowbridge	57
Twigworth	280

U

Upavon	97
Upper Apperley	260
Upper Lydbrook	295
Upper Minety	135
Upper Swell	219
Upper Woodford	18
Upton Lovell	37
Upton Wraxall	144
Urchfont	93

V,W,Y

Vaggs Hill	56
Warminster	46
Watledge	187
West Amesbury	95
West Ashton	52
Westbury	46
Westbury-upon-Severn	321
West Crudwell	158
West Grafton	105
West Kennet	100
West Lavington	94
Westwood	55
Whaddon	273
Whiteway	197
Whitminster	180
Willesley	167
Wilton	22

Winchcombe	242
Wingfield	56
Winson	210
Winterbourne Monkton	117
Winterbourne Stoke	21
Woodchester	185
Woolley Green	64
Wootton Bassett	118
Wootton Rivers	104
Wortley	169
Worton	91
Wotton-under-Edge	169
Wroughton	116
Wylye	21
Yarnbury Castle	21
Yatton Keynell	140